American Architecture

Ideas and Ideologies in the Late Twentieth Century

American Architecture

Ideas and Ideologies in the Late Twentieth Century

Paul Heyer

VNR *VAN NOSTRAND REINHOLD*
New York

Copyright © 1993 by Van Nostrand Reinhold

Library of Congress Catalog Card Number 92-18415
ISBN 0-442-01328-0

I(T)P Van Nostrand Reinhold is a division of International Thomson
Publishing. ITP logo is a trademark under license.

Printed in the United States of America

Van Nostrand Reinhold
115 Fifth Avenue
New York, NY 10003

International Thomson Publishing
Berkshire House
168-173 High Holborn
London, WC1V 7AA, England

Thomas Nelson Australia
102 Dodds Street
South Melbourne 3205
Victoria, Australia

Nelson Canada
1120 Birchmount Road
Scarborough, Ontario
M1K 5G4, Canada

16 15 14 13 12 11 10 9 8 7 6 5 4 3 2 1

Library of Congress Cataloging-in-Publication Data

Heyer, Paul
    American architecture: ideas & ideologies in the late twentieth
century/ by Paul Heyer.
       p.   cm.
    Includes index.
    ISBN 0-442-01328-0
    1. Architectural design. I. Title. II. Title: American architecture,
ideas and ideologies in the late twentieth century.
NA2750. H48 1993
729—dc20   92-18415

To my mother and the memory of my father.

Contents

Acknowledgments

My years of teaching have brought me into close relationships with countless dedicated and talented students. I have been fortunate in that they have continually forced me to expand and challenge my knowledge and understanding of architecture and design, and to prioritize and structure how I presented and discussed this information. The first thoughts for this book and its organization came from such contact.

I have been privileged in my career to know many great architects and designers, especially in the United States. The work of many of these people is included in this book. Without them and their generosity in sharing their thoughts, as well as their generosity in the more mundane aspect of providing graphic materials, this book would not have been possible.

Finally, thanks are due to many of the staff at my publisher, who worked with such conviction to produce this book: Wendy Lochner, for her total commitment to this project and its myriad of details; Bernice Pettinato, who so diligently handled the editing and production aspects; and Michael Suh, for his tireless efforts to ensure a quality design. Their care, patience, and faith could never adequately be rewarded by any expression of gratitude.

Preface

■ THE IDEA FOR this book originated in the mid 1970s when modern architecture was accelerating into a crisis of self-evaluation and lack of confidence in the more transparent theories of modernism. With everything possible, everything—and anything—was seemingly being realized. Certainly in the 1980s we saw sweeping changes in architectural attitudes as different as Bauhaus Modernism was from the Beaux Arts. While the vigor has been without question, often the results have raised many questions. The advent of Post Modernism, for example, can readily be attributed to the so-called failure of Modernism. But where has Post Modernism, for many architects another saga of failure, and the legacy of earlier Modernism left us? Clearly with a need to again reestablish valid basic questions rather than dwell too religiously upon our more ephemeral conclusions.

One thought, however, seems apparent and reasonable: The present dilemma of modern architecture is the failure to develop a cohesive body of theory or set of disciplining criteria within which parameters of form derivation can evolve. The Gothic period had a notion of structure that dealt with it not only as a support system but with structure as essence, as the container of all aspects of a building even to the idea of light penetration both permitted by the methodology of structure while in turn deriving its own fundamental presence from this very dialogue with light. During the Renaissance more variable, hierarchical, and connective ideas of space by intention led to more sequential ideas of space and generic form varying the overall organization and exterior volume. With these two very particular attitudes toward design, theory and idea basic to the approach set the framework for the conclusion. Theory supported conclusion, conclusion evolved from theory.

The Modern period, growing out of Beaux Arts notions of order fused with new technological potential, began within the dual influence of these strong ideas where method of building and organization of space promised to be one. The beginning was strong because the promise was inherent. The essence of structure—or methodology of building—would be the container, the evolution of space would be the contained. Theory held the promise that components would be relative, that an order would exist. Instead, we have evolved in the tendency toward approaches to architecture that are based on ideas of form as personal and idiosyncratic. We are even inclined to evaluate architecture within personalized parameters where everything has its own rules, its own standards, its own obligations. The result is an architecture of singularity where personal preferences reign without connective tissue to elemental theory. Finally, we decorate our personalizations, which further underscores their isolation. Within this climate is the challenge to once again connect to supportive theory. This we can only redefine from reemphasizing the importance of fundamentals and the attitudinal theory deriving from our response toward them. This establishes the spirit and framework of architectural effort. The essence of architecture can never more than fleetingly be touched through idiosyncracy.

Consequently, this book presents the idea of building design, basically from the perspective of problem solving within the cultural climate and physical context in which the architect functions. Hence, the framework of design becomes a process that is itself suggestive of form, conditioned and modified by the architect's overview toward social and cultural factors, which collectively culminate in architecture.

The "framework" of architecture is presented in three chapters: Form, Function, and Concepts of space; Structure, Technology, and the New Means; and Site as an Imperative. These fundamental architectural determinants are modified by the architect's "overview," which is documented in the subsequent three chapters entitled: Idea as Catalyst; Order as Context; and Coherence and/or Inclusivity. The introductory chapter entitled Problem and Process acquaints the reader with the nature of design and some of the more pertinent cultural factors that influence the way the architect thinks, works, and conceives of architectural solutions. The concluding chapter, The Inevitability of Style, discusses how architecture results, inevitably, from reasonable responses within the framework of designing, as these are modified by the architect's attitude or overview.

Style, therefore, is not taken to imply an arbitrary aesthetic imposition or preoccupation with formal organization, but how an architecture based on purpose, context, and idea, upon reason and reasonableness, can result in design responses that, as they develop denominators and expressions in time, manifest themselves as style. Style is then fundamental to buildings that are shaped by ideas. Buildings, in turn, impose their own laws that transform and enrich ideas. Process is one of interaction, just as the "framework" implies the "overview," or the overview modifies the framework. The world of practice and the world of ideas become one in actuality and process, bringing determinants, skills, interpretations, and attitudes together as architecture.

1

Problem and Process

■ ANY CREATIVE WORK of consequence is essentially an expressive statement that aspires beyond the ordinary. The proposition is one beyond mere existence. With architecture it is a personal and social idea that in addition to presenting itself expressively represents an approach toward life, a consciousness of responsibility. Deriving from a sense of logic, of cultural evolution, and appropriateness, architecture gains its legitimacy and sense of directness as patterns and processes of life are heightened and as the essential nature and quality of a design problem is revealed. It also is the passion to originate form, provoked by selectivity and an informed intelligence. It is the pursuit of excellence and the clarity of rational response, combined with compassion for the social context and the touch of the artist.

Intelligence plays a role in the art of architecture, but it alone cannot create a work of art. It enables the architect to select, reject, explore, develop, and scrutinize facts, but, whereas intelligence sharpens and refines the art an architect brings to the creative act, it can never be a substitute for that magical synapse between rational realism and sheer inspiration that prompts art and architecture. Beyond intellectual insights, fortunate accidents, sudden intuitions, detached interpretation, all of which, too, constitute this art, a project brings its particular logic, an environment its particular implications, a time its particular technology, a society its special needs, and the architect an individual sense of art. With purpose and principle a synthesis is effected which expresses the aspirations and serves the needs of a time. Thus a concensus is formed upon which the architect bases decisions and combines the many attitudes and aims that are pivotal to the design process.

In more homogeneous periods in the history of architecture, with agreement on standards that were themselves high, excellence in building was seemingly easier to attain. Today, our disciplines are largely derived from economic and technological factors and, in our time of wide choice, personal restraint, rather than cultural values. There is a sense of a need for a synthesis which will reach beyond confusion and contradiction toward a feeling of the interdependence of new solutions, a flexible order to the diversity of our built environment. As such ours is a period of reassessment and consolidation.

How, and in what direction, and with what implication is the nature of architectural thought involved in this intellectual climate?

Some architects hold the belief that in this technological age we should, in response to our social challenge, embrace technology and its highly systematized, industrial construction processes, but in this pursuit there are also reasons for caution. Even to Ludwig Mies van der Rohe, a major advocate of science and technology in the early days of the modern movement in architecture, technology was simply a newer means to older ends. He created designs which were sophisticated, rationalized studies, formal architectural statements in the classical sense, never moving far from such priorities as order, space, and proportion. Technology can obviously not be a singular priority or aim today. Even engineers who have produced some of the poetic, technological/functional statements of twentieth century potential, have never been entirely oblivious to appropriate compromise and judgments of the eye. The emphasis on technology can be misleading when considered a panacea. An architect who believes in working with the technology of the time also does not by implication necessarily produce a building that is itself a slick technological artifact. Often this may be the last thing a design wants to be for its purpose. It will mean, however, that a work will not move in a direction contrary to a respect for technology, or, more important, to the basic implication of a method of building.

Many architects today see the effort to control, refine, and produce a distilled and restrained, contained and quite resolved solution to a problem to be an architecture of exclusion achieved at the expense of other equally important factors. Contrary to this more neoclassic approach, they see contradiction, equivocal and hybrid elements, a desire to often incorporate attitudes toward history, or conversely a somewhat expressionistic response to purpose as a more intense, even reasonable embrace of a design's insistent will or letting something essentially be, to use Louis Kahn's expression, "what it wants to be." Or, what we could image it to be within context. Or, what we desire it to be. The idea *is*. Design being arrived at by guidance and pragmatic eclecticism rather than elimination and abstraction. In this area Robert Venturi has been the most impassioned and articulate advocate of a "nonstraightforward" architecture with "richness of meaning rather than clarity of meaning."

This direction has particularly evolved into a reassessment of attitudes toward history, because the struggle to establish design priorities today is not one of supplanting outmoded historical attitudes toward architecture with a moral, visually crisp and clear foundation as it was in the "heroic" early period of the modern movement. Architects are simply tending to take our moral base for granted as they search for an inclusive framework for architecture beyond the narrowness of this early period. We no longer feel defensive about looking into history for a sense of continuity, even inspiration, as we now can laud such classical Beaux Arts devices as the organization of circulation within a building as an abstract structuring system and admire their highly structured continuity of compositional, sequential space experiences for both meaning and beauty. To have seen virtue in such scholarly, geometric space-movement abstractions would have been somewhat anathema to the so-called progressive thinker a few years ago. Clearly, this attitude or awareness is too encompassing with too many avenues being explored to be simply or conveniently labeled into post-modernist or neohistoricist camps. Any such simplification is against the very catholic nature of the search for spirited meaning in architecture that is germane to this new sensibility.

Architects are of necessity questioning, too, the premise of their professional responsibility. How should we as a society confront a sealed, artificially lighted, heated, cooled, and ventilated building in view of psychological and physiological factors, pollution, and energy consumption concerns. Certainly, regardless of architectural priorities, in a world of finite resources presumptuous waste becomes increasingly conspicuous. A new awareness of environmental factors, with the full range of concern implicit therein is one of our brighter hopes for a better, more sensitive and more responsible attitude toward environment. We may in the end "humanize" our built world by the need to reinclude the natural world if only for ecological reasons, as we of necessity place humankind in closer harmony with this Earth.

With the architect no longer the aesthetic moderator of an academic art, even the nature of professional responsibility has become confused. Pivotal decisions at a broad conceptual scale are made by planners, economists, and politicians. Even the direct field of practice has been encroached upon by developers, builders, and engineers who often see the architect's concern for aesthetics and other "nebulous" ideas as a liability. Consequently, some architects have become more inclined to view the design process as primarily a social responsibility where design is secondary. Others, taking the opposite stance, see architecture as an ART form, and disenchanted with the whole climate of professional opportunity have retreated to theory rather than the practice of architecture. Here, in postulating thought form, they often tempt the intellect with visions of what might be.

In our period the architect is clearly struggling to find a role amid contradictory tracts. The range of choice is broad, more so than in any previous time, because of the options technology has revealed and the range of ideas that we are grappling with as a culture. Even the very idea of art is more complex. It has, for the first time in Western culture for example, embraced the enormous shift of consciousness from object to experience. The easel painters of a century ago certainly could not have conceived as art Carl Andre's placing bricks upon the floor in a straight line, nor Christo draping a curtain 26 miles through the California landscape. These are manifestations of our technological culture, just as experience has from ancient times been part of non-Western thought.

Based on complex interactions and sensitive value judgments, architecture in such a climate is naturally open to interpretations. Assuming that a central and imposed discipline should not resolve and control conflict in the design process and that a building should be allowed to exercise a freer "insistence will," then even irrationality may be conclusion. If our sensitivities are obscure, however, tenable knowledge to solve problems need not be. If rules for design can always be challenged at some level within the framework of what is possible and appropriate, the architectural process should be a search for the possible without a prior determination of what is possible. The creative door is then left open and the nature of the problem and its uniqueness become the inspiration for originality. Piet Hein, the Danish philosopher and designer, superbly clarified the enigma: "Art is solving problems that cannot be formulated until they are solved." In one of his aphoristic poems, which he calls Gruks, entitled *Ars Brevis,* he even defines the spirit of the effort.

There is one art, no more, no less;
to do all things with artlessness.

Art is not a question of fashion, nor of composing things into a favored, preconceived form, nor should a building of any complexity be designed abstractly. Although a building can become sculptural, architecture is not pure sculpture.

Emanating from the spirit of the sixties, American art and architecture have paralleled each other in that there has grown an increasing disregard for the old rules and restraints. Ordinary things have been looked at for their own merit out of pragmatic contact with daily life. Curiously from the Pop art movement, which at first seems so personal, we get a sense that the vitality of any creative effort comes when personal preferences and notions have not ruled but have been polarized within a proper discipline leading to an appropriate form. It is also rather revealing that Pop art, one of the more playful and whimsical movements in the art world, should have been responsible for some of the most perceptive social commentary.

Like art, the nature of architecture is a problem-solving confrontation, striving for the essence of a problem, trying to make things work in relation to other things, trying to continually build through a dialogue with the problem aspects of its solution, where the problem itself is the source of knowledge and inspiration of its own nature and being. It is a process of accumulation and taking away, of seeming endless testing and reforming of ideas. Pablo Picasso said, in a talk with André Malraux, "I begin with an idea; you can't begin with nothing. It has to be vague. If a painter isn't quite sure of what he wants, it's of no great importance. So long as he's very sure of what he *doesn't* want." The idea is the trigger, the fact that it is vague is the area of latitude, the definition of what the designer is excluding helps to narrow the design effort. The act of beginning is predicated on an attitude with which the designer draws upon accumulated knowledge and a problem's resources. The approach is to state an objective, it is the search for an object's correct form. In itself it is not a design, although it sets up the direction for the process of designing. The process is defined by the approach.

Historically architects have attempted to define an approach or a philosophy to clarify a set of ground rules that might serve as measures.

The Roman architect, Vitruvius, pointed to commodity, firmness, and delight as measures of architectural quality.

Le Corbusier, expressing the utopian spirit of the new age in the twenties, published in the *Oeuvres Complètes 1910-1929* in collaboration with Pierre Jeanneret, his five points for a new architecture: *columns,* or pilotis, whereby a building could be raised up from the ground and the landscape penetrate its mass; *the roof garden* to "replace" ground taken up by a building, to provide a different type of leisure space, and technically to protect the roof surface from damaging extremes of temperature; *the open plan,* affording a new flexibility to organize space not possible within the limitations of traditional load-bearing wall systems; *the wall of glass* liberating the window, which can run continuously from wall to wall of a building; *the free facade,* with columns set within a building and its exterior walls no longer load bearing, the skin opened or closed to satisfy functional and aesthetic aims.

Eero Saarinen in the late fifties defined his three pillars of modern architecture as functional integrity, structural honesty, and awareness of the times. After the potent architectural influence of Mies van der Rohe he felt that three more needed adding: a building must make an expressive statement, must be concerned with site and environment, and must express itself throughout as a unity.

Entering into the spirit of this game it is not difficult to expand the list with further "pillars": expression of the integrity of material; particularizing design demands including psychological and symbolic tenets; expressing appropriate form and space relationships, (monumental, pastoral, recreational, etc.). Such definitions would hardly fuel any efforts today because they represent little more than simplistic commonsense denominators. They are generalities that are open to personal interpretation, not process.

In Le Corbusier's example the measures had little in the end to do with social reform and the healthful happy life, but in architecture aspired to high art abstract compositions out of interlocking geometry resulting in rich statements of free form. At a planning level his theories, visions of free-floating apartment slab blocks in a clear new landscape of sweeping scale, became misinterpreted by developers, planners, and "convenience" architects and were the inspiration for the sad era of ruthless, stark building in nightmare, barren landscapes. Of course, the Jaoul Houses in Paris (the catalyst for the influential New Brutalist movement in England of the early 1950s) and Le Corbusier's subsequent Chapel at Ronchamp, were a direct shift from these earlier visions.

With critical judgment as the impetus, purpose initiates, design supposes, form evolves. The process stems from a hierarchy of ideas that are social, functional, structural, technological, environmental, and formal, and their priority changes with each design problem. Formal is the most nebulous factor because this deals with the architect's feeling—what he or she wants to do—toward design, taste, and expressive factors such as a concern with the nature of space, the introduction of natural and artificial light, notions of geometry, articulation, and detail, and attitudes toward continuity and context.

Throughout history there have been devices for confronting some of these questions, at least within an aesthetic idea. *The Rules for Drawing the Several Parts of Architecture* published in 1732 by the English architect James Gibbs documented, for example, systems for relating the classical orders of architecture into harmoniously conceived and proportioned building configurations. They were that period's system—presented with a meticulous and scholarly level of aesthetic refinement—comparable with a manufacturer's window system or the steel-section catalog of today. They were parts toward a whole.

The nineteenth century architects working under the academic tradition established by the Ecole des Beaux Arts in Paris also had a system, or rather a methodology: They fabricated a problem, invented a schedule of detailed requirements defined in a program, and then, through the study of the classic buildings of antiquity, fabricated the rules of composition to solve it. This limited projection of need was very seductive simply because the process of resolving defined problems into finite, contained solutions is in itself so absorbing and gratifying. It was rich in attitudes, a sense of a direction based on an idea of total imagery, supported by stylistic notions carefully selected as to the treatment of elements, which set the scene for the conceptual framework of the architecture.

The emphasis of the Beaux Arts training method is of interest in another respect today: During the actual design process when a project has brought its logic and technology has brought its means, the designer then brings the sense of art through critical judgments of the eye, when elements are shifted until desired relationships are achieved. Since in most design processes the objective factors will not clearly suggest a design path, the designer having to rely on a heightened sense of intuition, the Beaux Arts system was excellent at developing an architect's sense of the ability to manipulate and select among ideas. It is the foundation of our own approach toward contemporary architectural problem solving. It also led in the mid-twentieth century toward an attitude in which some architects resolved difficult problems in the design process by simply never allowing them to arise. We can refer to this attitude as design by avoidance. Mies van der Rohe, for example, with single-mindedness and selectivity always sought the formal clarity of a meticulously refined architecture, ignoring or placing in a secondary role, as did the Beaux Arts classicists, anything that might compromise this. If the placement of a window in a wall might compromise the perfection of the architecture, his solution would be to make the window part of the overall wall treatment, or simply to move the room to another space where the window was not required. Design problems were solved by allowing the conceptual idea to set the framework for the solution, the emphasis being on solutions rather than problem solving. Such governing ideas, even if they were based on notions of exclusion, did permit the refinement of an approach or a particular language, as the surety of classical buildings demonstrates; but as any movement moves closer to a stage of perfectability, the artist and architect by temperament and instinct also sees limitations and the natural inclination is to explore wider possibilities. This inevitably leads, as it has increasingly done since the 1950s, to the expanding of a vocabulary and of developing new attitudes and expressions.

One reality, however, tends to anchor our judgments; we ultimately respond to something because it appears to make a statement, seems to have a certain rightness, appropriateness, and inevitability. This is close to the true nature of any art, and this is a constant. The architect is then not responding to extrinsic change, actually the process of change itself, but rather the intrinsic quality of significant and/or new directions. Durable ideas are continually reborn through the response of new and fresh infusions of imagination. The Greek myths and Shakespearian themes touch deep values and consequential aspects of life and therefore have an ongoing relevance. Then there are the new ideas and directions, which contain a sense of where our culture is evolving.

Following these paths, as in all the arts, instinct becomes the force to transcend the measurable; but inevitability, as a measure of great architecture, ultimately reflects a consensus of opinion on principles and priorities where these in turn become the prerequisite for authority of action. This idea is reinforced by the ability to think conceptually, to seek to discover the signifi-cant forces within a problem and then state them unequivocally and poetically. In this context there is a basic difference between great art, which is brilliance and imagination in the solving of a problem and giving clear expression to the forces dormant within that problem, and great innovative art, when a culture takes a step into the future. It is the occasion when the artist's origination is preceded by the statement of a new question, How can I fly? How can I build to a great height? thereby establishing a new plateau of knowledge and under-standing, both factual and aesthetic. The social need and cultural opportunity is fundamental to this notion of innovation. The architect's initiative and sense of a moment in time, however, is the entrée.

Architecture is also by nature environmental and the most accessible of the arts to our sensibilities. It embodies the full cultural, technological, social, and psychological momentum of an epoch. As such, the architect is not trying to be *modern* for its own sake, but gives expression to the real cultural forces of a period, with buildings developing form characteristics from the historical context and condition. Architecture is also the pursuit of a vision, a synthesis that might project an image of what a better life might be. The expression of a life-style was the fundamental, social promise of modern architecture. This idea remains pertinent, if not yet realized, when we recognize that the needs of a people are tied to architecture; there is little meaning in the occasional *good* building if our cities are sterile and our resources and landscape are depleted.

The need today is for synthesis, to see things in context and as a totality. The Greek intellectual's intention was to strive for beauty, but also to go beyond this to show a culture's true moral and social nature. The intent was to be inclusive and not atomistic in the application of knowledge; art was not valued purely in aesthetic terms. To the Renaissance architect, believing in the idea of the "universal man," knowledge also appeared as homogeneous. Art and science were one. Not surprisingly, architects facing the enormous technical challenges of the nineteenth century, could not keep architecture on such a broad and unified base. An important challenge today is to reintegrate art and architecture with technology, with a sense of inevitable direction and momentum as the great artist-architects of the Renaissance endeavored to do. Since we question the political, social, and moral foundation of society and probe the riches of science while remaining intrigued by the myths that underlie our civilization, understandably the world of our actions and of our thoughts represents a fragmentation of collective and individual interests, of intellectual and emotional reactions. If historically some architecture has been great because it has transcended the contradictions and inconsistencies of life, in our time much of our architecture has come alive in their specific embodiment. As the architect strives to bring order and form to the forces that are distinct in an era, success becomes a measure of the timeliness of the design effort. We are at best a vehicle of a cultural and pragmatic imperative as we seek to create an environment that will express our visions. In our inner struggle with the known and the tangible we come alive as we conceptualize and give form to the unknown! As Carl Jung succinctly said, "The work in process becomes the poet's fate and determines his psychic development. It is not Goethe who creates Faust, but Faust which creates Goethe."

2

Form, Function, and Concepts of Space

■ FORM IS THE container of function. The effectiveness of a design might be described as a measure of its "perfect" function. While function is pivotal for form, it is anything but a direct, straight, or narrow avenue to form. Since symbolism, idea, and environmental continuity are also vital considerations in architecture, form is the expression of these as they too amplify our understanding of function. In addition to how things act, form is also what they imply. Existing form presupposes how we use buildings, potential form is a vision of how we might.

The Bauhaus in the twenties was fundamentally associated with the idea of "functionalism," or the supposed expression of function as the determinant of form. But the Bauhaus idea of functionalism went beyond a strict utilitarian attitude to see design not as applied but as intrinsic, and present in the appropriateness and vitality of the total scope of design, from object to building. Proportion, color, relationships in space and psychological considerations were as vital as structural and technological fact in the search for pertinent form. It is sad, and also indicative of the self-doubt typical of our time, that Walter Gropius, before his death in the late sixties, should have felt compelled to defend one of the powerful influences of recent design history against accusations of narrowness.

Even before Walter Gropius proselytized functionalism at the Bauhaus, Louis Sullivan, embroiled in the Beaux Arts climate of Chicago at the turn of

■ Adler and Sullivan, Auditorium Building, Chicago, 1890 *(Photo: Museum of Modern Art, New York)*

the century, reasoned that in a tall structure where the function remained constant, the form should not change; he then enunciated one of architecture's classic quotes: "Form follows function." Sullivan, like Gropius, was much too sophisticated to mean a strictly literal interpretation leading to a singular idea of design. He saw function as an organic avenue to design and an act that was certainly mindful of the eye's need for delight and the architectural need to organize forms and elements toward an articulated whole as evidenced by such designs as that for his Auditorium Building in Chicago. He wrote, "That which exists in spirit ever seeks and finds its visible counterpart in form, its visible image—a living thought, a living form."

Function is not a simplistic idea, nor is there a duality between form and function. Although they are simultaneous in architecture, one does not necessarily literally follow the other. Form is in itself even instrumental, not static nor a singular reflection of function. Form is something that moves us. The form of a building can itself be suggestive of function—the form of a container suggests ideas about its function.

The architect in the search for form has always had to expand on a narrow idea of function. Obviously Mies van der Rohe's essentially symbolic 1929 German Pavilion in Barcelona was involved with ideas beyond use, as was Le Corbusier's Villa Savoye of the same vintage (a building also expressive of his five points toward a new architecture referred to in Chapter 1) and these were

■ Mies van der Rohe, German Pavilion, Barcelona, Spain, 1929 *(Photo: Museum of Modern Art, New York)*

among the outstanding buildings at the high point of the so-called Functionalist Movement.

Philip Johnson, one of the early advocates of the Modern Movement in the United States and one of the first architects to point to its shortcomings in the fifties, designed, in his own Glass House, one of the world's most beautiful yet least functional houses; it was never envisioned as a "home" (house) to live in but a life-style stage to live with. Ostensibly entirely in *l'esprit nouveau* of the Modern Movement, it was a building really expressing many concerns of classic design, from the elevated placement of an object in a space, to its serene proportion, general overall symmetry, and combining of a balance of elements with a meticulous refinement of detail. The building is a further instance of whatever the period, whatever the "banner," the architect bringing certain "fixations" to a project. Here, the glass-walled room, a minimalist artifact suggesting a definition of space, is serene and composed in its space. It also expresses Johnson's proclaimed interest in the measure of architecture as being remembered in the presence of great one-roomed buildings.

The idea of functionalism is synonymous with pragmatism and this notion of Henry James and the Instrumentalists is very much a part of American philosophy. Deriving from this is the idea that because an object functions and is true because it works, it is beautiful. This was a motivating thought in the early days of the modern movement and indeed beauty as a reflection of truth has for centuries been coupled by philosophers. Literacy of function, if such could exist, is no guarantee of beauty. Correspondingly, there is no reason to separate utilitarianism and beauty—an equation that is integral in nature.

Pragmatism was the platform for another pillar of architectural philosophy articulated by Louis Sullivan: "It is the very essence of every problem that it contains and suggests its own solutions." Ultimately in the design process this is seeking to express suggestion. It is an assertion that form lies within a problem

and it is especially interesting that Sullivan should have pluralized solution, the implication being one of interpretation, of variable conclusion. It is also a personalizing idea and as such a position that is antiabstract; the correct response in a particular place rather than a universally tenable response valid for any place. This idea is important in considering the direction of architecture; whereas personal concepts may open horizons, universal concepts tend to consolidate directions. Progress is an amalgam of both. Valid personal visions are obviously few. Cultures are built through the strength of collective acts that incidentally have invariably followed more personal visions. A profusion of personal acts, especially those "less" than visionary are, however, the indulgent road to chaos. The authority of a collective and acceptedly valid discipline has the inherent possibility of order.

A direct reflection of this idea, and opposing attitude to the functional input, is clear from the comparison of Mies's approach to design with that of Frank Lloyd Wright's. Crown Hall, the School of Architecture at Illinois Institute of Technology represents Mies's principle of universal space. It packaged function, and as such moved historically back to embrace the neo-classic idea of resolving varying functions within a unified envelope. Contrary to Sullivan's idea that "form follows function," Mies said that while form cannot change, function does: "We do not let the function dictate the plan. Instead, let us make room enough for *any* function." In not establishing a predetermined

and contained allocation of space to accommodate the functional necessities of a building but by providing a space adaptable to changing space requirements, Mies created a flexible space supposedly capable of continual modification and thereby designed to counteract obsolescence. Mies concluded that the scale of our society, with its technological and scientific forces tended to negate the specific solution. He was fond of quoting the physicist Erwin Schrodinger: "The creative vigor of a general principle depends precisely on its generality." To Mies, these forces suggested the universal solution: a flexible response to the need for space at a vast scale and a more anonymous background. Again Mies was alluding to another neoclassic notion, that of form as idea, form as a higher and applied order.

Although Wright was also obviously preoccupied with ideas of form, to him these were totally alien generalizations. He saw the universal approach as an abstraction synonymous with the anonymous man, and the personal space as the proper response to individual needs in a fixed time and place. The comparison of his own school of architecture and home, Taliesin West, dramatizes their differences. Clearly, Wright saw design as a personal act deriving from particulars, with functional complexities as integral means of form and expression and loosely connected open forms and the articulation of volumes

■ Frank Lloyd Wright, Taliesin West,
Phoenix, Arizona, 1938 *(Photos: Paul Heyer)*

as the result. Crown Hall is architecture regardless of climate and context, Taliesin West is architecture relative to both. Herein lies the impetus for the increasing reawareness of Wright's importance to the architecture of today.

Mies approached building as a type rather than an individual problem, with functions resolved within larger constructs where diagrammatic space divisions were subject to an external discipline. The vulnerability of Mies's belief was the subjugation or exclusion of natural forces, an idea of reduction that simply eliminated too much. Ultimately, as Robert Venturi has pointed out, architecture came to find that less is not more but (unless exquisitely executed and even then sometimes too) simply a bore. Wright's noble thought that if art and individual liberty endure they can resolve all became a position that we are also forced to treat circumspectly in the arena of today's libertarian environment.

Whereas Mies's design for the Gallery of the Twentieth Century in Berlin is another objective in the diagrammatization of glass-walled space and a

■ Mies van der Rohe, Gallery of the Twentieth Century, Berlin, 1962–1968
(Photo: Hedrich-Blessing)

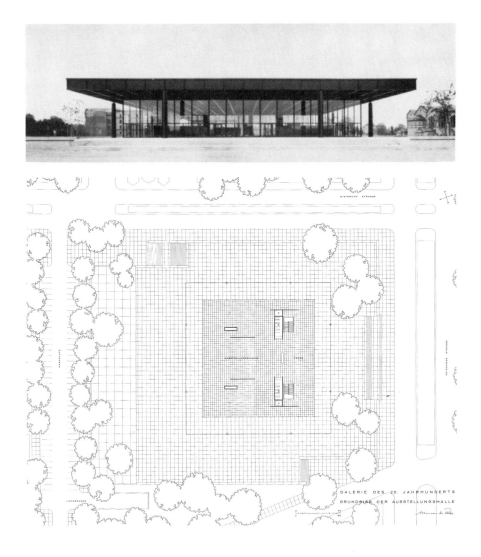

■ Frank Lloyd Wright, Guggenheim Museum, New York City, 1946
(Photo: The Solomon R. Guggenheim Museum)

■ Marcel Breuer & Assoc., Whitney Museum of American Art, New York City, 1966

further example of his preoccupation with clear-span, open space structures, Wright's Guggenheim Museum continues his desire to create drama in space or drama out of space—the spiral that had appeared in earlier sketches and projects awaited its grand moment! Rather than responses to functional necessities, both designs again reflect their architects' intellectual preoccupations. They are detached designs conceived in the grand manner and, if function is a measure of good architecture, both fail sadly. They are simply of interest as consummate objects.

Other American architects in recent years have looked at space, movement, and form as an expression of the museum function in a less singular manner.

In the Whitney Museum by Marcel Breuer and Hamilton Smith, the architects asked the questions: "What should a museum look like; what is its relationship to the New York landscape?" The response is a stepped form, an idea preoccupying many architects in the past quarter of a century as a formal organizing device. Clad in dark gray granite with open, rectangular, loftlike gallery spaces, the building's exhibition spaces can be flexibly arranged by floor to ceiling partitions whose placement is architecturally delineated by a concrete ceiling grid. Windows, unrelated to functions of light and air to the interior are sculptural points of contact with the outside. The building does not have Mies's reductive poetry nor Wright's singular flamboyance, but it is undoubtedly a more sympathetic space in which to exhibit art.

Michael Graves's controversial designs of the 1980s to dramatically expand the Whitney Museum proposed an addition exemplifying our more historically catholic search toward architectural solutions. Breuer's succinct and chaste modernism is architecturally clearly a generation apart from Graves's classically spirited and romantic, Post-Modern extension. The pastel colors, columned arcades, and upper floors spanning old and new, are an impassioned and romantic vision constituted from classically inspired elements. If form is relative to scale, and it most clearly is, the scale of Graves's extension relative to Breuer's original remains its most disturbing aspect. In subsequent revisions of his first design, Graves has endeavored to make it less contentious for hard-core modernists, somewhat compromising the design's original impact.

■ Michael Graves, Whitney Museum of American Art, Scheme 1, 1984 *(Photo: Paschall/Taylor)*

■ Michael Graves, Whitney Museum of American Art, Scheme 3, 1988 *(Photo: Paschall/Taylor)*

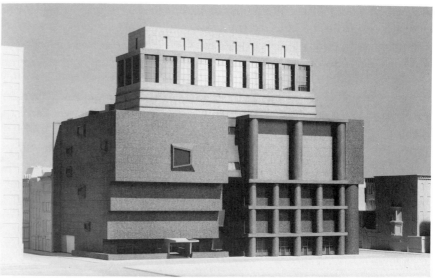

Johnson/Burgee's museum at Corpus Christi was designed to accommodate the more nebulous needs of a community arts center, rather than exhibit spaces to house a permanent collection. It is a sequence of spatially defined rooms expressed on the exterior as a loose arrangement of irregular, hard-edged, and angular white masses. The principal upper level gallery is approached across a long bridge which traverses a main hall, a versatile exhibit space experienced from various levels and viewpoints. The functional attitude is based on one of the central themes of Johnson's work, "the organization of procession," where processionalism is the drama and control of sequential movement relative to spaces that themselves have geometric and architectural definition.

Johnson/Burgee, Art Museum of South Texas, Corpus Christi, 1972 *(Photos: Ezra Stoller)*

The Johnson Museum at Cornell University by I. M. Pei & Partners is a teaching facility containing study and storage reference areas for individual research, lecture, lounge areas, meeting rooms, and public gallery space. The site, a grassy knoll with sweeping, panoramic views, led to a vertical design where the various elements are separated and strongly articulated within the building's overall rectangular mass. The lounge and study gallery areas at a projecting fifth floor level create a "cornice" plane that aligns with the older

■ I. M. Pei & Partners, Johnson Museum, Cornell University, Ithaca, New York, 1973 *(Photo: Cornell University, Russell C. Hamilton)*

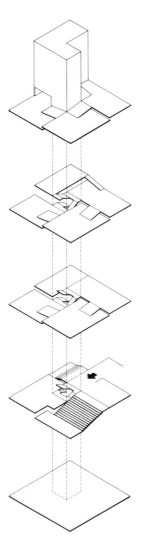

buildings of the campus, while the open sculpture terrace above the building's 2-story entrance lobby creates an overall mass which, while forming a visual edge to a campus quadrangle does so through a volume that is visually penetrable and therefore seeks to retain the campus character of extended landscape vista.

The Walker Arts Center, designed by Edward Larrabee Barnes, another 6-story structure, is a cluster of boxes veneered with plum-colored brick on the exterior, enclosing white-on-white, airy in feeling, and more anonymous loft spaces with varying ceiling heights for changing exhibits. Galleries ascend in a three-plane pinwheel plan connected by a broad staircase where landings are the galleries, an organization that permits a variety of vantage points of the works of art. The spatial organization is continuous more in the spirit of the Guggenheim without the liability of continually sloping planes and the absence of defined spaces, yet more spatially interconnected and sequential than the Whitney's loft exhibit galleries.

■ Edward Larrabee Barnes, Walker Arts Center, Minneapolis, 1969–1971 *(Photo: Walker Arts Center)*

Louis Kahn's Yale Center for British Art, based on a repetitive 20-foot-square grid, was formally conceived as a series of highly structured "roomlike" spaces. Organized around two inner courts which, like the fourth and top floor, are beautifully naturally lighted from above through a coffered skylight system, the whole ambiance of the building is rich, seductive, and well-scaled to the mainly eighteenth and early nineteenth century paintings. The exposed concrete structure with oak paneled inserts has led to a warmer, more sedate

■ Louis Kahn, Yale Center for British Art, New Haven, Connecticut, 1969–1974
(Photos: Paul Heyer)

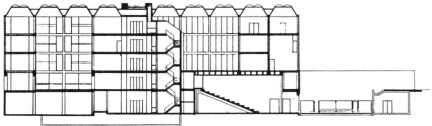

feeling, appropriate to the art displayed. As Kahn asked himself questions about light to the interior he made openings in planes, as he broached questions of exhibit he devised systems to place planes in space.

The preceeding examples clearly indicate the need for a response to the subtle nuances of different functional needs and character of sites. They demonstrate how another level of design consciousness is engaged immediately when the architect leaves the strict programming of functional requirements, and how the architect must have convictions and an objective, where the act of design itself extends function. The moment the architect places people in space, a social program begins to be defined; as circulation is considered the thought is to translate movement into experience; as history is regarded as continuity of process, the adaption of form becomes the precedent for form.

How the architect "sees" function and uses it as an organizing device is elemental in any function-to-form equation. In a building type such as a museum, restraints and interpretations are more of a self-imposed nature than problem implied, or function is an adjunct of an architect's sense of art. Looking to buildings in history, of essence what remains is their art. We can never truly feel the function because we are not a part of that civilization. We see building as a reduction to the essential of the idea where the abstract quality is of more concern than the preciseness of function. Function as a departure and not conclusion is the lesson of history. Form, however, is not, or should not be, arbitrary or whimsical but should derive directly from architectural elements—physical and intellectual elements that are, in themselves, response to and expression of purpose and hierarchy of movement that both articulates divisions and unites elements. It is unnatural to separate functions with a planner's mentality into "conveniently" manageable packages when the architectural context demands definition in terms of pertinently abstract relationships. All forms of life are based on growth, change, and the variable, the complex and interdependent. Function must find form expression in relationships that can incorporate such interactions. This does not mean that every design has to result in a highly animated and overall variable building form. Where a building naturally contains varying elements, even to services and equipment that are an essential part of its function, the architect can express these and may use them where appropriate to reinforce the architectural image, as in the Pompidou Center by Renzo Piano and Richard Rogers. However, in the personal search for formal relationship and a certain clarity and control, the architect, again in the desire to express a sense of organization, might move to clarify complexity without its negation. But, where a structure is a repetition of elements, for example, the cellular in nature apartment building, the design challenge becomes the control yet enrichment of a repetitive expression without falling into monotony. The Casa Mila, an apartment building in Barcelona by Antonio Gaudi, is a natural amplification of the potential in the manipulation of repetitive elements, or form generating naturally from a sophisticated understanding of function.

Whereas certain structures can be focal in the urban matrix because of their significance and associative importance and their symbolism can be more uniquely expressive, the majority of buildings are "background" in

■ Renzo Piano and Richard Rogers, Pompidou Center, Paris, 1977 *(Photo: John Pile)*

nature and establish urban continuity and cohesion and it is not appropriate for these to become too expressionistic. Where there is a strong common denominator to buildings, it is perfectly natural for them to develop similarities. Arbitrary variety in the inner organization of a transient occupancy office building is obviously senseless. Historically, architecture has always progressed based on form ideas that have been capable of repetition. It is also easier to permit change and flexibility within more repetitive and anonymous frameworks. Townhouses in the elegant crescents of England to the brownstones of New York, originally conceived as one-family residences, have remained viable as a form in that they have been capable of adaption to new demands, from conversion to multiple dwellings, or to professional spaces. The recycled shell of a structure itself even brings a unique atmosphere, context, and potential to the new idea of adapted use, which can also be very supportive of an architect's creative intent. This is a further instance where the attitude to functional expression is tempered by factors beyond strict use consideration.

Associative ideas of expression and symbolism can also derive from the analysis of purpose. The Fire Station at Corning by Gunnar Birkerts & Associates is inspired by such a *sense* of function. "I am not imposing a form on a program," says Birkerts, "I am trying to symplify it through finding relationships that mesh." The triangular form was prompted by the housing of different size fire engines for fast exit. With the facade treatment of polished fire-engine-red metal panels, aluminum checkerplate base, stainless steel coping, and red gyrolights that flash at the corners to signal an emergency, the image of the analogy is both obvious and playful. Located in a barren floodplain, the building becomes a minimalist object expressive of a highly stylized, distilled, machine aesthetic. In a positive sense, its symbolism is a continual visual reassurance of functional efficiency to the community.

■ Gunnar Birkerts and Assoc., Fire Station, Corning, New York, 1973 *(Photo: Paul Chu Lin)*

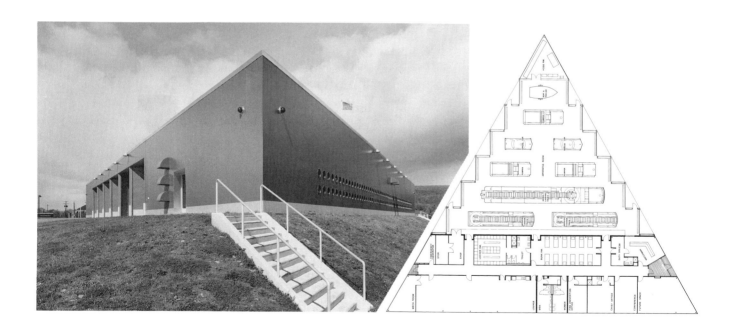

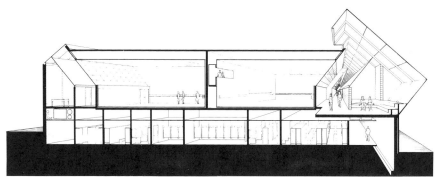

■ Gunnar Birkerts and Assoc., Dance Instructional Facility, Purchase, New York, 1971 *(Photos: Joseph W. Molitor)*

Rather than any notions of symbolism, in the Dance Instructional Facility at Purchase by Birkerts, it is the simple, yet strong linear organization of the plan and the introduction of direct and reflected light to the interior that becomes the building's expressive force. Two skylight circulation spines, visible in the exterior design, angular in profile and running the buildings length are both organizing device and character element. Studios are illuminated by indirectly reflected light from a tilted plane in the corridor spine that also forms the roof of office spaces. This tilted plane is paralleled by an outward canting glass plane which, while admitting light, also adds form interest to the studios' rectangular interiors. Function almost resolves as planes in space as are dancers choreographed in motion.

In these buildings by Birkerts function is *used* as an organizing tool and although there is a certain integrity of structure there is no particular allegiance to it. The dominant thought is one of *overall* organization and this is a major filtering notion in questions of function in today's architecture. But still it is not organization imposed as in classical architecture and the turn of the century Beaux Arts approach, but organization emerging out of considera-

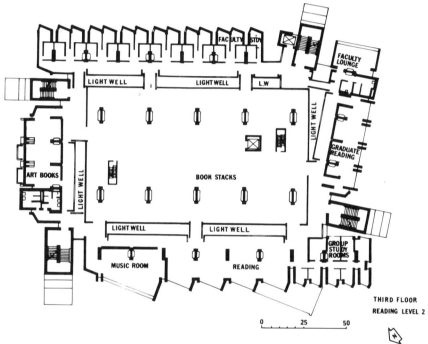

LIGHT WELL   LIGHT WELL   L.W
FACULTY STDY
FACULTY LOUNGE
LIGHT WELL
GRADUATE READING
ART BOOKS
LIGHT WELL
BOOK STACKS
LIGHT WELL   LIGHT WELL
MUSIC ROOM   READING
GROUP STUDY ROOMS

THIRD FLOOR
READING LEVEL 2

0   25   50

■ John Johansen, Goddard Library, Clark University, Worcester, Massachusetts, 1970 (Photo: George Cserna)

tions for the variable elements of a building. Concepts that are a response of poetic license rather than literal truth.

John Johansen also thinks of building as the organization of parts and a synthesis in the ordering of programs, but in his architecture the elements are freely assembled and the design process is one that the architect presides over rather than uses to pursue a predetermined idea. Control is to assemble and combine rather than discipline and refine. "Vitality is sought after," says Johansen, "architectural composition is given little concern." Although the architecture appears machinelike, there is no attempt to "look like a machine," but merely to reflect its principles of organization, with the accommodation strongly based on expressed methods of construction. Johansen's approach is one of space as enclosure, connection as access, and support as structure, where imagery, hopefully, is an expression of these and the flexible design process through which they are combined.

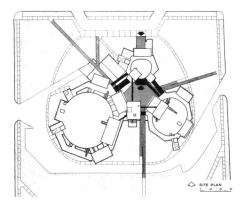

SITE PLAN

■ John Johansen, Mummers Theater,
Oklahoma City, 1969–1970 *(Photo:
Balthazar Korab)*

The Goddard Library at Clark University was for Johansen the beginning
of the idea of an accretion of noncompositional forms, of "rigging instead of
composition." A central element is flanked on each side by four different
structural configurations where the horizontal layering of varied elements fits
within a vertically uniform structure. Although the combinations are loose and
the consequent building expression quite variable, the antiperfection, anti-
masterwork philosophy when literally applied becomes suspect in light of the
skillful resolution of design aspects of the library. As the late critic Sibyl
Moholy-Nagy stated, "There is nothing accidental, haphazard, unresolved in
these side-views. They are simply excellent design."

With the Mummers Theater in Oklahoma, referred to by Johansen as a
"fragment, not a building," structure, function, and circulation are referenced
by more fanciful electronic terminology. Components (the functional elements) have attached subcomponents where the attachment is intended to
modify or extend the effectiveness of that function: structure, as in the electronic framework, is referred to as a chassis: circuitry is the connection and
services. Whereas in the Beaux Arts, circulation was expressed by a hierarchy
of movement systems of different widths and prominence according to the
importance and amount of traffic and organized with respect to centrality and
balance, Johansen's movement notion is one of tubes that support flow. Spaces
are static, tubes express movement. The architecture is "anti-geometric, deals
with the imperfect—never design elevations, they are a resultant of a system of
building—you feel proud of having found your way by discovering you have to
find your way, you are part of a process as you complete it," says Johansen. The
theater is an overlay of five circuit systems performing separate roles each

■ Johansen & Bhavnani, Staten Island Community College proposal, New York, 1975

disregarding the organization of the other. The first and uppermost, the distribution of chilled water from the cooling tower; next, theater goer tubes connecting lobbies to auditoriums: then bridges connecting sidewalks to public gardens; then automobile circulation connecting to parking entrances, and the fifth and lowest layer, basement corridors connecting understage areas.

As the Archigram group in the sixties in London explored notions of "clip-on and plug-in" architecture as a more realistic and functional response to the need for change, flexibility, and growth within the format of buildings, in the Staten Island Community College design, Johansen & Bhavnani endeavored to move beyond the early Clark Library and Mummers Theater premise to an architecture even more an accretion of elements both fixed and clipped-on, a grouping and assembling of parts, a reshuffling and finally in the search for a "kinetic" architecture, the movement of parts: "Take out a plane of glass and plug in an element." Where elements in the Clark Library were moved only in the process of design, the intent in the community college is that elements can be moved after the building is completed. Taken at a broader planning level, the importance of this approach is that the theory becomes one of generalized structure, functionally supported by and in turn supporting an accretion of changing, connected elements where, ideally, there is no distinction between architecture and urban design. Design determination is more open-ended, changeable and accommodating of subsequent additions rather than predetermined and geometrically excluding by virtue of organizations of complete and finite geometry.

To consider architecture at place in an environment and as an extension of its context is again to extend any concept of function to a more encompassing level. Varying functions are combined, or reconciled, to achieve a higher purpose and more encompassing sense of scale, where literal function is hardly the direct route to form. In Le Corbusier's 1930s Algiers Plan, for example, apartment buildings were proposed above and below a major highway snaking through the landscape, where the rhythm and speed of movement itself became the suggestive and cohesive design system. The notion of several different functions and different movement systems unified within one essential framework—a megastructure—is a level of complexity in architecture that is basically a product of the drive toward urbanization of the last century. Functional compatibility and reconciliation is the design prerequisite. Within highly variable structures great potential exists for space itself to inspire activity. A culture creates new functions, for which we create new spaces, which in turn suggests new forms, as for example the shopping gallerias of Europe, which became precedent for the late twentieth century climatically controlled shopping malls of North America.

As the architect looks to expand and heighten a sense of function within a structure the vehicle to this end is space and the concern is the psychological implications of the use of space. Gathering in a church is hence more than the act of assembly. The intent is to elevate and dignify the act of worship, which at its most eloquent expresses an essence of religion: Then, space is symbolic, ambiance and memorability. Space is also attitude, and this has developed through history. The pyramids of Egypt were elemental geometric forms on a flat landscape. The Greeks, in a sense, inverted the Egyptian temple, surrounded the walled cell with columns thereby animating the exterior temple form, again developing powerful external relationships. The spatial concern was primarily that of the interplay or visual tension created in the relationship of static volumes. The Romans, however, started to give emphasis to the hollowed-out interior volume. The exterior form of the Pantheon in Rome resulted from the dominance of the centralized space within manifesting itself as exterior form. The continuity of interior space was highly developed in the Middle Ages, only limited by techniques of masonry and the subordinate idea of our relationship to our world. In the Renaissance and Baroque periods, form deriving from inner space was carried to a sophisticated degree of refinement. As we moved under the dome in the Renaissance and occupied the central space, so the walls pushed outward during the Baroque period as we gained a new sense of awareness and self-determination. Such enriching of complex space was only to be surpassed as a result of our present structural possibilities and a more subjective questioning of our own role as twentieth century shapers of space.

Architects began a major break with the past when they started exploring the relationship of volume, space, and transparency rather than depending upon mass and solidity as means of expression. The potential for a new architecture was born. The Industrial Revolution, the most explosive and formative development in the entire history of architecture provided the means to this vision, one consonant with its own intrinsic potential—and imagery.

It was a vision that painters had begun to explore too. At the beginning of the twentieth century, exterior and interior space became the interpenetration of continually flowing space. The single viewpoint of perspective that had dominated art and architecture since the start of the fifteenth century was superceded by the recognition of the implications of a three-dimensional comprehension of space with asymmetrically related forms and volumes that could be appreciated from multiple vantage points. The perception of space was no longer a passive transfer of images but an organic process where motion and mass itself initiated a way of perceiving and experiencing. The Cubist painters pursued this idea at the beginning of this century. Picasso's *Les Demoiselles d'Avignon*, painted in 1907, freed pictorial space from any limitations of time sequence. Cezanne in his still lifes, sensitive to the weight of an object and its ability to break the line of the supporting plane, sought not a fractured cubist vision as seen through a prism or crystal but a dividing of planes and of imagery in response to volumes as a more thoughtful and decisive control of form. Solid objects were painted transparently, overlapped and fragmented to represent simultaneously their external and internal appearance. By showing an object from several viewpoints at once, the dimension of time was introduced.

While the Cubists explored space penetration, the Futurists sought to dramatically represent the idea of forces in motion through the simultaneity of movement. Although Umberto Boccioni was the leading painter and sculptor of this movement, it was Marcel Duchamp, closer in spirit to their ideas but using Cubist forms, who was able to more powerfully state them. In his *Nude Descending the Staircase,* detachment and anonymity led to the expression of an unrecognizable, unidentifiable figure symbolizing an abstract figure in motion. At that time, the new science of photography allowed painters to technically capture motion as sequential, hence technology expands the artist's awareness and interpretation of his or her world.

In the early 1920s the Dutch De Stijl group brought art and architecture together within a universal aesthetic principle and gave potent architectonic expression to the dynamic fluency of space. The elemental simplicity of the geometric abstractions of Theo Van Doesburg and Piet Mondrian pursuing form and color relationships more forcefully demonstrated the new spirit as they moved painting and architecture far away from derivative involvements with history or representations of nature. Overlapping planes were suggestive of space without a seeming conscious effort to form space in the classically contained and defined sense. Frank Lloyd Wright's Robie House, built in 1909, with its interest in the interlocking of masses, intersection of planes and interpenetration of space was suggestive of an idea to be realized in the 1920s by Rietveld designing the Schröder House in Utrecht in an expression more compatible with the machine in the open, light, airy, and transparent aesthetic of the De Stijl.

■ Frank Lloyd Wright, Robie House, Chicago, 1909 *(Photo: Museum of Modern Art, New York)*

■ Gerrit Rietveld, Schröder House, Utrecht, Holland, 1924

Attitudes have developed out of this new sensibility that have led us to highly variable and divergent ideas as to form and the shaping of space. Today our concept is of a complex and panoramic space-form potential of which the "hotel" architecture of John Portman is one example. In the focal space of the hotel, Portman has created a contemporary version of the grand salon, sustained by the lively bric-a-brac of light, color, and especially visible movement-mechanical elements, architectural forms, and people on levels that have made his hotels a commercial and popular success. In these central spaces Portman has progressively moved into richer and more flamboyant plays of forms, developed always within geometrically predictable envelopes. The Hyatt Regency Hotel of 1967 in Atlanta, the foreunner of Portman's hotels with the theatricalized central atrium as the organizing element, is a simple rectangular focal space ringed by hotel rooms rising the full height of the building. The Embarcadero Center in San Francisco has rooms converging on one of its sides, which is also staggered inward toward the roof skylight, dramatically narrowing and changing the overall form of the central space. As the central space subsequently became more compact in projects it has become enriched. The Peachtree Plaza in Atlanta has its hotel rooms organized into a single and more conventionally compact tower, "sitting" on ten circular columns penetrating a 7-story base where the central space is terraced outward to skylights, again to bathe the atrium in natural light and dramatize the circular shaft in the square opening. The central space at the Renaissance Center in Detroit is a multifunctional and circulation core area that serves as a focus for the cylindri-

■ John Portman, Hyatt Regency Hotel, Atlanta, 1967

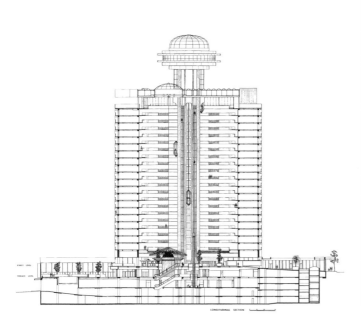

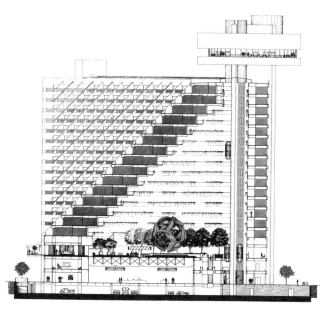

■ John Portman, Hyatt Regency Hotel, Embarcadero Center, San Francisco, 1974 *(Photo: Alexandre Georges)*

■ John Portman, Peachtree Plaza Hotel, Atlanta, 1976

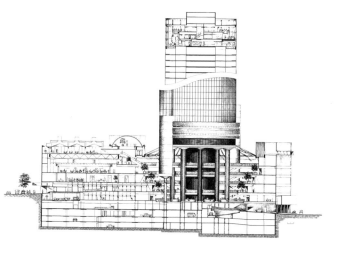

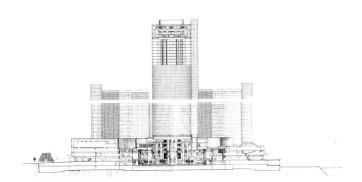

cal central hotel tower and its four flanking office towers. The highly orchestrated play of interlocking form is here expressive of what Portman refers to as his "natural evolution toward Baroque space." The intent is to create space that will be lively, exciting and appealing, within an organizational idea that comprises straightforward configurations, balanced relationships, and repetition of form.

The concept of Renaissance space was of essence clear, organizationally "clean" and, upon knowing the placement rationale, basically predictable. The sequential image and experience that forms and reforms as we move around and through it was basic to the defined, related sequence of carefully disciplined and geometrically phrased spaces. This, too, was the Beaux Arts approach to design. Louis Kahn, firmly schooled in this tradition in his formative design years in Philadelphia, a sensibility that was to remain with him and become increasingly dominant in his later years, was able to draw strength and profundity out of this tradition as he moved beyond the frozen attitudes of the past to a manipulation of forms and elements codified into lyrical totalities where the whole became a flow, leak, penetration, and definition of geometric space. The organization of Kahn's buildings did not subjugate space, function, and structure to patterns; rather configurations evolved from these measures as space was born in a new image of traditional or timeless notions. Space and form organizations were monumental but not remorseless, abstract yet not detached. Kahn's site plan for the Indian Institute of Management in Ahmadabad, a business college on a 66-acre site, is an organization of disciplined geometry,

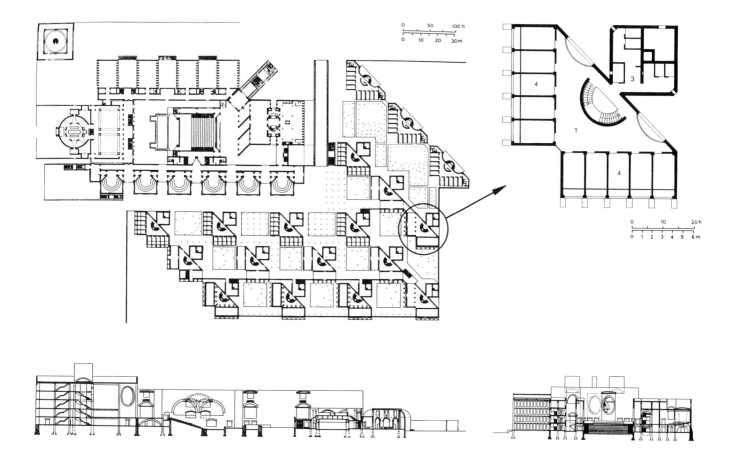

where buildings to catch the breezes are pierced and interlocked, achieving "tight" configurations of exterior and interior related spaces. "Free-flowing lines are most fascinating. The pencil and the mind secretly want to make them exist," said Kahn. "A stricter geometry lends itself to direct calculation and puts aside the willful particular, favoring simplicity of structure and space, good for its continuing use in time." With Kahn, space was always under strong control and, especially in his larger scale projects such as the Indian Institute, was conceived to be encircling and environmental rather than, as in classical buildings, more linear and directional. Further, function and space as form statement became dramatized through notions of transparency, with the use of "screen" walls to shade and protect and break the sun in front of walls to define occupied space, where natural light and its changing effect within the inner volume of a building would enhance space as a sequence that impels one forward, arouses the curiosity, and instills anticipation. Psychologically changes of pace are reinforced, the aspect of surprise and variable character heightened. Spaces are in light and conversely light is in space.

Concepts of Baroque space, while focusing on elements both in enclosing mass and defined space, sought a more gentle and sensuous flow of space companioned with the desire for the more mysterious rather than tightly articulated. Paul Rudolph's buildings are an expression of this idea. His work opens up new vistas in that he seeks to preserve complexity in a building and indeed uses it as the vehicle to architectural expression. His method is to relate space loosely yet quite positively in a powerful and highly variable drama.

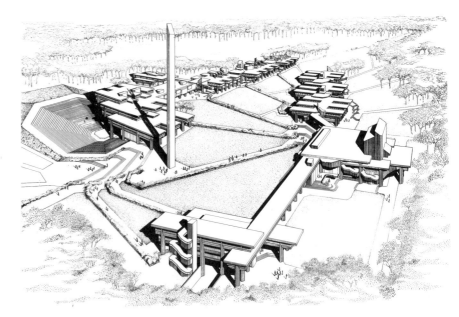

■ Paul Rudolph, coordinating architect, Southeastern Massachusetts University, North Dartmouth, Massachusetts, 1963

Rudolph is far removed from any classic intent. Whereas Mies tried in an open volume to give the suggestion of function in space around and between free-standing space dividers, and antithetically Kahn used geometry in a classically poised way to bring a quite different and more visually structured order of clarity to his architecture, Rudolph projects loosely defined volumes of space into larger, also loosely defined volumes of space which the smaller volumes in turn partly define, the whole brought together in very personal terms and expressed in the exterior fractured sculptural mass of the total composition. Explicit control of function and clarity of structure is replaced by the location and character of space as the organization method.

At the Southeastern Massachusetts University, within an evenly spaced and strongly articulated structural system which incorporates much of the building's mechanical systems into its hollow column centers, Rudolph interlocks vertical and horizontal circulation combined with projecting balconies and seating areas for a strongly orchestrated, variable and dynamic sequence of space that breaks to the exterior, almost seeming to slide out between the

■ Paul Rudolph, Earl W. Brydges Library for the City Niagara Falls, New York, 1969–1972 (Photo: Donald Luckenbill)

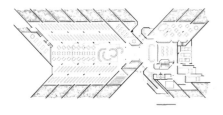

vertically ribbed structure. The projection and recession of elements, a vigorous surface modeling within the strongly expressed, vertical lines of structure, creates a powerful variety in a large complex of buildings whose basic organization is essentially repetitive. The central open area continues the flow of space as in a gentle and broad, radial spiral of terraced planes it fans downward and outward to distant views of trees and a lake.

In the Central Library at Niagara Falls a diagonal flow of space controls the building's entire configurations in plan, section, and exterior form, where each is in spirit a reflection of the other. The diagonal planes of the building's structure slope inward as its mass progressively diminishes through its three floors, reflecting a subdued quality of glare-free light off the sloping planes to the interior. A cleverly conceived clerestory system introduces a further type of light to the building's 3-story central core space while also dynamically punctuating the broadly sloping exterior roof plane of the building.

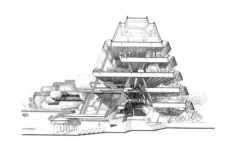

■ Paul Rudolph, Burroughs Wellcome, North Carolina, 1970–1972 *(Photo: Joseph W. Molitor)*

The dynamics of diagonal, tapered space are further explored in the more complex program for the corporate headquarters of Burroughs Wellcome. Here, within the diagonal movement of interior space, Rudolph says that "growth and change is implicit in the concept. It is the idea of a building never finished where one can pull out parts." Architecturally it is a delineated and tightly resolved attitude that, in spirit at least, somewhat parallels that of Johansen's more "as-built," loosely conceived and less-seemingly-manipulated and open-ended approach. The building's diagonal volume is an upward extension to the crest of a ridge on which it is built. The set back floors allow a continuous system of skylights at each floor to pull light deep into interior spaces while enabling ceiling heights to be raised to fifteen feet at the building's exterior edges, increasing the sense of space in movement within the interior. As the linear planes of the building are bunched in an end expression of solid, shifting, tubelike elements, they visually evoke the idea of modular elements, although in fact they are the product of conventional steel frame construction. The grouping and combining of modular elements as an expression of a technological capability, a sound idea if one not so economically possible in reality, is a notion that continues to preoccupy Rudolph and in many ways gives impetus to the shifting planes that impinge upon rather than elementally define space.

A further and quite different notion of the manipulation of space, one that embodies through simpler means a complexity that incorporates appropriate "contradiction" is evidenced in the architecture of Robert Venturi. Spaces are organized not on an abstract order like Kahn's, but are more flexibly manipulated for humanist, functional, associative, and less monumental reasons. Although elements are given suggestion of formal disposition, they are loosely manipulated and gently plied rather than formally controlled. Their monumentalism is not that of Kahn's classical vision and tight, lyrical play and counterplay of geometrics, but a monumentalism that grows out of an august seriousness that, while it incorporates inferences of forms and elements past, does it with seeming spartan awareness. Architecture appears systematic but again the geometry is quite apart from any purist theory or organizationally disciplining control. Elements such as windows are of modest scale and freely placed for functional reason rather than as the result of a design approach or infilling a structurally defining framework. At times the placement, because it does not subscribe to immediately obvious rules, seems often perverse in its outward lack of organization. Indicative of this is the small house for the architect's mother by Venturi & Short. Its antecedent, with its nooks, small grouping of elements, stair wrapping upward and around an overscaled central fireplace and mouldings applied to infer further shifts of scale and breaking and definition of building plane, lies in the tradition of the "sheltering" houses of the Shingle style. As if by contradiction, though, the house is stuccoed and its angled and ascending roof line is interlocked and cut in echoes of a Palladian past that create its detached, monumental presence. Says Venturi, "It contains things within things in plan: an interior multiplicity

distorted to fit its rigid bounds and forced to accommodate its exterior symmetry. It contains things behind things in elevation: an interior multiplicity appropriate for a house protruding beyond the parapets of its two parallel walls and manifesting itself in the irregular positions of its windows." As Rudolph uses the built elements of architecture to heighten the drama of function in space, Venturi looks for a more flexible, eclectic and incorporative conceptual base for his designs.

Charles Moore's architecture is an overtly playful and an even more referential variation than the Venturi theme. He looks beyond questions of space, form and organization, more expressly for image. Where Venturi's inspiration has Pop art overtones in its insights and juxtapositions, Moore creates more spontaneous and intuitive in feeling, stage-set allusions. "A good house," he says, "is of the intangible rhythms, spirits, and dreams of people's lives. Its site is only a tiny piece of the real world, yet this place is made to seem like an entire world." The Burns House in Los Angeles is in the spirit of the colonial style architecture of Southern California, yet architecturally it is also a composite of slant-roofed forms that also evoke the imagery of the New England shingle house and the Italian hill town villas. Like the house for Venturi's mother it is finished in stucco for a more monolithic appearance which, coincidentally, evokes a more "faded" villalike impression. The winding stair becomes a device for overlapped and sensed spaced; an implication of flow rather than a simple notion of circulation. The client's baroque pipe organ became a focal element as the major living space was conceived around it. Again, furnishings and decor are eclectic, as personalization, response to lifestyle, and client interests and idiosyncracies become the impetus beyond any synthesis of uniformity. It is the incorporation and collaging of elements that is a formidably significant shift of focus from the more succinct attitudes of the earlier modernist tradition.

Kahn and Venturi, both in their own way were also looking to explore beyond the leaner synthesis that the modern movement had been impelled

■ Charles W. Moore with Richard Chylinski, Burns House, Los Angeles, 1972–1974
(Photos: Charles W. Moore)

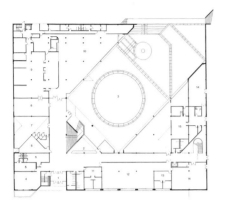

toward as its reductive appropriateness came to be shackled by economic imperative, were the leaders of the so-named Philadelphia School of the 1960s. Romaldo Giurgola, the next most celebrated member of the 'school' in importance, closer in kin to Kahn's classicism probably by virtue of his Italian heritage, is a bridge between their interests. The purist notions remain by virtue of the elegant detail, formal clarity, and geometry as design device, yet present, too, is the notion that different programs imply different solutions that demand complex resolution in the design process and, in confrontation, shift the emphasis from ideology to more elemental questions of program resolution and the method of building. The allusions to historic traditions are there but within a context that is unequivocably modern. The Student Union at the State University College at Plattsburg, with a central courtyard dynamically breaking into its rectangular overall form from one corner, and the Tredyffrin

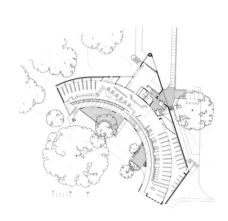

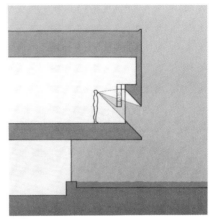

Public Library in Strafford, a gracefully curved building opening through a freestanding arching arcade for sun protection onto a southern parklike setting, are rich examples of this harmony. Function and building method become impetus and geometry which in turn become the medium to form. "Form must not be confused with shape," aptly states Giurgola in Kahnsian overtones! "Form resists time, shapes are transient and ephemeral."

In a similar spirit, Birkerts in the Law Building at the University of Iowa and the Museum of Glass at Corning develops designs based on the different possibilities inherent in the purest geometric form, the circle. To Birkerts the circle means "concentration; study and seclusion, it maintains its affinity with the universe and the law of the universe." A characteristic of the circle is its competeness as a form, its absence of sides and ignorance of exposure. Birkerts deals with this by bedding the large limestone and metal trimmed form into the top of a sloping site by cutting away from the circle. He also cuts away at the building's upper levels to form indentations thereby bringing sun and light into the interior volume while responding to internal functional dispositions. Where exploiting the completeness of the circle is elemental to the Law

■ Gunnar Birkerts and Assoc., The Corning Museum of Glass, Corning, New York, 1976–1980 *(Photo: Balthazar Korab)*

■ Gunnar Birkerts and Assoc., University of Iowa College of Law, Iowa City, Iowa, 1979–1986 *(Photo: University of Iowa)*

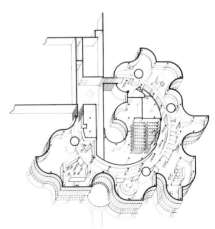

■ I. M. Pei & Partners, East Building, National Gallery of Art, Washington, D.C., 1971–1978 *(Exterior elevation photo: Ezra Stoller)*

Building, the Museum of Glass, a flowing extension to an existing building, wraps a central circular form with an exterior glass membrane of basically interlocked quarter circles. Fluid when molten, structured and crystalline when solid, Birkerts appropriately exploits these characteristics of glass while also cleverly dealing with its liabilities as an exterior skin: The exhibit floor has two bands of 45-degree angled mirror terminating in a continuous band of clear glass, above which the exterior wall is surfaced in an opaque, reflective glass skin—material and geometry, detail and section, function and attitude deriving from the idea of glass itself.

The clarity and power of form that is beyond shape is eloquently manifest in the National Gallery of Art in Washington, D.C. designed by I. M. Pei & Partners. It is a persuasive reiteration in the style we have come to identify as

"modern classicism," of the power of geometry coupled with streamlined logic to create a reductive and lucid architecture. As such it is a powerful statement of one of the positions of architecture today—at its elegant, and cool, abstract parameter. Totally modern, engineered and monolithic in its taut interlocks, it is classic to the full extent that modern architecture can parallel the classic intent of the monuments of history in detail, organization, clarity of designating idea and, without a strong functional determination, organizational synthesis. Its restraint and rigor is the antithesis of Paris's Pompidou Center. Yet both persuasively express aesthetically the vastly different potential of twentieth century engineering and building methods. The concept of the National Gallery is embodied in a geometry as bold as it is simple. The awkward trapezoidal site is cut into two triangles, the larger isosceles triangle—whose major axis appropriately lines up with the main axis of the original West Building, housing the main exhibition spaces—and the smaller slender triangle—with its unequivocably modern 20-degree knifelike edge—contains the reading and study center. A third triangle, overlaying and connecting the former two, forms a huge tetrahedronal space-frame skylight over a multilevel central court. A geometry derived from the initial site logic is here rationally elevated to the total disciplining method of approach.

It would be impossible to deny the importance of geometry as an organizing medium that has been a catalyst toward lucid form configurations and a richness in the concept of space. It has been particularly a major force in architecture since the early sixties. Geometry, as the modern movement has been reassessed in the search for a richer synthesis, not to create shape as we have seen, but as an idea to articulate function and to open up form. Geometry not to create patterns of circulation, but to interlock systems of movement in space and the relationship of planes to define that movement both literally and visually, while also dynamically juxtaposing forms in space. Within a broadly based and different aesthetic intent, the previous examples illustrate the pertinence of geometry used as a tool to stimulate presence within a building as opposed to repeat overdone predeterminations of shape. Clearly, the curving line or the shifting plane moving in space can be both a gracious and aggressive statement of dynamic motion; as a continuous connective it has the power to evoke a functional suggestion of space that has gone, with consequence, beyond the simple overlapping of the De Stijl aesthetic of the early days of the modern movement. High technology with its sophisticated implications of communication has likewise moved us away from the narrowness of the defined space. Today, an arena for machinery can replace the salon for discussion.

The idea of using the delineation and definition of sequence in space, then going beyond it to embrace the implied has become one of our most potent avenues of contemporary expression. The architect can start the design process with a clear geometric form and gradually cut away and shift the exterior membrane as interior space is shaped, where at the design conclusion the original exterior geometry does not in reality exist. Only the sense of the beginning remains to give an implied clarity, which in its complexity poses a richer hypothesis than the usually more elemental form of the design's origin.

The Futurists and Expressionists proposed a vision of the world that provoked us to see what might be. What is, is invariably of essence more interesting than what might be simply because it *is*, and by simple implication has to work and challenge response. And in the end this is the reality of function: Purpose as space, or, more important, purpose in space, sequence and implied idea in space, it remains in essence one of the most potent initiatives to architecture.

3

Structure, Technology, and the New Means

■ ARCHITECTURE HISTORICALLY WAS a "from the ground upward, element upon element" form of building producing essentially indigenous structures. This seemingly durable tradition was dislocated by the excitement of employing new technological possibilities, companioned by the advent of a "new worlds" inevitable drive toward industrialization. In the light of the clear and pristine image of modernism, handcrafted and traditional aspects of building seemed antiquated and, in terms of a new vision, to a large degree inappropriate. As we now strive to find greater sensitivity to materials and building methods, a sense of individual worth and to reestablish a basic relationship with archetypal forms, we have gravitated into a revisionist period that questions the dependence upon our technology or indeed any brave new world vision. We have learned by hard experience this past half century that there are no panaceas.

The appeal of craft architecture is that it is indigenous and based upon what is directly possible with natural materials. Its persuasion is as an alternative to the grinding anonymity of universality: the fallacious idea that anything can be all things to all people, in any time or place. Its strength is local resources used in a natural—traditional—manner, the immediacy of effort transmitting a pertinence and effortlessness: a building precise for location with material, texture, and color responding to and becoming environment, harmony deriving from continuity. Our instinct is to feel comfortable when seeing the "touch of the hand."

Architecture has always gained expression from its measurable content. It displays, or basically should, logic of technique. But the world of architecture today is a more complex synthesis than that of the traditional craft world because, pressured by great economic, social, and political forces, we have moved beyond the capacity of the craft world's potential to be responsive at our vast urban scale. For the architect, too, new means derived from advanced technology have created structural and technological possibilities unknown before. This presents the challenge of trying to employ these new means in a manner that is pertinent locally and in a spirit that recognizes the individuality of human need and effort.

Where preindustrial society found its inspiration in the natural craft world, ours understandably finds its stimulus in our scientific mechanical one: The major historical shift in our culture in the last century has been the influence of technology, undeniably one of the fundamental forces at work in our time. As we struggle to provide for our increased mobile and urbanized population that avariciously devours the natural landscape and despoils the environment, it appears to be the only realistic means to engage our problems.

When the architect or craftsman, confronted with new problems on an expanded scale, denies the technological fact, the work is cast adrift from our main cultural force and consequently tends to lack immediacy, certainly with respect to our problems. There is evidence that even the craftsman is trying to redefine a cultural role; to see an exquisitely hand-finished wood version of Eero Saarinen's 1953 plastic formed "Tulip" pedestal chair is a total cultural reversal. In the early technological era the machine was frequently used to copy the effect of handmade products but those were the days of search for a new language or expression. Clearly when the craftsman today tries to beat the machine at its own game there can only be questionable success. When the craftsman tries to use mind and hand to skillfully work *with* the machine, capability and effectiveness are dramatically extended.

The architect is often forced to look to a craft vision of architecture for inspiration rather than to the beautiful use of technological innovation. Pragmatics dictate this circumstance. We all too frequently find traditional methods to be the only means to cut construction costs and operate effectively within the framework of labor unions, labor skills, product availability, and that professional nemesis, insurance liability, where oft proven fact becomes plausible defense, even the last bastion of self-preservation. At a subjective level, we are all familiar with the marketplace attitude toward natural material as "warm" and the yearning for simpler and what now appear as more humanly scaled and conceived environments. Given the scale of our technology and its too frequent monotonous and insensitive application, it is easily understood why we would look back to simpler, supposedly more stable patterns and processes where individuality seemed present and secure—such emphasis is intrinsic to the Jeffersonian tradition. Having the means, however, should not necessarily make us the means. The classic symbol of mass depersonalization, the computer, has not only eliminated huge areas of mindless, dreary tasks, it has given us the power to synthesize facts and data in amounts and at speeds that were inconceivable a generation ago. The electronic calculator, inexpensive and as available as the toothbrush, fast and nonjudgmentally accurate has replaced the slide rule. Production methods, in changing the position of the traditional craftsman, have brought the promise of new potential if we can only more effectively bridge the gap between process and production, the designer and the machine.

A stunningly persuasive example of the power of early industrialized methodology to shape a new sense of space at a new scale was the Crystal Palace. Designed by Sir Joseph Paxton and built for London's great exhibition in 1851, it was a prefabricated and quickly erected structure at a huge scale. It

■ Joseph Paxton, Crystal Palace, London, 1851

had an airy transparency and machined elegance that was a beacon of technology to the Victorian age and clearly demonstrated that the beauty of the industrial process is based on two important ideas: that it has the potential to eliminate waste, and that it is entirely precise. In contrast to a handcraft architecture, it fits or it is wrong, it is exact and nonvariable with all that this architecturally implies. Extending this idea, each act of putting together of elements of itself suggests further and new contributions. The process suggests its own evolution. This notion of assembly is the route to a technological vernacular and its appropriate personalization.

Just as craft architecture developed its own sense of coherence out of limited means and construction techniques, so our architecture today can develop its own coherence and attitude out of technology and the preciseness of component assembly if we develop appropriate methods that respect materials and their structural and space-defining characteristics. Especially in the area of architecture where efforts are generally one-of-a-kind (buildings are not tested production line items like automobiles) with contained financial returns to the investor and where construction is generally financed by conservative banks, there is a considerable time lapse in the employ of new means. The space age is clearly advantaged over our building age when we consider application. But today we have a shift of potential in that science, technology, and industrialization have given architects the power to *lead* rather than follow its development.

In the past new materials and/or new methods led to new approaches to building design. When the Romans used wedges of stone to make an arch instead of flat beams of stones as lintels to span openings, a completely new space potential became possible. Our concrete and steel construction has allowed us to make similar great advances in the shaping of space. Our technology is such that new concepts can focus needs and we in turn can initiate methods and materials with new capabilities to realize them. This concept is built into industry in general rather than architecture in particular. Architecture clearly needs a formative research and development approach rather than a passive application role. Again, the exploration of space better demonstrates processes of attainable cause and effect. The absence of enough creative building research based on technological potential is one of the great shortcomings of modern architecture and it is a role that can never be sufficiently undertaken by the individual practitioner but requires the resources and power of our industry.

Historically we have had different attitudes toward the machine. In England in the 1860s William Morris led a strong movement back toward the handicrafts. Examples from this period and its subsequent influence are admired by many Post-Modernists today. The Futurists, with a singular, romanticized view, recognized the machine as a poetic life force. The Bauhaus saw in it a moral implication requiring social awareness; an instrument toward change, rather than an objective in itself.

The impact of the early modern movement came from the dramatization and contrast of technological potential with historical buildings. It gave many early modern buildings with a machined imagery a revolutionary feeling. In turn, it produced a variety of images and a new scale that brought a special

quality to the architecture of the twentieth century. The Johns Manville headquarters by The Architects Collaborative is such a building. It innovatively
employs long-span steel members whose weight is reduced by taking advantage of the plasticity of steel simultaneously with the composite action of steel
beams and concrete slabs for a direct and economical structure. The building
is clad in a beautifully detailed, prefabricated aluminum skin curtain wall that
enhances its simple, long and powerful form, it is dramatically—and reflectively—
placed right at the base of and against the natural backdrop of the foothills that
ring Denver. The parking of thirteen hundred cars is judiciously an intrinsic
part of the design as it is carved into tiered layers behind the building and
hidden from view on the roof of its long, low mass thereby helping to maintain
the singular presence of the uncompromised machined object. By not employing natural materials, it is clearly an architecture of contrast without any
intention of blending with the landscape.

For different reasons the sleek and polished-object-look of Johns Manville
is in contrast to the imagery of technological interlock of the Columbus Occupational Health Center by Hardy Holzman Pfeiffer Associates. Here, the
primary circulation defined by a skylit L-shaped spine is at a 45-degree angle
against the main building mass, while the exposed steel structure, with mechanical systems threaded through and suspended between, is overlapped again by
employing opposing geometry, an idea further dramatized through strong,
differentiating, and contrasting colors. The distinction between structure, infill
panels, and mechanical systems is the aesthetic device that leads to a strong
expression of the building's elements. The combination of overhead natural
light to the interior and the juxtaposition of black and mirrored glass at the

■ The Architects Collaborative, Johns
Manville Headquarters, Colorado, 1977
(Photo: © Nick Wheeler)

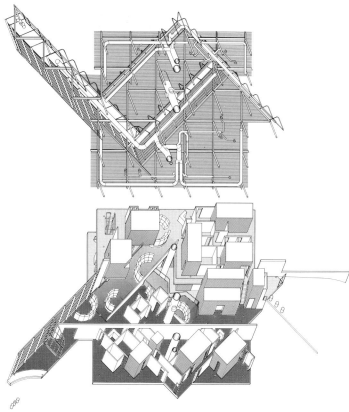

■ Hardy Holzman Pfeiffer Assoc.,
Columbus Occupational Health Center,
Columbus, Indiana, 1974 *(Photos: Norman
McGrath; isometric drawing: Robert Mangurian)*

exterior further changes the building's ambience from night to day. The Health Center's assembled, industrialized, and hybrid look is an example of directed spontaneity far apart from the Johns Manville building's technological yet classical-type refinement, yet both buildings are an effort toward a vernacular that seeks also to embody the durable values in architecture that can derive from and account to technological fact.

The architectural implication of advances in technology can also be illustrated in the way the architect responds to new means by in essence developing new form responses. In the case of materials, there is an inseparable relationship between material, structure, and form. In addition to searching within new problems for a new and pertinent sense of function and idea as it is the generator of form, the architect naturally seeks to express the intrinsic potential and characteristic of the material employed. Hence, the new building configurations that become indelibly associated with various epochs in history, of which Modern architecture is also rich. Our present-day glass structures have achieved configurations in their exterior membrane far away from the early historical stylistic vocabulary of the Crystal Palace. Such transparent, airy and clear span structures are just one of the dimensions of accomplishment in our epoch. In recent years their form has been both varied and potent of image.

Such a structure, employing glass on the grandest of scales, is the Garden Grove Community Church by Johnson & Burgee. Seating four thousand celebrants, it is a subaqueous environment—a reflective glass building allowing

■ Johnson & Burgee, Garden Grove Community Church, California, 1976

only 14 percent of heat and light to penetrate to its interior—a "light-world" apart from the traditional Gothic church interior of punctured stone walls and dimly lit ceilings. Its 400-foot length, 200-foot width and 120-foot height is greater in all three dimensions than Notre Dame in Paris.

Also at a grand scale is the 6-story, three quarters of a million square foot Pacific Design Center by Victor Gruen Associates, with Cesar Pelli as designer. Its blue, glass-clad blunt forms and vaulted silhouette is indicative of a new scale or scaleless monumentality that does not join the urbanscape by association but echoes and fuses it into its own shimmering facade. It does not attempt to bridge history or establish dialogue, it simply is. Even its skin is intentionally neutral and has a mechanically repetitive pattern where volume replaces mass as the design emphasis.

In contrast to the presence of these two buildings and their celebration of space within a taut membrane at a grand scale is the hexagonal glass modules of the Plants and Man Building by Edward Larrabee Barnes for the New York

■ Roche Dinkeloo & Assoc., Deere West
Office Building, Moline, Illinois, 1975

Botanical Garden. Each of the 45-feet-across modules can be clustered to create space of variable width, height, and flexible grouping and are consequently not static and rigidly confined like traditional glass-domed or shed-roof greenhouses. Each cluster or biome can also be contained to have its own particular climate. The hexagonal concept is a nesting form that can be combined to grow in any one of six directions and since it is not a closed prismatic form or finite object like the dome, affords the possibility of an undulating and highly varied glass structure interlocking into, through, and around the landscape.

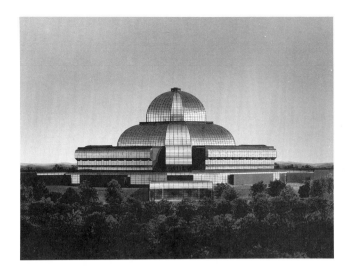

■ Roche Dinkeloo & Assoc., Corporate Training Center, Moline, Illinois, 1980

The dramatic presence of glass in the Deere West Building by Roche Dinkeloo & Associates is primarily in the use of a series of long, gambrel-shaped skylights that both shelter and filter light into the central multilevel garden area of the 3-story building. The external envelope of the building is a meticulously detailed linear assemblage of columns, beams, mullions, and sun-screened devices of exposed Corten steel that will eventually naturally rust to a deep brownish-purple hue. The buildup of tracerylike steel elements is as carefully and meticulously conceived as the external elements of the traditional Japanese house with its linear, panel, and rectilinear organization and open geometrically related interior spaces.

In the subsequent design of a corporate training center also to be located in Illinois, Kevin Roche, in yet another glass-enclosed structure, has returned to a more classically centralized, rather than linear, form. A 100-foot high central atrium covered by a steel ribbed glass dome, is supported by four, steel star-shaped columns. In a 3-story structure encircling this space, which is purposely sparsely landscaped to facilitate its use for exhibits and meetings, are recreational, dining, and meeting facilities and inward-facing guest bedrooms that overlook the skylit atrium from balconies. The nineteenth century garden conservatory dome is a recognizable iconography for this structure whose centralized buildup even has precedents in the temple forms of the Middle East, the spirit of the observatory in a slightly unreal or prophetic space epic, whose tracery has an art-nouveau–like sensibility. Roche was not seeking the historicist references or precedents; he says, "in trying to find a suitable and exciting way to enclose the central garden volume, the search happened to follow a traditional path."

While these structures lead our imagination to consider new concepts such as transparency and being able to live free in the landscape, a new sense of environmental potential, and the drama of our evolving technology dramatically applied, they also pragmatically focus our thoughts on the implication of the use of glass in future architecture. Energy, or the expense and limitations of it, is increasingly forcing architects to further explore the use of natural forces rather than to continue a dependence upon mechanical means to make buildings habitable: to use glass to collect solar energy rather than reflect it; to use design to create gardens that can heat or cool interiors and be an environmental interface between the built and natural environment, especially in adverse climates; to look for more sophisticated and design sensitive methods of sun control and better sound insulation for interior spaces. Nature is a resource to both enjoy visually and bring factually into our architecture as a means to support and sustain our life styles. It is the Japanese traditional sensibility that a building draws its validity from the natural world, as building and its garden are a complete form as a single unit. Such fusions are also necessary as advances in our technology and sense in design application are of necessity concomitant.

The National Commercial Bank Tower in Jeddah, designed by Gordon Bunshaft of Skidmore, Owings & Merrill (SOM), is obviously an expression of Saudi Arabia's affluence and its urbane and technological aspirations, but in

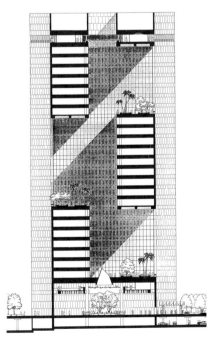

■ Skidmore, Owings & Merrill, National Commercial Bank, Jeddah, Saudi Arabia, 1978 *(Photo: Wolfgang Hoyt/Esto)*

turning the building inward related to a system of natural protection and ventilation, the design attempts to be a marriage of sophisticated thought and indigenous traditional principle. Cut back from two sides of the building's basically solid and triangular, marble-clad form are three grand landscaped courts. These bring natural light and views to the interior while shielding the large glass areas from direct exposure to the effects of sun and winds. They are pivoted around a core open space that acts as a central, natural ventilation shaft for these courts, extending from the skylight ceiling of the main, ground floor banking room upward through the center of the building. Here garden is not as a unit with the building as in the tradition of Oriental understanding, it is paradise on Earth (the word *garden* in Arabic is translated as paradise on Earth). It is land claimed from the desert as a sanctuary of a sacred space belonging to Allah.

A less monumental and more technological application of design in response to energy conservation is the Madeira School Science Building in Virginia by Arthur Cotton Moore & Associates. Here the building is nestled beneath a 4,600-square-foot single pitched and southeast-facing solar collector roof. The collector is a parallelogram in shape both to minimize the impact of its size on the environment and to afford beneath its steep slope a good sense of scale and proportion to the building's interior. The roof's upper edge is a skylight to the interior and its lower edge a glazed colonnaded entrance to the building. It is a modest application of solar energy that intelligently resolves

■ Arthur Cotton Moore & Assoc., Madeira School Science Building, Virginia, 1975

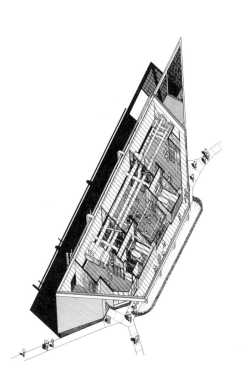

■ Skidmore, Owings & Merrill, Enerplex, Princeton, New Jersey, 1982 *(Photo: Wolfgang Hoyt)*

technical needs with relation to architectural form, entirely appropriate to a science building.

Conservation techniques and the harnessing of natural energy sources are also the form generators of Enerplex, a speculative office venture by the Prudential Insurance Company that brought together the Princeton University School of Architecture and the office of Skidmore, Owings & Merrill to design two 3-story buildings flanking a central mall, from which they are entered and across which each develops a different organization and facade treatment. The exterior of the south building, by the Princeton team led by Alan Chimacoff is of limestone-clad walls, with ribbons of windows and a colonnade theme at the ground level. The largest expanse of glass is the central north atrium facing to the entrance plaza, which is solar heated from south facing rooftop skylights. A further U-shaped corridor, topped with skylights oriented to minimize summer heat gains while permitting direct, warming sunlight to penetrate during the winter, diffuses natural light to interior offices. The exterior of the north

■ Alan Chimacoff and Princeton team,
South Building, Enerplex, Princeton, New
Jersey, 1982 *(Photo: Paul Heyer)*

building by Skidmore, Owings & Merrill, with Raul DeArmas as the design partner, is in direct contrast to the predominant solidity of its neighbor. It is sheathed in a double layer curtain wall which is separated by an 18-inch air cavity; the outer membrane is a continuous single-glazed weather resistant skin, the inner has windows from sill height to the ceiling. Here, a large atrium, gathering light and heat from the sun's rays, extends the entire length of the south facade. Similar to its neighbor it is vented and shaded in the summer. Since light loads often consume up to 30 to 40 percent of a building's energy costs, then a further 10 percent to cool their heat emission, the attention to the distribution and diffusion of natural light is pertinent both economically and environmentally. The corollary of winter heat is summer cooling and again there is an ingeneous solution: An ice pond is frozen during winter with water recirculated until it is solid ice, a cover seals the ice for summer use, when "melt water" is drawn from the pond bottom and is used to chill heat exchange coils within the building, which is then returned as spray to the ice mass. At many levels the appropriateness of the architecture has derived from the attention to natural, environmental elements and the richness of design potential is embodied in the contrasting, yet equally energy efficient, flanking facades. While we are developing energy-related technology into comprehensive and efficient systems, many simple design moves can prevent us from ignoring intelligent ideas of conservation and exposing buildings in climatically vulnerable ways. Such is the strength of this design.

■ Craig Ellwood Assoc., Airport Business Center, Irvine Industrial Complex, Newport Beach, California, 1968 *(Photo: Glen Allison)*

Questions of technology and its application can often be an effective means to smaller and design supportive applications as well as overall and conceptual postures, or, the elements of a building can serve a multiple architectural role. In the Airport Business Center at the Irvine Industrial Complex by Craig Ellwood, the concept is a light, prefabricated for fast on-site erection, steel-bearing wall system of structural mullions 5 feet on center, glazed with solar bronze glass. The mullions are filled with water for fireproofing, eliminating inches and thereby maintaining a light and visible structural system, which is of a natural self-weathering steel that is self-oxidizing. Hence the wall system serves the multiple functions of being both columns as structure and glazing mullions, while it is also self-fireproofed and self-weather coated.

In contrast is the more robust, additive and expressive in feeling, concrete structure of the Tougaloo College Library by Gunnar Birkerts & Associates. Here the 30-foot-square structural module organizes the building plan. The poured concrete columns have cylindrical precast capitals that act as seats for precast beams. These support precast, prestressed hollow-core floor planks, spanning in opposite directions in alternate bays to equally load the floor beams, which themselves have openings at their center depth through which mechanical equipment can pass. Both buildings derive a different aesthetic from a conscious intent to allow the system of building to develop a specific architectural character.

■ Gunnar Birkerts and Assoc., Tougaloo College Library, Tougaloo, Mississippi, 1966 *(Photos: Balthazar Korab)*

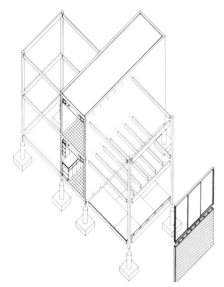

■ Booth & Nagle, Magnuson House,
Vashon Island, Washington, 1975
(Photos: Christian Staub)

Architecturally such buildings increase our understanding of prefabrication as developing not only building elements but also entire service components, such as bathrooms and the interplay between structure and more sophisticated mechanical systems, where heating, cooling, lighting, and even maintenance can enhance our architecture as they are expressive and more organically integral—and conserving of time, labor, and energy. Building less expensively and more efficiently even in itself continues to pressure such advances. Many of our labor union increases are paid for by cheaper materials and faster installation, for example sheetrock wall systems as a substitute for plastered walls. Systems building does not imply the mass production of entire buildings, nor preclude any flexibility of assembly to inhibit the fulfillment of design interests or social awareness. It means the employ of our technological potential to maximize these, leading to new systems of building and organizing the urban matrix based on denominators of collective need at the new scale that technology implies. Industrial processes may even not be monotonous but

Paul Rudolph, Green Residence, Pennsylvania, 1968 *(Photo: Donald Luckenbill)*

highly variable and surprisingly do not really need to be arranged in predictable modules except for considerations such as distribution and catalog publication. They are not limiting to the individual except in the more whimsical aspects of personal expression.

In reality, however, much of our industrial expression to date remains in principle a handcraft approach with machines simply performing tasks that traditionally would have been done by hand. The Magnuson House by Booth & Nagle, endeavors to apply a component-module approach with its central 8-foot by 36-foot core containing bathrooms, stairs, and mechanical spaces abutted by 12-foot-square modules housing prime living spaces. Built inexpensively and largely at the site, its modular conception anticipates factory-built and site-assembled structures of prefabricated components.

In its initial concept the Green Residence by Paul Rudolph envisioned three factory-assembled, prefabricated units flanking a large, aluminum tube and glass, standard catalog greenhouse structure. The size of the units (the largest was 12-feet by 54-feet by 9-feet with fold down panels increasing the basic size by 6 feet 6 inches on each side and a 15-foot sloping tilt up roof panel forming a glass clerestory) was determined by the size limitations of highway trucking to the site. Unfortunately at the time of construction, the prefabricated units became uneconomical and the design was executed at the site with steel cantilevered beams. It remains nevertheless an interesting study for designs of the three-dimensional and prefabricated, expanded module approach. The systematization of building method preserving the individuality of components with a certain whimsey, but within a philosophically cohesive whole—a system that permits within its strictures also the concept of formal architectural clarity.

The intent to channel technological reality toward a machined and visionary idea is in no way new. In the late twenties the French architects Pierre Chareau and Bernard Bijvoet designed the Maison de Verre in Paris to be prophetic of an industrialized feeling. With that epoch's visionary belief in the social pertinence of the machined artifact, such a design attitude was seemingly easier to achieve then than at present. The result was a beautifully crafted, cleverly eclectic (some of the furnishings had strong traditional and luxurious overtones) and romanticized structure where the machined imagery became in detail as much a lyrically symbolic assemblage of fashionably sophisticated taste, as functional and industrialized. But then the paths of architecture are strewn with visions of a new future achieved through employing new means within the context of a new imagery that, while they may not result in the finite precursors of a new vision, have resulted in many interesting buildings however incidental to or apart from their design premise. Clearly the impact and image of a machine aesthetic—which of essence must be beyond a purely technical aesthetic—has been established as scientific and industrial fact, but its reality as systematized design in building, as it remained a half century ago with the Maison de Verre, still lies ahead. Although the vision is tremendous in impact in our "all things are possible world," we have a tendency to forget how difficult a goal the pertinent technologically industrialized artifact is to achieve, even if it is attainable at all in view of the varied responses to different inputs that we require of our architecture.

New materials and their structural potential in assembly have also totally changed construction possibilities since the late 1900s. Before the Industrial Revolution buildings were essentially an accretion of elements one upon another, discontinuous structures primarily supported in compression. We are accustomed to these sturdy structures that are visually "earthbound" by building mass and weight. The traditional post and beam structure, because it is discontinuous, is basically wasteful of material since it is not stable at the connection. Structures with continuity of material are capable of greater performance both within the structural members as stresses are shared and transferred at the connections by virtue of their continuity. This idea is fundamental to our contemporary building methodology. With the development of steel, reinforced and especially prestressed concrete, all with the ability to be economically employed both in tension and compression to form continuous structures, came greater structural efficiency with less visible effort, the possibility of greater heights and spans—the potential of the most dramatic symbol of tension, the cantilever—the enclosure of more space with less mass and greater flexibility in the enclosure of that space. The poetry and aesthetic economy of the suspension bridge with the drama of steel and steel cables is that of the immediately visible and correct employ of a tremendously strong and aesthetically persuasive material. The delicacy and transparency of the geodesic dome, as seen in the U.S. Pavilion by Buckminster Fuller at the 1968 Montreal World Fair, achieved the maximum enclosed volume with a minimum enclosing surface, the strut support elements defining the shortest distance between points on a curved spherical surface. It is as much a reflection

■ Pierre Chareau and Bernard Bijvoet, Maison de Verre, Paris, 1931

of the structural potential of our epoch as the dome of St. Peter's was of the Italian Renaissance. Steel also led to the slender structural skeleton and liberated us from the need to build directly upward off the ground, affording the opportunity to hang even buildings from slender elements in suspension.

In the Federal Reserve Bank in Minneapolis, Gunnar Birkerts & Associates were able to achieve a column-free space of 275 feet with two catenary members, 60 feet apart placed on either side of the building facade. These support the office floors and are suspended from two great concrete towers housing stairs and bathrooms at either end of the building. The tendency for these towers to be pulled inward is restrained by two 28-foot-deep trusses at the top of the building, which contain mechanical equipment areas between them. The catenaries, clearly delineated on the facade because the glass above is recessed while below it is at the outer edge of the curve, creates an elegant design solution through the structural idea.

By contrast, the U.S. Tax Court Building in Washington, D.C., by Victor A. Lundy and Lyles, Bissett, Carlisle & Wolff, in concept and detail does not structurally reveal how its central drama of a 200-foot-long granite-faced courtroom block, cantilevered for 53 feet over the building's glass entrance wall is achieved. The 4,000 ton "floating" box of prestressed concrete, connected to the rear block by a "compression" bridge at the ceremonial third level and a tension link at the roof level, is supported by 145 post-tensioned, 3-inch-diameter steel cables buried within transverse, vertical concrete shear walls. Similar to the Reserve Bank, it is a sculptural idea derived from bold engineering, the former striving to make visible its construction methodology, the latter, the opposite, the impact of a "look no hands" attitude.

■ Gunnar Birkerts and Assoc., Federal Reserve Bank of Minneapolis, 1968 *(Photo: Balthazar Korab)*

■ Victor A. Lundy and Lyles, Bissett, Carlisle & Wolff, U.S. Tax Court Building, Washington, D.C., 1976 *(Photo: Paul Heyer)*

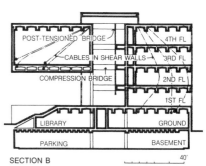

SECTION B

STRUCTURE, TECHNOLOGY, AND THE NEW MEANS | **63**

Such structural examples, regardless of their functional pertinence, are clearly no mean feats of construction. The continuity of material through the sophistication of connection, allowing our buildings to visually defy the forces of gravity, has moved our vision of the contemporary world of architecture to the apocalyptic. It has meant our becoming accustomed to the idea that a building no longer of necessity needs to seem earthbound but of choice can be soaring and light. The "it could not have been done before syndrome" has also brought with it the sharp realization that technology is no panacea, but only a means: the "how" companioned philosophically by the "why."

Where steel construction is linear in nature, reinforced concrete is a plastic material with the potential to change in shape as it expresses the exact flow of structural stresses within a building. The expression of these stresses in effect becomes architectural form. Precast concrete for precision and speed of

■ Marcel Breuer & Assoc., IBM Building, Boca Raton, Florida, 1967–1970 *(Photo: Joseph W. Molitor)*

assembly, systems of pre-tensioning and post-tensioning for greater strength, improved methods of formwork for better and more durable finished surfaces with a variety of aesthetic possibilities, these are among the refinements that have further expanded the potential of reinforced concrete, both in structure and as facade treatment. In the IBM Building in Boca Raton by Marcel Breuer and Robert Gatje, the exterior facade is a 34-foot tall, 5-foot deep precast concrete panel, suggested by the repetitive nature of the project, which is both structure and the principal component of the exterior. Its deep modeling is mainly load bearing, where the rhythm of ribs and canopies stiffen the elements while also shading windows. The precast panels are carried on Y-shaped "tree columns" that are poured in place concrete.

With the exception of expansion joints, reinforced concrete has also the potential to be "endlessly" continuous, where the enclosure of space and structure can be immediately one, with individually responsive forms resolved into a single mass. Strength is even derived from shape in statistically indeterminant shell structures of continuous, warped and folded membranes, and systems of spraying concrete onto steel mesh has even overcome the limitations of the wooden formwork into which concrete is poured. Instead of structural skeletons, structural skins have also freed architectural form from containment

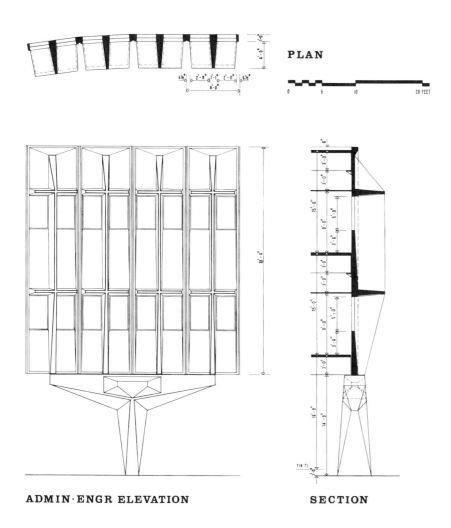

PLAN

ADMIN·ENGR ELEVATION   SECTION

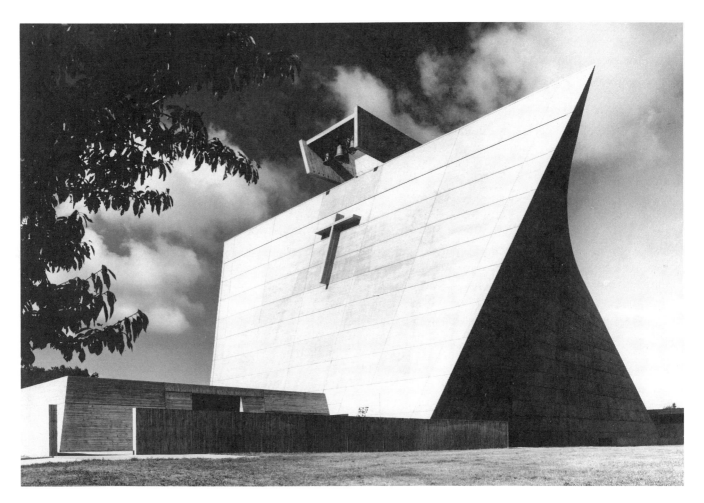

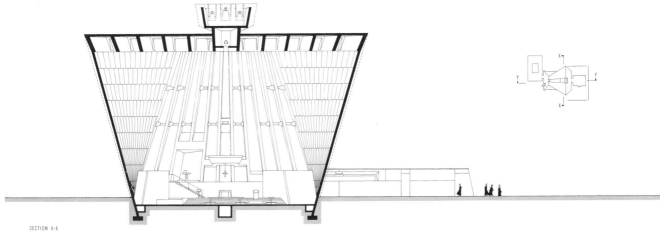

SECTION X-X

■ Marcel Breuer & Assoc., St. Francis de
Sales Church, Muskegon, Michigan,
1961–1967

within structural grids, giving the architect further freedom where it is needed
within a problem to organize space. It has also pointed beyond the skeleton to a
planar architecture based on the strong relationship of solid to void, preserving the historical interest of architects in the combination of structure, surface
texture, and the play of light and shadow. The form of the Church of St. Francis
de Sales by Marcel Breuer and Herbert Beckhard evolves directly from side-

walls that turn in plane as they rise to a 75-foot height from a rectangular base, in the process describing the geometric shape of a hyperbolic paraboloid, whose properties are a continuous curved plane formed of straight lines. In church architecture at its best, be it through the medium of stone lintels and columns, Roman or Gothic arches, or dome and barrel vaults of the Classic period, the enclosure of space was synonymous with the structural logic of that enclosure. Here the rhythm of space remains the poetry of structure, but instead of stone upon stone held in place by weight, it is one of flowing line of concrete and a continuous web of integral steel bars: a planar architecture.

Even the most commonplace and traditional structural system of bearing walls with a beamed roof ceiling has taken on new realms of possibility. The central space of the Lyndon B. Johnson Library designed by Gordon Bunshaft of Skidmore, Owings & Merrill is defined by two parallel walls 200 feet long, 65 feet high and 90 feet apart. The walls curve upward to a thin point at three quarters of their height and then are gently splayed outward to receive and distribute the weight of the concrete roof's massive hollow girders cantilevering 16 feet beyond the side walls. The girders seem to hover above the supporting walls as they are carried by steel pins that, with a strip glass infill, allows the roof to seemingly float above and appear detached from the support walls of Roman travertine.

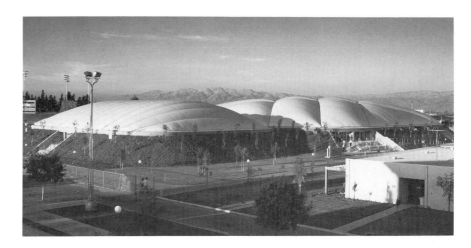

■ Caudill Rowlett Scott, University of Santa Clara, California, 1975 *(Photos: exterior, Julius Shulman; interior, Balthazar Korab)*

Air itself has even become a method of support. In the Student Activities Center at the University of Santa Clara, Caudill Rowlett Scott designed two air-supported structures, one covering the main activity area, the other retractible over a pool. Both employ a teflon-coated fiberglass membrane with steel restraining cables, supported by a 5-pounds-a-foot pressure differential that is maintained by an environmental control system. A subsystem of steel supports for lighting protects against the total relaxation of the system.

The U.S. Pavilion at Expo '70 in Osaka by Davis & Brody also used low air pressure within a single membrane, to span 274 feet by 465 feet for the largest overall clear span air-supported roof built at that time. Weighing only one pound per square foot including cables, it is also the lightest roof of such span. The elliptical, translucent roof of a single 100,000-square-foot piece of vinyl-coated fiberglass is secured to a concrete compression ring that forms the rim of a hollowed-out earth berm. The fabric, developed out of the Apollo space program, has a melting point of 1,000 degrees Fahrenheit making it virtually fireproof. Air rising out of the structure at any point of fire would cool the surface to a point where it could not support combustion and hence, effectively extinguish itself. Similar to geodesic domes, such environments look toward a future where entire areas or complexes can be encapsulated, be in 24-hour use, and be environmentally controlled. They are also new ways of creating column free space that is enclosed at a grand scale.

■ Davis & Brody, U.S. Pavilion, Expo '70, Osaka, Japan

■ Skidmore, Owings & Merrill, Haj Terminal, Jeddah, Saudi Arabia, 1982 *(Photos: Jay Langlois-OCF)*

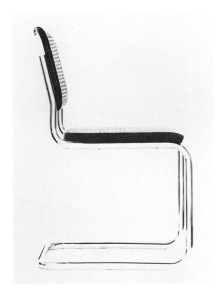

■ Marcel Breuer, Cesna chair, 1928

The image of the nomad in a hostile climate and the tent as a sheltering, open umbrella, is the inspiration for the vast, teflon-coated, fiberglass-covered, long-span, steel cable roof of the Haj Terminal in Saudi Arabia. It is designed to receive between a half million and one million Moslems arriving by air for the annual pilgrimage to the holy cities of Mecca and Medina. To quote structural engineer Fazlur Kahn of Skidmore, Owings & Merrill, who was central to the project's design, referring to the symbolic and religious presence of this initiation or arrival point: "It creates the spirit, it gives you a feeling of tranquility and a sense of continuity, of transition into the real place, which is Mecca." This is realized in a terminal consisting of two identical roofed halves, each 1,050 feet by 2,250 feet with airplane docks running their outer lengths, separated by a landscaped central mall that responds to the great scale of the problem in an appropriate "vernacular" without denying the scale, functional necessities, and universality of the airplane. Beneath the fabric roof—a series of semiconical modules supported by steel cables suspended from tapered columns spanning to open steel tension rings at the top of each unit—pilgrims rest, sleep, and eat food purchased or prepared by themselves. The means have been employed for a compatible presence and pertinent imagery, to culturally and symbolically derived ends.

In addition to concepts derived from our new structural potential, the variety and combination of new materials has itself also enlarged our architectural vocabulary. In Marcel Breuer's Cesna chair, designed in 1928, the innovation of chrome steel as cantilevered structure, beautifully contrasts with its traditional, wood framed, caned seat. As a Louis XIV chair reflected the spirit of the French Renaissance, the Cesna chair epitomized the new spirit of early Modernism. The precision and discipline of the design resulted from a consistent attitude and its restrained execution, while richness and durability derived from the elegant use of quality materials. Mies van der Rohe believed that one of the strong factors in the acclaim for the German Pavilion in Barcelona was precisely such a juxtaposition of elegant, rich traditional materials like marble, onyx, and travertine contrasting with chrome and tinted glass, especially since this was at a time when modern architecture was more austerely conceived.

The elemental idea pertaining to material in architecture is that it is used for its own inherent physical character and quality in a manner respectful of its natural properties, a forthright employ for structural, durable, and even sensual reasons. As the structural use of new materials has become greatly developed, we are finding the finish materials as the challenge. Many traditional materials like brick and stone undoubtedly look better and weather more harmoniously than steel or concrete. It is no accident that Henry-Russell Hitchcock's excellent book on the buildings of Frank Lloyd Wright 1887–1941 was entitled *In the Nature of Materials.* Mass and space in Wright's buildings was strongly a product of natural and usually traditional materials, with material itself plied, faceted, or juxtaposed to become essence. Beyond traditional materials, one of our many challenges in modern architecture is to look outside the now cliché of the glass skin or the travertine clad structure, toward the incorporation of new materials into our architecture. Materials that might both generate as well as encase form; to sense and liberate qualities both literal and symbolic within new materials. For material, as the sculptors realize since their work derives

■ Mies van der Rohe, German Pavilion, Barcelona, Spain, 1929 *(Photo: Museum of Modern Art, New York)*

from expressions within the nature of materials, does not itself possess any intrinsic, aesthetic content. Michaelangelo said of his own sculpture that there were figures trapped within the stone struggling to release themselves, his task being to chip away the excess stone to release the essential nature of the block. Concern for material and its "proper" use, although fundamental in application to architecture is also psychological in derivation.

Structural honesty also fits into this category. Even if an architect does not finally feel the need for a clear expression of structure, it is a principal form determinant and method of approach to the design of a building. It is as elemental as circulation is to the city or the skeleton to our body. The idea that the architect is obligated to express a clear structural system in a building may well have its origin in the modern period in the Chicago era when the concern, both aesthetically and emotionally was an underlying, candid directness of function resulting in proper and right form and expression. This drive, for example, led to the "Chicago window" where structure was developed as a cage, within which the voids were filled with horizontal expanses of glass. Beyond the practical aspect of admitting a maximum of light to a building interior, it was a seductive idea because, as in nature, function, form, and structure became one. Interior and exterior developed a visual simultaneity. The beauty of structure as an idea is that through it relationships are established that can bring a sense of logic and control to the entire design of a building.

Although it is natural for the architect to want to express a well-proportioned and handsome structural system, there is no reason to believe that this will automatically result in good architecture. Obviously an exposed structure in some building types might be a severe limitation to an architect's creative intent, and any building can have the integrity of its structure preserved without it being visible and nakedly expressed on the surface. Even then, there is no such thing as exact appropriateness of structure, but judgments about various systems to use, and intelligent comprises about sizes of members considered as relative parts of a whole. It would be as naive to believe that a building could be built without certain compromises in its structure as it would to believe that an architectural structure is not motivated by certain aesthetic ends. Even with such functional problems as bridges there are judgment variables and also psychologically motivated expressions to be weighed. Bridges have an immediate appeal because they express the struggle to take powerful materials and use them to not only achieve the seemingly impossible, but to do so from the most heroic stance where method and technology seem most succinct. But, with even such a singular design problem as a bridge, where function is a relatively simple "from here to there" equation, there are many nebulous factors to reconcile in the pursuit of exactness. There are live and dead loads, impact forces and wind loads, erection and temperature change stresses, centrifugal and longitudinal forces, all combined into factors of compression, tension, and stress transfer. What appears as rationale based on information, apportionment, and calculation also in the end must, and where great bridges are concerned does go beyond mathematics to the realm of compromising and balancing variables and expressing the poetry of strength combined with economy; the clarity of the 'right' move dramatically made. To the idea of variables and compromises the engineer August Komendant, best known for his structural design work on the buildings of Louis Kahn said, "There are three basic criteria to evaluate structures rationally—expressiveness, aesthetics and end-means relationship. But the final product has only one criteria—good or bad. Also these three must be balanced to obtain the single quality."

Questions of structure have invariably been approached by architects within the context of a broader guiding attitude or theme idea that often grows out of a notion of, or toward, structure. Overlooking Long Island Sound, the Deane House by Paul Rudolph gains its design presence from a wood frame seven-sided figure cut and bolted together with its side walls set back from the edges of the frames to allow them to become clearly expressed. The capacity of the material is "released" into an original set of configurations. The frames are double-cantilevered from wood posts built up from 2-inch by 12-inch members, and are juxtaposed inside and out against heavily textured cementitious and

■ Paul Rudolph, Deane House, Long Island, New York, 1969

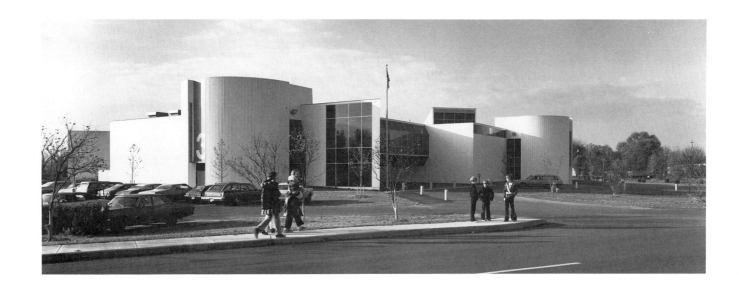

■ Caudill Rowlett Scott, Fodrea
Community School, Columbus, Indiana,
1972–1973 (Photos: Balthazar Korab)

pebble finished wall surfaces, trowel applied to lath over plywood. The openness and staggered interlocking of the structure became the opportunity for space to flow and diagonally interpenetrate between it. The inventive expression of structure is clearly a product of a dramatic, architectural space intent where each complements the other.

The notion that an idea of space can derive from an idea about structure, or even that structure as the strong design element of exposure and enclosure can be conceived in such a manner that it can bring a new dimension to the architectural presence, that it can complement, even decorate, a building, as lines are "drawn" in space through the medium of structure is not new. Such a notion was elemental to the Gothic period and its cathedrals and such contemporary structures as the geodesic dome and other space-frame type buildings. At a more intimate scale and as an expression of structure as enclosure used to generate space, the Fodrea Community School in Columbus by Caudill Rowlett Scott creates, as its major design theme element, a flexible interior space by roofing the two-level open plan with a Unistrut theatrical grid and metal deck supported by exposed concrete columns. Mechanical systems, threading between the space frame, are painted bright colors. Continuing the industrialized aesthetic approach, the exterior skin is a prefabricated, foam-filled panel clipped onto the steel structure, with an integral baked enamel finish on both sides for easy maintenance. Structure, at least in the interior, gives presence and form, although the punctuated triangular rhythms of the interior have not appeared as an influence upon the exterior expression.

Roof as defining element takes on a more dramatic and conceptually persuasive note at Gund Hall, the Harvard Graduate School of Design by John Andrews, as its raking lines parallel and cover an open terraced sequence of overlooking studio spaces. The angled, steel and glass stepped roof, where again the exposed structure and mechanical systems are functionally and aesthetically elemental to the design concept, is a series of 134-foot-long by 11-foot-deep primary trusses. Built from round tubing, they are treated with fire retardant paint and covered at the roof level and upper chord of the truss

■ John Andrews, Graduate School of
Design, Harvard University, Cambridge,
Massachusetts, 1969 *(Photos: Paul Heyer)*

by a fiberglass enclosure. The tiered interior of studio spaces is built over a
"hill" of its own creation which contains offices, library, and workshops. The
concept derives from a social and pedagogical idea of learning that strives to
create a layering of space that is both universal in its singular totality of
presence and personal in that it provides students with more individually
defined working areas. In this sense it is an idea conceptually between Mies's
School of Architecture at Illinois Institute of Technology and Rudolph's at
Yale. The introduction of light to the interior, filtered between and highlight-
ing structure, is as powerful a complement to the concept of space as it is in
Rudolph's Deane house. Again, we can discover precedents in the tracery of
Gothic arches set linear and sinewy against their infills of glass.

The fundamental idea that there is some virtue in exposing structure is
comparatively recent and is being especially questioned today by a culture
challenging the last vestiges of its early modernist puritanism. The Greeks
were more concerned with the refinement of proportion, detail and optical
correction, so that it is often difficult to distinguish which of their expressed
elements were structural. Although the Gothic period developed from a new
principle of construction, with elements pared down to their slenderest, many
of the supposedly structural features were without function and indeed decorative to dramatize the mass. Renaissance architects concentrated their energies on architectural features, pilasters and the like so that even if they did
emphasize certain facts of structure they were in themselves nonstructural.
Baroque architects freely revealed or concealed structure purely for architectural effect and the drama of space. However, structure is a major discipline
and means of design approach. The historical references emphasize that considerations of architecture and structure are inseparable. For example, in the
neoclassic uniform envelope approach architects created a structural system
within which the elements of a building were resolved. It is often necessary,
however, to think in terms of structural systems that can accommodate a flexi-

STRUCTURE, TECHNOLOGY, AND THE NEW MEANS | **75**

bility appropriate to the differing functional organizational elements of a building. Facades often need to vary in response to different views, solar conditions, and existing urban contexts. Such an attitude has been the conceptual force behind the architecture of Jose Luis Sert. In responding to important factors that a more formal structural directness is inclined to ignore, in his Holyoke Center at Harvard University, while running the risk of losing a simplified clarity, he derived forms and surfaces that potentially better reflected the life of the building and its environmental relationships. The building evidences that structure itself is, or should be, beyond graph-paper-like divisions and it does not have to be repetitive.

Although nature simplifies, in nature structure is anything but simplistic. Systems in structure can be based on flexible groupings, distilled as in nature for significance, where they define and articulate a hierarchy of spaces. A sense of structuring within a work is more important than any pristine, inflexible structural expression—an idea implicit in the composer's approach to music. The structuring as such extends to connection, detail and interlocking systems of suggesting, defining, or enclosing space, creating themes and variations within them. Command in this area is often most persuasive in the technological vernacular because the fact of precision itself can be so compelling. Even within the more neoclassic approach of the overall, defining envelope the notion of structure and its expression is anything but simplistic and the exterior membrane can be both revealing and variable. The shaft of the skyscraper is the new, classic example of this, as three quite different and distinctive structural concepts by Skidmore, Owings & Merrill show. The 54-story tower for U.S. Steel in Manhattan, rises straight upward based on a 45-foot bay structural steel frame. Steel flame shields cladding and extending the steel floor beams as a fire protection system, create strong shadow accents while shading the interior. These rise above the floor level to provide window spandrels dividing the facade into an unusual, equal proportion of horizontal solid to glass banding.

The tapering upward thrust of the John Hancock Center in Chicago is a sculptural object in itself. The tower is basically a bearing-wall structure where columns and spandrel beams are part of a structural grid over the entire exterior, with diagonal bracing against wind loads, which are absorbed at the building's facade rather than more conventionally through a tower's central, structural service core. The structure is clad in black, anodized aluminum, with bronze colored aluminum frames and bronze tinted glass windows. The taper through its vertical height lightened the steel in the tower both by angling the structure into the wind forces it is resisting, while also reducing the total impact of wind loads on the tower, appropriate in the "windy city." Before our era of computer sophistication the possibility to calculate structural stresses within the three-dimensionally designed frame would not have been possible. The tower is also interesting for its mixed use concept within one overall form; the lower floors house a retail store and parking, the middle floors offices, the smaller in area upper floors apartments, with the building terminating in a rooftop restaurant at the 95th and 96th floors. Because the walls have an inward slope of 6 inches per story on the north and south, and 3 inches on the east and west, the apartments have five changes of layout between the 46th and 92nd floors to accommodate the diminishing floor area. The questionable philo-sophical validity of placing such diverse functions within one rigorously logical structural envelope resulted in the building's economy. It is a statement in the spirit of the idea that from structure in essence is derived architectural form. Here, functions are resolved within a framework predicated upon the logic of building with a structural derivation rather than the resolution of functions within an urban context becoming the initial catalyst for form. Nevertheless, allowing for this it is one of the most exciting buildings of the skyscraper genre built in the United States in the past three decades.

Where the U.S. Steel tower was an imaginative solution to the economy of a more conventionally and repetitiously framed building, the Hancock Tower was a rigorously pursued and empirically logical structural resolution where this itself became the architectural expression. The Sears Tower in Chicago, however, is a structural, cluster idea that resulted in a fragmentation of the overall tower envelope, with more flexible, functional possibilities. As such its form is somewhat more prophetic because, although this tower contains only office space it has longer range urban implications if we are to anticipate a future of building at heights and concentrations. In the design of skyscrapers there are enormous shear stresses induced by gravity and wind loads which becomes critical in single, monolithic tube shapes that rise above 400 feet. Above this height the shaft must resist stresses that subject corner columns to inordinate shear loads. This was resolved at the Hancock Center by the brac-ing of the entire height of the shaft with sheer resisting diagonals. At the Sears Tower, whose 1,450-foot height accommodates 110 stories, the shear is absorbed incrementally, rather than simultaneously at just a few points. This is achieved through a configuration of a nine tube cluster each 75 feet square, with tubes dropping off at the 50th, 66th and 90th floors, for a tower base dimension of 225 feet square. Forces are dissipated groundward as each tube acting inde-pendently assumes its approximate portion of shear, each tube having a perimeter of 15-foot-spaced columns connected by deep steel beams at every floor. A system of 2-story-high trusses, where mechanical equipment is located, connect columns to pick up wind and gravity loads at the 90th, 66th, and 29th to 31st floors, acting as vertical shear diaphragms to transfer the loads from

■ Skidmore, Owings & Merrill, U.S. Steel, New York City, 1973

■ *Left:* Skidmore, Owings & Merrill, John Hancock Center, Chicago, 1966–1970 *(Photo: Ezra Stoller). Right:* Skidmore, Owings & Merrill, Sears Tower, Chicago, 1974 *(Photo: Ezra Stoller)*

upper levels to the increased number of modules below. These trusses smooth out shear stresses enabling the building to act as a real cantilever of interdependent tubular design. Since all the tubes have their own structural integrity it is theoretically possible to eliminate groupings of tubes as desired to obtain floors of variable area, while preserving the integrity of the overall structure. The Sears Tower has four quite different overall floor areas through its height, pointing toward the possibility of variations in floor size and configuration that might permit different functions all within feasible economy because whereas the traditional skyscraper averages 50 pounds of structural steel per square foot, the Sears Tower required only 33 pounds.

Although the previous towers illustrate the incredibly increased possibility of engineering to permit new feats of economical and conceptual design,

they also raise questions about such dominant and singular elements in the urban context. The 60-story John Hancock Tower in Boston designed by I. M. Pei & Partners with Henry Cobb as partner-in-charge, endeavors through its rhomboid shape to relate to the buildings and define the spaces around it, and by the tautness and the pale reflectiveness of its skin to respond to its context by acting as a foil to the adjacent smaller scale historic structures of Copley Square. Irridescent and ethereal by day, brightly animating the skyline with its luminous presence at night, its color and tone dependent upon the light and atmospheric effects of its surroundings, it attempts an accommodation or fusion of the new urban scale of large and imposing forms in an uncompromising but sensitive manner by deference to its surroundings in that it reflects and fuses them. It is ironic that this, one of the most elegant and poetic of the reflective tower genre built in the United States, should have been plagued by its ½-inch tempered reflective glass windows being repeatedly sucked from their aluminum frames by wind loads and movement. A technical problem now resolved, it makes architects, as I. M. Pei comments, questioning or wary of innovation and suggests tried and more conservative methods. In contrast to the SOM towers, except as it too reads as an object in the skyline, it strives for a dialogue with its urban context. Its own presence while also obviously sleekly engineered makes nothing aesthetically of structure using only its intentionally impersonal and regularly repetitive skin as its expression.

The United Nations Plaza Hotel by Roche Dinkeloo & Associates also relies for the aesthetic expression of its 39-story mirrored glass facade upon an anonymous glass membrane but here, as a variant, it is a diagonally cut and faceted prism in response to zoning and in an attempt to make its overall form

responsive to surrounding buildings. The faceting is also clearly an effort to break down, in a nonmechanical and less predictable manner, the overall monolithic quality of its exterior membrane form.

In his design for the Bank of China I. M. Pei carries the idea of the faceted prism to a new plateau of relevance. Here, similar to SOM with the Hancock and Sears skyscrapers, he brings form and structure together in a design tour de force, one also of persuasive structural expression. The tower rises from a 170-foot cube at its base as a group of four triangular quadrants. Basically every 13 stories, or one quarter of its height, the tower is incrementally diminished by one quadrant. Reinforcing the tower's pure geometry, the quadrants themselves are also angled at their roof profiles, until the 70-story tower terminates

■ I. M. Pei & Partners, Bank of China Tower, Hong Kong, 1982–1990 *(Photos: Paul Warchol)*

against the skyline as a final triangle of space, containing the bank's penthouse lounge, affording sprawling views of Hong Kong's harbor and mountains beyond. The building, without internal columns, is supported by diagonal steel truss frame systems clearly expressed at the exterior skin, which transfer loads and stresses to four massive reinforced concrete corner columns, and a fifth column at the center of the tower. The structure is hence a composite of steel and concrete, the former to diagonally resist lateral fierce wind loads—twice as strong as those of the "windy city," Chicago—and the latter to transport vertical loads earthward. Clad in silver-coated heat reflective glass, the tower seemingly changes color, blue under sunny skies and gray against Hong Kong's brooding clouds.

The glass facade and overall envelope technology-wise also raises questions of energy response and control. The idea of windows placed for view and the psychological need for variety in it, even respite from view as an unrelenting presence; high windows make sense near ground level but less so as one is above the surroundings and tree level where glare, sunlight penetration, exposure and energy consumption become increasingly critical factors. Of course the whole idea of glass in architecture has less to do with view and more to do with the fact that it remains, certainly initially, the least expensive way to enclose a volume and to date is probably the most subjectively succinct expression of a machined technology. It also has a mystique or powerful image coefficient as evidenced by Gruzen & Partners, with Der Scutt as consulting architect, completely sheathing the masonry facade of Manhattan's old 1400-room Commodore Hotel to transform it, with a veneer of glass into the "new" Grand Hyatt. If the existing facades were not so distinguished, they did have a certain historical anonymity and character of permanence that is fast disappearing in our cities. Here the intent was presumably to contemporarize in its more

marketable and sleek image the Hyatt Hotel chain as "identifiable and modernly efficient." The renovation, although most skillfully executed in its detail, does raise the philosophical question as to whether this is an appropriate exterior use of a material that has its own integrity and characteristics, one of which, incidentally, is transparency. Here what we usually equate with a more neutral skin has ironically resulted in a glass-faced building with a hue and reflectivity more visually assertive than its predecessor. Clearly we are already looking nostalgically back to the quiet and composed richness of the skyscrapers in Sullivan's turn of the century Chicago and New York's own fine towers built through the 1930s.

If the correct employ of our technology remains a premise requiring on-going interpretation, our large, clear span structures and skyscrapers could not have been realized without our new technology. If within its own capability, it has created problems for many designers, technology has also given us the potential for their solution. Things are harder to control but correspondingly the means of control are more sophisticated; automation, for example, has far reaching implications way beyond technological technique or economic policy. In implying less specialization—or conversely even more specialization—greater collaboration and people who have the adaptability to learn new skills, it has already begun to dramatically reshape society and the pattern of our lives.

A fundamental idea of the modern movement in architecture was that of uniting art and technology through understanding and principle to improve the human condition. If we can learn from historic precedent, learn from the wonderful past accomplishments of the craftsman and use our technology with sensitivity and purpose we can then afford a sense of still youthful optimism. For the basic fact is, at least at any degree of urban scale, as we struggle through technology to solve the challenges of the post-Industrial Revolution, so we undoubtedly will shape our legacy to the twenty-first century.

4

Site as an Imperative

■ IN THE RELATIONSHIP between the constructed element and nature the architect in some manner always seeks a dialectic contact or "support" between nature and object, an attitude toward the relationship of one to the other. For Le Corbusier this was a harmony born of the Cartesian concept of universal order, the unity of the object in the landscape: "The unity which is in nature and in man is the law which endows his works with life." For Le Corbusier the building placed in the landscape still retained a sense of containment, but it also had a sense of pulling inward and back from the surface plane, of pulling nature within its overall volume, as it, too, replaced the ground occupied by building with a roof garden, while it remained an element distinctly placed on and even locked with the landscape, but not embedded in it.

Mies van der Rohe and Frank Lloyd Wright, with their own very different attitudes, also sought a dialogue with nature. "I don't feel site is *that* important," said Mies referring to his proposal for Chicago's convention hall, but also obviously making a general statement of philosophy, "I am first interested in a good building; then I place it in the best possible spot." A harmony between architecture and landscape was sought through emphasizing their differences by making architecture in a way recede and by allowing landscape to become a further definition of suggested space beyond a building's glass skin. In contrast with Le Corbusier's treatment, the skin was regarded as a diaphragm or

■ Mies van der Rohe, Farnsworth House, Plano, Illinois, 1950 *(Photo: George H. Steuer)*

transparent veil "barely" defining a separation, where the building remained a volume in the landscape not penetrated by it as it visually invaded the building's interior. Consequently, there was the greatest distinction—or the ultimate unison—between the built object and its natural setting. In Mies's architecture the space was a defined, linear skeletal framework with reflective "taut" glass surfaces, a tendency toward quiet, classical balance of composition, even the added sense of containment by such traditional devices as raising the total form of a building above the landscape, "floating" or by the use of a podium, all creating a sense of poised detachment from the environment. The idea is contrast, but with total awareness.

Wright's attitude was the antithesis. He sought a harmony with nature, to be "organic," of time and place, of the land, to see the touch of the hand, of nature worked with and transformed. From Ralph Waldo Emerson to Walt Whitman it was a seductive theme to American intellectuals of the period. "No house should ever be 'on' any hill or 'on' anything. It should be 'of' the hill, belonging to it, so hill and house could live together each the happier for the other." So Wright defined his approach: an attitude toward site that set the framework for problem solving that was an indigenous response rather than a context of theoretical formulation. "We may deduce laws of procedure inherent in all natural growths to use as basic principles for good building." Wright's

■ Frank Lloyd Wright, Taliesin East, Spring Green, Wisconsin, 1911 *(Photo: Museum of Modern Art, New York)*

approach was to group individualized parts built of natural materials, with connected and orchestrated interlock over and through the landscape. The exterior membrane of the building, as in the architecture of the De Stijl, was broken as planes, volumes, and spaces thrust outward into the landscape, almost in motion, penetrating nature to establish dialogue. The goal was a oneness of architecture and site, a romantic growing up and out of the land, but still in a *bauen*—or built—manner. Wright always remained the clear and articulate architect in command. There was never any effort to merge with the landscape like Mykonos in the Greek Islands, or other vernacular and indigenous contexts. Using discipline and control, the language of architectural elements and the act of shaping as an act of design set the scene. Clearly, in any mainstream attitude toward architecture there always remains a fundamental quality of form by virtue of the method of building, the nature of structure, and even the type of anonymous clarification that our technology has reinforced as part of our total architectural language. Wright, Le Corbusier, and others have shown that from these determinants architecture can still be rugged, responsive, and simultaneously eloquent; that architecture does not have to have a finite, neoclassic type containment, but just as existential philosophy demonstrated that thought can and must embody ideas of flexibility and spontaneity, that life—and architecture—can and must move beyond the preordained.

The pristine quality in built architecture, as the previous buildings exemplify, comes from an attitude toward nature that is highly variable. The artist does not of necessity copy it, but has a degree of rapport with nature that becomes a departure for abstraction, is a new insight, and can expand our level of wonder and understanding about nature. Wright harmonized with nature more in the proximity of oriental and primitive cultures to which he responded, rather

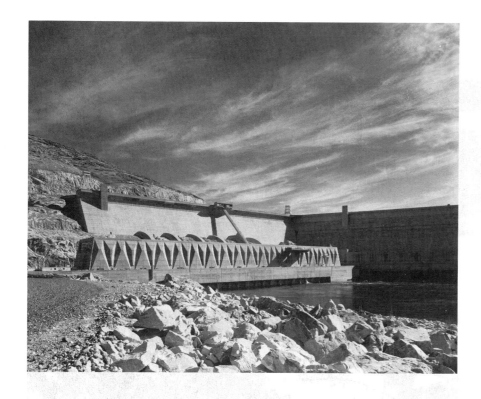

than the spirit of modern art, which he generally found distasteful. But nature as incentive and inspiration can be equally powerful in what might at first appear as tertiary stimulus. At an extreme, in the horizontal stripe and totally abstract paintings of Kenneth Noland there is a whole, wonderful panoramic drama of color that powerfully evokes an expansive and inclusive landscape; there is always a phrasing and tempering of attitude toward nature, through abstraction. Even if the image is intrinsic to the culture of technology, the philosophical reaction is to evoke and respond to the vastness of our landscape, to bring to it human associations and understanding, to make its impact relevant. The expression is of the limitlessness of scale and the horizon as frontier, as opposed to the classical easel painter of the nineteenth century, inspired by the intimacy and inward-looking charm of the European countryside. This new awareness of scale deals with nature as expansive and lyrical through a sense of grace: The suspension bridge soaring above and connecting the land or the dam embedded to transform what land and water together can do for our lives—the abstract element and its dialogue with nature.

The Grand Coulee Dam complex by Marcel Breuer and Hamilton Smith is such an example—an engineered element as a physical adjunct of the land and an obvious and dramatic example of dialogue through a functionally derived abstraction. The combination of aesthetic presence and refinement of the faceted planes of the folded-plate concrete wall construction of the power plant, is a dynamic of light and shadow against the more static, unbroken concrete mass of the dam above, whose smooth and unbroken plane is a further foil to the surrounding rocky landscape. The 1,100-foot length of the power plant's observation platform, approached by a descent from the dam rim in a glass-enclosed inclined elevator, is in itself a spectacle and displays an

■ Gunnar Birkerts and Assoc., IBM
Computer Center, Sterling Forest, New
York, 1970 *(Photos: Balthazar Korab)*

instinctive sense of relationship to purpose with the dam wall, sheer and
all-powerful behind.

A more detached, intellectually derived and technologically executed
abstraction, and stylistically appropriate since the building is for a computer
center, is Gunnar Birkerts's IBM building overlooking a lake in New York. The
building is a highly machined object with an exterior of polished aluminum
separated from reflective glass by brightly colored, red enameled metal panels.
With little disturbance of the landscape, the building's rectangular form cleanly

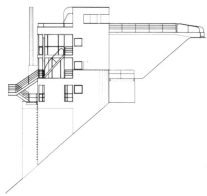

and abruptly meets the ground. Totally precise and hard-edged from afar, upon approach the building begins to assume the romantic, lush characteristics of its surroundings within its reflective surfaces.

The crispness shown in the IBM building takes on a different, but again entirely *bauen* spirit, in the pristine, white painted wood spatial interpenetrations of the Douglas House by Richard Meier. Located on a spectacular, 45-degree sloping and densely wooded site overlooking Lake Michigan to the west, it is a sophisticated statement of clean, abstract lines in direct contrast with nature. Instead of terracing down the hillside into the natural terrain, the design layers a house, respecting the verticality of the site, on a series of four strongly expressed and stacked levels, where the horizontal layering in turn reflects the shore line and the approach road at the top entrance level to the house. Solid surfaces in combination with transparent visual penetrations to the interior, curved elements and terraces interconnected at every level whose edges are delineated by the nautical-like lines of white metal handrails, all create a penetrated volume poised on the slope, framing spectacular views; an object in the landscape that elects to recognize the rich color of nature in its contrast of white solid elements and planes, and a white depth revealed by transparency and terraces against it. The compositional abstraction of crossed bands again is in the modernist spirit of the De Stijl.

■ Roland Coate, Jr., Alexander House, Santa Barbara, California, 1974 *(Photo: Jesse Alexander)*

The Alexander House by Roland Coate, Jr., was designed not to poise delicately above the land, but conversely to cut deeply into the top of a rolling California hillside and, with grass covering its roof, to unite building and site as a dignified monolith. At the entrance level approach, which is on top of the house, three circular concrete chimneys and a lookout tower visually linked by the parapet edges of walls from below, form a lyrically surreal, concrete and grass "landscape" garden. From here a brick-paved court leads downward via an open stairway to a rectangular inner court, which affords entry to the living

■ Caudill Rowlett Scott, Salanter-Akiba-Riverdale Academy, Bronx, New York, 1975

■ John Andrews, Graduate School of Design, Harvard University, Cambridge, Massachusetts, 1969–1972 *(Photo: Paul Heyer)*

spaces which in turn fan expressively ouward in a radial and broken geometry to views over brick terraces, a pool, and the Pacific Ocean. As the Douglas House is a white and linear penetrated abstraction "read" against a backdrop of green, the Alexander house is an exposed concrete episodic structure embedded and breaking into and from the land.

Similarly, on a series of layers following the natural contour of the hillside, is the Salanter-Akiba-Riverdale Academy located in the sedate, residential Riverdale section of New York City by Caudill Rowlett Scott. Its 1-story raking profile minimizes the school's impact on adjacent buildings and its exterior of buff-colored block masonry and bronze-coated, aluminum-clad roof harmonizes with the treed slope. Clerestory windows, located within the depth of the steel roof trusses, afford views of the river from all tiered levels of the interior. Its quiet, compatible unobtrusiveness for a comparatively large school facility is as much a product of pertinent response to site as is the detached, ocean liner iconography of the Douglas House to its splendid, water's edge isolation.

Such comparisons underlie the necessity for response-to-site criteria as a design fact. Architects having a style or attitude toward solving problems as an abstract theoretical process, to a degree can preempt considerations of the individuality or necessities of location. Also, the object isolated on a site only in relation to nature is quite different than buildings in the context of other buildings. In the former, the sense of abstraction can be more dominant. It is interesting to note that the sloped terraced form of the Riverdale Academy, deriving essentially from site considerations, has a similarity to the Harvard Graduate School of Design where the form generation of the terraced slope was more an educational and theoretical-idea response. An inclined terrace of overlooking studios, a clustering of office and seminar spaces beneath, all ending in a recessed colonnade of high profile to the street on one side, physically angled down to a lawn on the garden side. It also shows how the roof line paralleling the ground and choice of materials leads to a harmonizing response in the Bronx, whereas the Graduate School of Design form becomes a

Mitchell/Giurgola & Thorp, Parliament
House, Canberra, Australia, 1980

monumental statement, closer in spirit to the detachment and containment of
the Douglas House. In the Bronx a design uses the natural slope, at Harvard
the other artificially creates one.

The building embedded in its site idea, which was explored in the house
designed by Coate, was developed in a "reconstructing the land" theme on a
contextural and panoramic connective urban scale in the design of the
competition-winning new Parliament House by Mitchell Giurgola & Thorp.
Sited on the crest of Capital Hill, it is a focal pivotal point that embraces, even
appropriately celebrates the Beaux Arts spirit of Walter Burley Griffin's 1911
radial plan for Canberra, as it receives his radial boulevard system functionally
and visually within a basic circular organization whose symbolism is in the
spirit both of the hill and Griffin's original organizing geometry. It is a building
perceptive to the surrounding order both natural and constructed. Also, it

somewhat spans two significant chapters in the development of modern architecture—its emergence out of the Beaux Arts to the present reassessment of our modernist legacy—which, in this instance, because of the dedication to order, governing principles and geometrically resolved organization, compatibly coexist. Not a monumental structure placed on the hill, the design is a union of land and built form where the radial road system, accepted within the geometry of the plan allows the building to exist as a presence from a distance, where the building's complexities are revealed as one approaches and where views extend through the complex, uniting it in a continuum with the landscape beyond. Two monumentally scaled curvilinear walls, landscape elements that demarcate the two legislative areas, flank a "forum" housing the formal spaces, which visually extends the major land axis uninterruptedly across the hill. Astride this central position and at the crest of the hill, giving a symbolic focus both to the urban organization and the legislative functions nestled within the slope, especially the two major government chambers, is the national flag, poised aloft on a triangulated mast structure to culminate the Parliament's centrality. Monumental in presence, the scheme is conceived to respond to a broad urban scale without bombast or pompousness, as scale is employed, with geometry, to achieve a sweep of land and built form, of landscape and monument, of vistas and definition.

More *bauen* in derivation and more essentially architectural in their definition, more technologically expressive and singular in their directness of purpose, are the likewise monumentally derived in spirit headquarters for American Can in Connecticut designed by Gordon Bunshaft of Skidmore, Owings & Merrill and the Art Center College of Design in California by Craig

■ Skidmore, Owings & Merrill, American Can Headquarters, Greenwich, Connecticut, 1973 *(Photo: Ezra Stoller)*

■ Craig Ellwood Assoc., Arts Center,
Pasadena, California, 1974–1975

Ellwood Associates. Elegantly linear as their structural, contained lines power-fully hug and parallel the earth plane, with both achieving their architectural drama through an elementally strong idea about relationship to site, which in turn lends drama to the architecture, the former dams a ravine, the latter bridges one.

The American Can Headquarters was sited to span a ravine with its primary 525-foot by 255-foot building, thereby creating a dam structure out of its 5-story lower-level garage, with an at-grade, or water level floor for terrace, cafeteria, and lounges, with three office floors above, looking out over the lake. Thus a 9-story facility with a formidable parking demand of 1,700 cars is quietly related to the site in a neatly packaged manner. Executive offices are in a 1-story, 165-foot-square building connected to the main facility underground but separated from it by gardens and terraces at grade level. Both structures have a landscaped central court, a device that brings light to the interior spaces of the buildings while minimizing their overall perimeter wall dimensions. The containment of a total area of 1,300,000 square feet created a complex that does not consume its landscaped 40-acre site and even by the effect of a dam permits the regulated flow of water, environmentally enhancing the swampy bird sanctuary at the foot of its site.

Maintaining the landscape integrity and minimizing cuts and fills to the rolling ridges of a 175-acre site at the foothills of the mountains overlooking Pasadena, in the Arts Center led to a narrow, 642-foot-long by 144-foot-wide structure whose central 196-foot portion spans a gorge. The upper, ground-hugging, and 1-story in appearance element, is connected to the land by a lower floor on either side which, in addition to providing required floor area tucked for two-thirds of its height into the land, also structurally serves as an abutment to the bridge, allowing a column-free span across the gorge. The building is interestingly approached from a roadway that passes beneath this bridge, leading to the main entrance of the center.

Despite their exterior difference, the off-white concrete frame and glass infill of the SOM building to Ellwood's exposed dark steel and bronze glass structure, both are "veil," planar facade buildings in the immaculate Miesian tradition, deriving their sense of singularity from the clarity and simplicity of their idea and its forthright execution. Their attitude toward site is in the classic, related-object tradition. The more insular posture of the built element, however, can be broken whenever the parts of a building are handled in a more fractured way in which the building breaks outward into the landscape, or conversely, exterior space invades or punctuates volume. Such is the corporate headquarters for Union Carbide by Roche Dinkeloo & Associates, where parking garages are a central and logically rectilinear spine paralleled by perimeter offices, which are linear and narrow in width with views of the landscape that they branch outward to embrace. Reminiscent in concept to the Salk Institute at La Jolla by Louis Kahn where perimeter offices for the researchers and scholars ring central and open loft-space laboratory areas, the clusters of offices further establish a noninstitutional atmosphere as they are grouped to reinforce a more personalized feeling of community within the whole. Set on a slightly elevated saddle of land, the first level of the 4-story building is continuous and unbroken, and the undulations of terrain are retained as columns of varying length project downward from this first-floor

■ Roche Dinkeloo & Assoc., Union Carbide Headquarters, Danbury, Connecticut, 1976–1982

■ Roche Dinkeloo & Assoc., Fine Arts
Center, University of Massachusetts,
Amherst, Massachusetts, 1964–1974

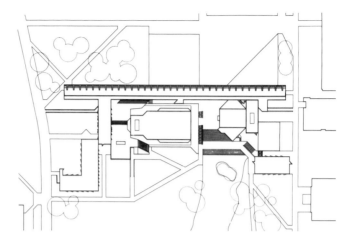

level to hold the building above the land, thereby allowing yet a further
penetration of the landscape beneath the periphery of the built volume.

Yet another "penetrated" building and, similar to Ellwood's, a bridge-idea
structure is the Fine Arts Center for the University of Massachusetts, also by
Kevin Roche. Here the "bridge" is formed by a visually strong, long "beam" of
art studios raised above the ground on a double row of V-shaped concrete

stilts that create, in this instance, a gateway to the campus of dramatic memorable presence—the traditional porte cochere at a new scale and meaning. Connected to it and on the north side of the bridgelike arcade are a 2,200-seat concert hall, a 750-seat repertory theater, and various other studio, performance, gallery, and library spaces, all more individually expressed and developing their own form in response to the specificity of function, yet aesthetically connected back to the master, unifying arcade element. Its relaxation of the overall imperative of guiding and containing lines permits a relationship of elements breaking out into the landscape, variably accentuated in changing patterns of light and shade as the sun moves around and shines through the composition of elements. Movements between the elements is fundamental to "knowing" such a building, as our mind's eye locates them in space through experience, rather than the intuition of "knowing" which is present in more predictable and formal relationships. The Fine Arts Center also confronts the

■ Roche Dinkeloo & Assoc., Creative Arts Center, Wesleyan University, Middletown, Connecticut, 1965–1973

landscape at two different scales; the formal, aesthetically predictable and grand sweep of long arcades, and the individual element scale of the more environmentally anchored and linked volumes.

The Creative Arts Center at Wesleyan University by the same architect is quite different in that its programmatic requirements are broken down so that they can be housed in a series of smaller buildings placed "in" the landscape, the separate parts carefully composed to preserve groves of trees, where the visual effect of space between buildings is the dominant thought—the "holes" in the Gruyère cheese enlarged to the point where they in effect become the matrix. The buildings, with bearing walls of limestone penetrated by simple, punched openings, reiterate the small-scale, countrylike theme derived directly from the residential scale of the site, which was a combination of gardens of nineteenth century houses.

The "pavilions" in the landscape is an opening up of the typical university quadrangle approach to let nature penetrate and play a stronger environmental role; reminiscent of the yards at Cambridge University, England, with their hard-lined and delineated courtyard spaces, opening through to the contrasting romantic and lush pastoral calm of the meandering River Cam at their rear. The Spelman Halls at Princeton University by I. M. Pei & Partners explores a related middle ground on these different dialogues of the connected or dispersed, between the built context and the landscape. Here 58 residential units for 220 students are disposed in eight triangular in plan and prismlike precast concrete and modularly repetitive, similar structures arranged along an armature of pedestrian walks. Connection becomes the theme as spaces have a sense of containment, but one immediately flowing into outward views through and beyond the structures. Their repetitive geometry provides individual predictability of form, but, especially because of their triangulated and cut form, simultaneously irregular shaping and relationship of exterior space.

■ I. M. Pei & Partners, Spelman Halls, Princeton, New Jersey, 1973 *(Photo: George Cserna)*

There is no sense of coming to rest as in the static and defined, traditional campus courtyard, but always the dynamic of movement through and between sliding planes. The walks are in an exciting dialogue with the structures, which are strategically cut back at the corners of their lower floors to allow spaces to penetrate beneath them. They become as persuasive a thematic element through reiteration, as do the modularly precast structural elements and the guiding design notion of connectability with penetrability also through organizational repetition. The tighter geometry that is logically implied especially in the cellular nature of a dormitory structure is adhered to, without resulting in the more standard row or courtyard scheme.

The traditional central courtyard, the university quadrangle, or convent patio as a building's landscape focus per se, can also take on new ideas pertaining to relationship, treatment, and definition as demonstrated in the Colegio de Mexico by González de León and Zabludovsky. Here, following the slope of its small 6.9-acre site, a central space on three interconnected and tiered levels affords various points of entry to the building, bringing the purplish pitted volcanic rock of the Pedregal del Ajusco and its picturesque vegetation in a spilling-down sequence within the space as a landscape focus. The court with its outwardly spreading west wing opens dynamically and diagonally beneath a 130-foot long concrete beam spanning the entrance, to dramatic views of the forest and mountains beyond, which encircle the valley of Mexico City. The shadows cast from overhead sunscreens create a sheltered intimacy of filtered patterns, an ambiance reminiscent of the grape arbors and trellised patios of Spanish-Mexican convents and haciendas. The view from, in this case a more dynamically and dramatically opening patio to the mountains beyond, and again beneath a space-defining beam is an idea further developed by Abraham Zabludovsky in his auditorium complex in the hills above Guanajuato.

In the Camino Real Hotel at Cancun, Ricardo Legorreta another Mexican architect, developed the courtyard idea into an aggressively linear expression. Open at either end and to the sky above, all the hotel's 256 rooms are entered from corridors overlooking this wonderfully landscaped atrium. The section of the building gains added drama from its sloping wing facing the hotel's

■ González de León & Zabludovsky, Colegio de Mexico, Mexico D.F., 1975 *(Photo: Julius Shulman)*

■ *Left:* Abraham Zabludovsky, State Auditorium, Guanajuato, Mexico, 1991 *(Photo: Peter Paige). Right:* Ricardo Legorreta, Camino Real Hotel, Cancun, Mexico, 1975

public facilities and a lagoon, contrasting with its vertical wing facing its ocean exposure. The atriums essence is that it suggests a definition of space in all planes while framing, at a grand scale, beautiful outward-looking vistas between articulations in its form structuring.

The courtyard concept is also basic to the Joan Miró Foundation in Barcelona, designed for the painter by his Catalonian friend Jose Luis Sert. Here it is conceived of less as a focus, more as a variable and loosely related sequence of spaces in the manner of a stage set taking full advantage of the existing features and grand landscaping of the old park in which the building is situated. A series of four different courtyards, one an old walled garden with cypress trees and hedges, another with panoramic, beautiful views overlooking the old city, a third central and interior, the last linked to study areas, auditorium, and cafeteria in conjunction with an exhibit roof terrace, form a variously interconnected series of exterior spaces. Much of their dynamic character comes from their definition by volumes of varied shapes, reflecting the different functions of the Miró Foundation, organized on a circulation system designed to lead visitors one-way through the entire exhibits. The varied shapes of buildings derive from changing ceiling heights, profiles, and prominent semicircular light scoops designed to bring overhead light to interiors, which also have different degrees of openness in response to the wish to develop various possibilities toward the exhibition and viewing of art, predominantly lighted by daylight. An auditorium, work, and research spaces are housed in a 3-story octagonal structure, having an affinity of shape to the local architectural tradition of the Romanesque and Gothic period and Islamic monuments left by the Moors in Spain. The white, vaulted, geometric volumes, lit by clerestories and oriented toward patios and gardens also draw heavily in spirit on the Mediterranean vernacular tradition.

So it is not only the form of elements and their relationship in and to the landscape that is fundamental in site considerations, but shapes and materials, methods of building character, and associative cultural and remembered image evocations are also important. Such is Thorncrown Chapel by Fay Jones

■ Fay Jones & Assoc., Thorncrown Chapel, Eureka Springs, Arkansas, 1980 *(Photos: Greg Hursley)*

in rural Arkansas, an architecture which complements and, in creating a special sense of place, "almost" completes the site. The character of the site dictated the method of construction, by "not using anything too big for two men to carry along a narrow hillside path." Jones's use of wooden tensile members in an overhead cross-lattice system holding the structure together, in contrast with the Gothic propped system of flying buttresses, emphasizes the fragility of the building and its surroundings, as life and nature itself is fragile and special. The rhythmic quality of the structure set against the calm magnitude of nature creates a sense of sacred space: The music of the fleeting moment, the rhythm of life, the seasons so clearly a part of the building. As the forest is a layering of vertical trunks and raking branches so is the building a canopy of layered and meshlike space. Thorncrown Chapel succeeds on yet another level, that of the symbolic: Using massing reminiscent of rural covered bridges, the image of shelter on the road of life is in keeping with the ecclesiastical understanding of nature. This is where regionalism through site and climate can play a vital role in making architecture not personally idiosyncratic in an ego or alternatively abstract-rule-applied sense, but special in a locally sensitive and relative sense.

Likewise, California-based architects have struggled through intelligent design evolution to express a life-style potential within a richly conducive, varied, and character-potent landscape. The classically derived but locally

■ *Left:* Bernard Maybeck, Christian Science Church, Berkeley, California, 1910 *(Photo: Museum of Modern Art, New York). Right:* Greene Brothers, Gamble House, Pasadena, California, 1907–1908 *(Photo: Wayne Andrews)*

inspired work of Bernard Maybeck at the beginning of the twentieth century, is very significant in the development of what subsequently became known as the Bay Region style. His imaginatively vigorous Christian Science church in Berkeley used factory sash windows, asbestos panels, and concrete in conjunction with local redwood, for a striking example of architecture born out of a local context and in the spirit of its time. The exquisitely made timber structures of the Greene brothers further developed a local tradition for cool and sheltered interior spaces, related to garden and patio areas through window and door openings. The honed craftsmanship and aesthetic totality of their Gamble House in Pasadena, thankfully preserved and put to good use as a facility for the University of Southern California, is a breathtaking testament not only to their design brilliance but also to the persuasive lessons of an architecture born of local pertinence and sensitivity. Even the furnishings were an intrinsic part of the idea, as was always general with the indigenous approach of Wright.

The crisp, cream-colored and sheer wall planes of the simple, volumetric buildings of Irving Gill at the beginning of this century were a combination of the frank spirit of the early modern movement from Europe and the poetic charm of the California-styled Spanish missions. This simplicity and local

■ Irving Gill, Scripps House, La Jolla, California, 1916 *(Photo: Museum of Modern Art, New York)*

■ Richard Neutra, Lovell House, "Health House," Los Angeles, California, 1928
(Photo: Paul Heyer)

persuasion moved inevitably into the architecture of R. M. Schindler and then that of Richard Neutra, with their opening up of volumes and the interpenetration of exterior and interior space. It was not coincidental that Neutra's airy, open, and terraced Lovell House was referred to as the "Health House." Such buildings evolved seemingly effortlessly into the industrial-like refinement of the slender steel and glass houses of the Case Study House Program sponsored, in one of the most admirable patron programs in U.S. architecture, by the Los Angeles based *Arts and Architecture* magazine publishing in the 1950s. The increasing imperative was toward interior volumes married to the exterior with illusorylike separation. Spaces vibrant from the changing patterns of natural light, as evidenced by Charles Eames's house and studio for himself, opening to terraces and patios and on to diffuse into a lush natural garden landscape beneath clear blue skies, the progressive and integral experience from the built world to nature. Taking full advantage of a favorable climate, they were a far cry

■ Charles Eames, own house, Los Angeles, California, 1949

from the sheltered, protective, inner world of the traditional New England saltbox house. The poetry of nature is inseparably part of their intensity and being, as much as it is in the different, handcrafted timber aesthetic of Maybeck and the Greene brothers. Interestingly, their boldly and finely carved structures clad with wood shingles, whose raking horizontal lines and overhanging eaves sheltered porches and cool terraces, were reminiscent compositionally and spatially of the less open, turn of the century Oak Park, Illinois, masonry houses of Frank Lloyd Wright. Curiously, in view of his inventiveness, Wright, designing in the 1920s in California, was much more interested in exploiting the lushness of its landscape by developing the sense of its romantic and pastoral tranquility in dialogue with the highly articulated, decorative, and cool surfaces of concrete block treated with the imprint of reliefs in a Mayan-inspired type of more theatrical aesthetic.

Confronted with designing the condominium complex of Sea Ranch on a spectacular Pacific Ocean site north of San Francisco, Moore Lyndon Turnbull Whitaker tightly grouped the units around a courtyard with traditional shed

■ MLTW/Moore Lyndon Turnbull Whitaker,
Sea Ranch Condominiums, Sea Ranch,
California, 1963–1965 *(Photos: Christopher
Noll)*

roofs and intersecting and towerlike wall planes, creating an overall commanding form but one of identifiably individual parts, at once casual and modest,
open to views and sun yet sheltered and protected from the wind. It was a
concept of cluster designed to preserve the openness of a rugged and beautiful
site, the California wood tradition projected into a mid-sixties leaner sensibility and aesthetic, with a builder's type awareness of economy.

It seems inevitable that the theatrical, stage-set type of environment would
be developed especially in the California setting. Gill and Wright were clearly
influenced by associative ideas of place, effects and sense of environment, even
a sense of romance and fantasy in many of their designs. Maybeck, at the

beginning of this century in the San Francisco Palace of Fine Arts, produced a classical, brilliant stage-set fantasy of stucco over chicken wire (now permanently reconstructed in painted concrete) of such evocative imagery that it would undoubtedly have inspired the likes of Maxfield Parrish or any twentieth-century yearning for a latent classicism.

In the late sixties, the Moore group designing Kresge College for the University of California at Santa Cruz, developed a totally theatrical-like painted stucco environment almost dancing in and through the landscape. For the College, Charles Moore and William Turnbull have designed a village street, one that is intimately defined by irregularly punctured false fronts of free-standing appearance and almost cardboard cut out feeling, of white painted stucco with accent planes of primary colors, where spaces are animated by social facilities and oriented to a sequence of plazas and gardens, all threaded, in what initially seems to be somewhat incongruously, through a redwood forest setting. Facades of buildings facing the trees are muted by being painted a dull brown color. The traditional college campus hierarchy of buildings and spaces, sequentially and predictably shaped and axially related, is rejected (the traditional sense of permanence and quality of detail and execution has also been surrendered) in favor of a 1,000-foot-long winding street rising 45 feet up the site to an octagonal dining commons and assembly, and a space looking toward a fountain at the ridge. The whole visually appears as a randomly disposed flow of space with shifting glimpses of views through facade cutouts of lanes and planes to woods; the converging juxtaposed to the diverging. Patterns of human association, the notion of students as a strictly transient and social population, sensitivity to site as a form potential both innately of its own characteristics and philosophically of the architects' intent to appropriately shape building in it in response to an objective, have led to a clever and stimulating, nontraditional response to the traditional campus problem. The lined-up courtyards and sophistication of Oxford and Cambridge, are replaced by the crooked mixes and cruder, playful forms of Kresge. It is a collage in search of dialogue, an attempt through site and association to create a highly personal and involving sense of place.

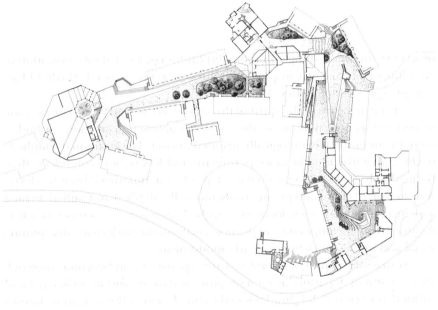

In a completely different attitude toward set and setting, the rural but sophisticated and relaxed chic of Sea Ranch and its timbered forms, takes on a tighter, crisp, hard-edged, and neat aesthetic in the more puritanically disciplined and New England inspired wood structures of Edward Larrabee Barnes, of which the residence at Mt. Desert Island on the spectacular, rocky Maine coast is typical. Composed of four, separate pavilionlike structures, a 2-story living unit for the owners, another a guest house, a high-ceilinged study library, and a studio above a laundry facility, they frame views between them from their unifying and connecting wood deck. The simple, elemental shed structures with roofs turning to wall planes without the traditional overhang or separation

■ MLTW/Moore-Turnbull with M. Buchanan, R. Calderwood and R. Simpson, Kresge College, University of California at Santa Cruz, Santa Cruz, California, 1966–1974 *(Photos: Charles W. Moore)*

■ Heckscher House, Edward Larrabee
Barnes, Mt. Desert Island, Maine, 1974
(Photo: David Franzen, ESTO)

of a fascia, are wood-shingled minimalist buildings, a persuasive evocation of
the value of a vernacular inspired and direct response to need. Maxfield Parrish gives ground to Andrew Wyeth.

Such extensions of the spirit of the saltbox house and barn have become
recognized as one antidote to the excessive abstraction of more orthodox
modernism or the technologically inspired artifact. The restrained simplicity
of the vernacular idea in more permissive and less rigorous architects than
Barnes has however often resulted in a type of contemporized "barn-modern."
A distortion of cubes and prisms, roofs and walls, all plied and pulled, twisted
and turned in their own form of detached abstraction, exercises in effect
divorced from the imperative of purpose, without the underlying disciplining
social and moral convictions of early modernism.

Vernacular *as* spirit, at its best, remains a persuasive architectural approach
idea, a point of departure as impetus grows out of site and its archetypal and
cultural associations. It is fundamental to the design of three separate houses
built for the same client, Peter and Sandra Brant by Venturi & Rauch. The
houses are radically different precisely because of considerations of association and context. The Greenwich house on a suburban and relatively flat
30-acre horse farm is in a natural clearing with a backdrop of trees. Its recall is
of the eighteenth century manor house with "Palladian" windows overlooking
the lawn. The front, says Venturi, has aspects of "WPA Post Office . . . Bauhaus
at the garage with its banded windows . . . Art Deco at the dining room alcove . . . a
Regency-like porch at the west side." The cited influences are as eclectic as the
owner's collection of modern American paintings, antique furniture, objects,
rugs, and artifacts. The house is far from the reductive presence as object and
furnishing of the previous Maine house and the influences are transposed in
the spirit of Venturi's philosophy of "complexity and contradiction" as an
incorporating synthesis. The intent is to roam, not focus, to blend and be

inclusive rather than eliminate idiosyncracies. The painter, Kenneth Noland,
for example takes beautiful colors and combines them into an equally beautiful whole, whereas Frank Stella takes strong, and often individually discordant
colors but through their juxtaposition creates paintings that are also beautiful;
one idea is more reductive in essence, the other more pluralist.

■ Venturi & Rauch, Brant and Johnson
House, Vail, Colorado, 1975 *(Photos:
Thomas Bernard)*

The Vail ski house, for the Brants and Johnson and their many guests, is a
totally different, 4-story structure on a steep mountain slope, its verticality
reflecting that of the stands of aspen trees in which it is ensconced. Entered on
the third floor where dining and other public spaces are situated, its vaulted
living room punctured by large dormer windows is above, bedrooms are on the
second level, with service facilities below on the first floor. Its cedar siding and
wide pine plank floors on the interior and cedar wood siding on walls canted
inward at the exterior, are capped by a brooding and broadly overhanging roof
of cedar shakes. The building is in the spirit of the Arts and Crafts movement
from England, which, transported to America in the early twentieth century,
became known as the Mission Style and in turn inspired the oak furniture of
master-craftsman Gustav Stickley, with which the house is appropriately furnished in conjunction with turn-of-the-century vacation lodge wicker.

The Brant house in Bermuda also exudes the architect's skill and confidence in transposing traditional elements into nonliteral configurations. The

■ Venturi & Rauch, Brant House, Bermuda, 1975 *(Photos: Thomas Bernard)*

elements of context are present; the sense of a white stucco eighteenth century style house seen through thickets of green foliage, the stepped roofs to catch rainwater and the dark painted shutters to screen windows from the penetrating sun. The house is a crescent-shaped cluster of wings to take advantage of ocean views and prevailing winds, each clearly articulated and capped by a disparate collection of roof profiles that read crisply and geometrically against clear blue skies. It is a house that looks as though it belongs to the sun-drenched beach but detached and poised above and looking down to it rather than an element of it, hence its crispness. The strength of the Venturi & Rauch example is that it adapts through new means and does not come out of outmoded nostalgia; the historicisms are always transformed and with great imagination, the way the Renaissance used classic architecture as a source filtered through Byzantine and Romanesque, or the nineteenth century revivals used the Classic and Gothic periods as precedent. The important point here, however, is that context and association as it emanates from location and site becomes form and idea determinant. A special place, a special solution.

Vernacular architecture of the Mediterranean hill town, the adobe or the saltbox/shingle genre, where the spirit is more closely pursued and less plied as in the architecture of Venturi & Rauch's or the Moore group, seems of essence more responsive to site simply because it is rooted in indigenous methods of building and tried and proven form approaches that respond to purpose in a manner purported to be unconcerned with fashion, the oblique, or the indigenously nonpertinent. This sophisticated distillation is the poetry of the Maine house by Barnes; it is a line held closer to the essence. The past is the present and alludes to the future through the timeless perfection of unaffected responses, of appearance seemingly spontaneously exercised.

Architecture as a texture response closely derives from the similar desire to be indigenous, pertinent, and variably attentive to site. Paul Rudolph, well-known for his predilection for dramatically interlocking space, variable form responses, and great interest in industrialized trailer housing (if a pluralist approach to architecture, one with its origins firmly in the heroic spirit of modern architecture), designed in a strong textural manner an apartment hotel for Jerusalem, one of his most interesting but not built or publicized projects. The whole intent to create architecture as a single act in time rather than an additive accretion of elements over a period as in the village precedent, did not compromise the project's essence whose origins seem to span two thousand years to carry a clear message of habitat as a timeless mode.

■ Paul Rudolph, Apartment Hotel, Jerusalem, 1974 *(Photo: Donald Luckenbill)*

■ I. M. Pei & Partners, National Center for Atmospheric Research, Boulder, Colorado, 1967 *(Photo: Ezra Stoller)*

In contrast to the Jerusalem project's accretion-of-cellular-elements-expression, a texture appropriate to the building's function, is the National Center for Atmospheric Research, southwest of Boulder by I. M. Pei & Partners. Conceived as a concentrated cluster of buildings in the more classically "contained" sense, impinging minimally on the vegetation and topography of their mesa site at the edge of the Rockies, it too is attentive to site in that it is almost an element of urbanity delicately lowered into nature, yet, like the previous project, monumental in presence while not axially monumental in concept. The crisp and angular masses of bold pinkish-brown concrete forms, resembling in color the backdrop of rocks, grow out of the mesa and its defining slopes. The forms are cut apart by vertical strips of gray tinted glass and sculpturally capped by concrete hoods and louvers, which act as sculptural accents in the overall upward thrust of the scaleless vertical wall planes. To quote I. M. Pei, "You just cannot compete with the scale of the Rockies. So we tried to make a building that was without the conventional scale you get from recognizable floor heights—as in those monolithic structures that still survive from the cliff-dwelling Indians."

In yet a different but again somewhat parallel vein is the proposal for an urban nucleus for the Santa Monica mountains outside Los Angeles, by Daniel, Mann, Johnson & Mendenhall with architects Cesar Pelli and A. J. Lumsden in charge of design. The complex is based on concentration, proximity, and the close interdependence of elements but in a more flowing and, by

■ Daniel, Mann, Johnson & Mendenhall,
Sunset Mountain Park, Los Angeles,
1967

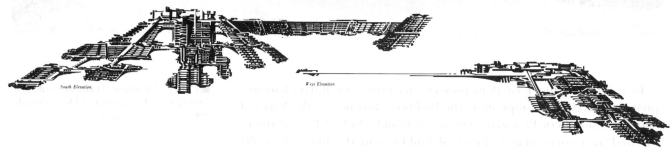

South Elevation   *West Elevation*

virtue of extending armatures, land-embracing megastructure type of solution. From a promontory at the edge of a bowl where all the urban core facilities and centralized parking would be consolidated, spurs of housing for a total of 1,500 units to have been built in stages and conceived as neighborhoods, located for view and privacy from other adjacent units, spill down the hillside as a connected series of concrete terraces. Moving sidewalks and funicular type cars would loop downward from the parking to houses. The whole community was conceived as a single building, a logical approach for solving problems of density without consuming the land. Tight and interlocking systems of organization at an urban scale have precedents in the work of Le Corbusier. It was philosophically elemental to the attitude of Louis Kahn, the urban studies of Sant' Elia, and the Beaux Arts architect Eugene Henard. It was in the spirit of the boulevard layouts of another Frenchman, Georges Haussmann, and elemental to the wonderful squares and crescents of Georgian and Regency England. Ironically, this project was conceived for sprawling Los Angeles!

In any consideration of site, using the land while conserving it is basic. A further example in this direction is the work and philosophy of Paolo Soleri.

Arcosanti, a prototype 25-story structure occupying 13 acres of an 860-acre land parcel in the high mesa country 70 miles north of Phoenix, is planned for an eventual population of 5,000 persons. The intent is for an urban form functionally sensitive to the ecology of the environment, three-dimensional and lively in its integration of elements. Its emphasis on proximity is a direction away from the consumption of time, energy, land, and human resources of the commuting type of suburb. Integrated with the town structure and sloping down from the town, will be a 5-story greenhouse on the mesa's south exposure that year-round will provide food and passively meet the space and water-heating needs of the town. It is Soleri's vision toward his idea of "the evolving consciousness of life in the mind and spirit of man"—a reference influenced by the philosopher Teilhard de Chardin of whom Soleri is a great admirer and for whom a cloister complex at Arcosanti will be named. With the increased complexity of our lives, Soleri's philosophical concept of conservation and an integrated life-style are increasingly timely.

The conclusion from the previous examples is that considerations of site must be of both building and context. Since locale influences thought and attitude, it is indigenous detail and the searching mind that is the best guarantee against the suffocating aspects of repetition and an anonymous technology. To protect a building against the heat and glare of a blistering sun, to quickly shed rain and snow, to express the memoria and the life-style pattern of a culture, to respect the continuity of historical context, to see building as a changing and not static and constant event, is to personalize a movement in architecture through following natural, evolving, and appropriate patterns. In terms of context and the quality of urban life it is entirely logical to see a building in a syntactical way relative to the urban or landscape matrix, a microcosm in or of a chain of events. The single building may be a measure of individual success but against the environment it is actually of little or relative importance. Then again, the urban environment is an accumulation of many "little" achievements. Few cities can rival the total architectural excellence of Paris, even though in terms of great individual buildings, especially of modern architectural merit, it has superiors. The lesson of Paris is homogeneity and respect, buildings coexisting, drawing strength and impact from a breadth of environment, thereby contributing, significantly, to each other.

In the early days of the modern movement in architecture, contextual relationship was of secondary importance. The masters of the modern movement had little to contribute beyond academic diagrams and the schizophrenic polarity of Le Corbusier replacing part of Paris with skyscrapers in a park, to Wright's agrarian and philosophically rationalized sprawl of an acre for every American family. Basic to the urban design consciousness movement emanating from the 1960s was the recognition that environment is design. Personality and context in the environment also brought with it a new grass-roots type of awareness of architecture as site and heritage, the relationship of the small to the large, and especially the old to the new. Even the epic Beaux Arts schemes that were so totally decried as devoid of merit until recently, sought in their own detached manner to bring a notion of inclusive form to buildings as elements in a total landscape. From this heightened sensibility and sensitivity to elemental patterns of architecture, echoing back to precedents as removed as the Italian Renaissance hilltown is from the English Georgian crescent or the Paris boulevard, our hope today is that within our cultural patterns, architecture and site can coexist as complementary drama, that building can gain in presence and individuality through and within context.

5

Idea as Catalyst

■ HAVING ESTABLISHED THE more definable parameters of a problem from the context of certain functional, spatial, structural, and environmental considerations, which have resulted in possible and usually variable organizational sequences, the architect begins to close in on a design solution. Having gained ground in comprehending and penetrating the realities of a problem, the architect simultaneously feels a murkiness of information, vulnerability of decisions, the grasp on a design just eluding intelligent probes. At this juncture the creative search is at its most intense, but also most questioning and frustrating. Out of the realities and an eclectic type of problem scanning, the architect hopes for an inspiration, for a triggering that will allow a leap beyond the facts. The grasping and panoramic search is for an idea. An idea that in itself can become a catalyst for the series of ideas of varied importance that will finally constitute the foundation of a design.

An idea in architecture points a direction but, more important for the architect, it actually becomes a point of departure. It is a commitment on which the success of a project depends, and without it a design will invariably be commonplace. The idea represents an insight or attitude that suggests an expression or hints at a form that is in itself beyond technique. A building that has the presence to move us has always gone beyond fact. It has derived from a strong idea about building, and like most strong ideas, it will invariably possess great clarity. In philosophy and all the arts such concepts touch at elemental truth. They can become like foundations to cultures.

The clarity of an idea in architecture can usually be expressed by a doodle, the smallest and most minimal drawing on a table-napkin-sized page. Such an idea doodle is a concept. It does not or should not come from dogma but a patient sifting through, about, and around a design. It is also often not a forceful, focused view of a problem, unless it is an engineering challenge like a bridge, and even great structural displays are of transitory interest in a building unless there is some stronger projection of meaning. Standing beneath the dome of St. Paul's Cathedral in London, we do not instinctively marvel at Christopher Wren's structural feat, which indeed it was—especially since he cut away the restraining tension chains, which had been added as a precaution, to demonstrate the great structural presence of his achievement—but we are moved by the powerful concept of space, the greatness of architecture transcending fact. The generating idea is clearly basic to the architectural statement and it is precisely such conceptual thinking that we recognize as the genius of history's master builders. The recognition that behind important architecture there is a structuring of clear and simple ideas, acknowledges that the essence of architecture is the unequivocable, poetic statement of these ideas. The power of architecture is not then in elaboration for its own sake, but in simplicity and directness of expression. Progress is idea.

An idea in architecture usually brings with it a strong image that can be seen as the motivating intellectual and architectural force in governing the concept of a building. Then, the various parts of a building complement the idea as they become dependent upon each other to constitute the fullness of the total expression. A building is then something from which nothing can be taken without weakening or destroying the concept. Detail supports concept. Elements and detail are integral to the whole.

In great classic architecture the parts are in harmony with and support the idea of the totality. The flying buttresses of the Gothic cathedral, for example, efficiently carry the spreading roof loads, directly resisting their outward thrust and transmitting it to the ground. They, too, are in the aesthetic of the lean, skeletal sense of a structural cage in stonework, reinforcing the drama and basic spirit of soaring that is the essence of the Gothic cathedral. Ribs of stone holding panes of glass, the idea of lines in and almost weblike dividing light is in unison. *Idea* is complemented by *fact* as column, wall, roof, and all aspects of decorative treatment to those planes, act to seemingly pull lines around and through space. The onward march of archways and the bellying out of transepts at the altar end, all are an episode of line and plane defining space that uplifts the viewers earthly sense of relationship to the notion of a supreme being. Here, architecture in all its detail reinforces idea, and idea is the drama of architecture.

Historically, an idea as the seminal influence in the design of a building usually meant that the idea was firmly imbedded in the cultural context of a period. There was still a certain continuity of clear philosophical directive from the early Italian Renaissance buildings of Brunelleschi, to those a century latter by Palladio, to subsequent designs by Michelangelo, Bramante, and Borromini. The arcade, the arch, the column in relation to the entablature, the window in the wall, were evolving steady developments and refinement of thoughts that grew out of an energetic and wonderfully imaginative rephrasing of ideas that had developed in classical Roman architecture.

This was dramatically dispelled in our century when idea in architecture became less related to the pattern of evolution within a cultural style, than to idea as a potentially abstract, intellectual act, which in itself carried or implied the suggestion of its own style, Le Corbusier's Visual Arts Center at Harvard University is clearly the product of a vibrant, authoritative inner force shaping

■ Le Corbusier, Visual Arts Center, Harvard University, Cambridge, Massachusetts, 1962 *(Photo: Paul Heyer)*

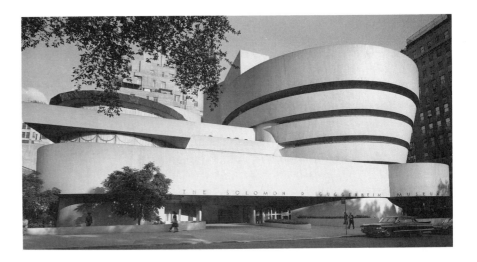

■ Frank Lloyd Wright, Guggenheim Museum, New York City, 1946 *(Photo: The Solomon R. Guggenheim Museum)*

space like sculpture that almost bursts outward to become exterior form. The cultural and environmental context and any thought of structural clarity or functional directness is clearly secondary. Likewise, Wright's dramatic spiral known as the Guggenheim Museum has little to do with New York's grid and brownstone pattern in which it is embedded, Central Park which it faces, or the display of art which is its supposed raison d'etre. Both remain forceful examples of architecture and where clearly prices have been paid for the demonstration of *idea.*

The most consistently idea-oriented architecture of the mid-twentieth century was by Eero Saarinen. Dramatically different buildings fundamentally derived their form and style from the pursuit of strong ideas, which were a consuming passion and preoccupation for his inventive and probing mind, whether the interlocking curves of TWA and the symbolic associations of the bird poised for flight, or the rusted corten steel of the Deere building, headquarters for the makers of farm machinery and itself in the spirit of their product. The swooping concrete shell clad with white penny-sized mosaic on the interior at TWA and the cinnamon brown assembled steel at Deere are intentionally both supported in their form idea by their material and construction method.

■ *Left:* Eero Saarinen, Deere Building, Moline, Illinois, 1957–1963 *(Photo: John Pile). Right:* Eero Saarinen, TWA Terminal, Kennedy Airport, Long Island, New York, 1956–1962 *(Photo: Paul Heyer)*

Kevin Roche and John Dinkeloo, who inherited the office upon Saarinen's death in 1961, continued the same attitude although in a gentler, more mannerly, stylized, restrained, and less frenetic manner. In the Ford Foundation, the oasis of an inner garden is a focus for offices and an attractive extension to the street while becoming the strong "idea" of the building and bringing to it its form, clarity, and aesthetic. It is an idea appropriate to the design problem, executed with taste and a singular directness, which of themselves are all basic to any successful idea in architecture. In its entirety the Oakland Museum

■ Roche Dinkeloo & Assoc., Ford Foundation, New York City, 1963–1968

■ Roche Dinkeloo & Assoc., Oakland Museum, California, 1961–1968

■ Sert, Jackson & Assoc., Married
Student Housing, Harvard University,
Cambridge, Massachusetts, 1962–1964

becomes landscape as the four-block area structure is conceived as a walled garden with galleries opening onto lawns, terraces, trellised passages, and broad flights of stairs. The roof of one gallery becomes the terrace of another, with planting in effect submerging and losing the whole building beneath a lush green veil. Clearly the TWA concept is more subjective and symbolic in derivation and the Deere building associative aesthetic and material motivated, whereas the Ford Foundation is more prestigious and imposing headquarters and environmental—the garden as grand salon—in origin, and the Oakland Museum, landscape as an urban presence oriented. Different forces and interests have pushed the architects to evolve and resolve different ideas that have in turn brought a pertinence and uniqueness to these buildings.

Where the Roche, Dinkeloo buildings were primarily derived from environmental ideas, the housing on New York City's Roosevelt Island by Sert, Jackson and Associates, a development of an idea imaginatively and cleverly pursued in the earlier Married Student Housing for Harvard University, is environmental in origin, but in an organizational and urban relationship sense. At Harvard a sequence of defined spaces, deriving from the quadrangle precedent, open via a brick-paved, tree-lined promenade, reminiscent of the adjacent Harvard "houses," to a grass space at the river, a solid and respectably traditional design attitude for academia. But the complex's interest stems from an idea that is organizational in origin: That of developing a stepping scale between low and high elements, thereby making a dramatic move beyond the limiting aesthetic of the tower apartment building "floating" in the landscape,

which in reality has done as much to destroy or qualify urban character as the suburban detached house. In the design, 3-, 5-, and 7-story horizontal volumes, relating to the low height of surrounding residences, rise up from the edges and are connected by bridges to the three, 22-story central towers. The elevators in the towers serve the fourth and sixth levels of the low buildings across bridges thus making 7-story walkups possible while the number of apartments in the low buildings in turn makes the slender towers economically feasible. The Roosevelt Island Housing, for a mix of incomes ranging from low to high, is conceived as a community with social services and commercial amenities integrated into the residential fabric. Here the form steps back from the waters edge on both sides of its island site to a high mass down the middle of the island. Developed as a central access spine, it is a profile derived from the elevator stopping only at every third floor in a skip stop fashion where, from an access corridor visible at the exterior, residents walk up or down one flight of stairs to their apartments or enter them at the corridor level. Since most apartments are floor through, with this system of organization most get direct sunlight, some even from two directions during a day, cross ventilation, and the majority a visual relationship with the water. The repetition of the 3-story step back, permitting sunlight to penetrate deeply into exterior spaces brings a commanding urban presence to the overall mass, but one which also respects the personalization and changing urban scale required within its own neighborhood fabric. As an idea in housing both projects evidence a contemporary logic with an affinity to the Greek and Italian hill towns, with height, ventilation, and view achieved without the medium of the hill.

The organizational, urban relationship and form idea of the Sert housing had a variant approach in Moishe Safdie's "Habitat" housing in Montreal, where the idea derived from an interest in mass production and the application of an advanced precast concrete technology, to create "boxes" that could

■ Moishe Safdie, "Habitat," Montreal, Canada, 1968 *(Photo: John Pile)*

be assembled structurally one upon another to achieve an even greater approximation to a modern hill town. This idea was explored in a different vein in the 1960s in the more playfully futuristic ventures of Britain's Archigram group, where projects had a sophisticated, comic-book-like idea of technocracy.

With the organizational stepping of the Sert projects, and the one element upon another stepping back effect of "Habitat," architecture as plane was more variable and—this is also conscious idea intent—a total departure from the neo-platonic and more simplistic geometric form of the aesthetically contained residential tower where all four facades are equally treated, and, because it is repetitive, has a more structurally economic, uniform envelope. Facades here, rather than formal clarity, can potentially vary in response to view, exposure, and sun, and structure is an accretion of elements rather than a predictable framework within which elements are resolved. The housing is also an idea move toward a connective aesthetic, an attempt to make scale overtures to the environment and to stress the linkage of masses. The idea of the stepped building, because it does fracture form and permit relational context ideas and can potentially be used to pull light into an interior while also making exterior masses less formidable and overshadowing, has become a popular form idea in our architectural vocabulary today. In the Harvard Graduate School of Design, for example, it was an idea functionally and socially derived and technologically executed in a linear manner, rather than the box upon box aesthetic of "Habitat."

■ Davis, Brody & Assoc., Waterside Housing, New York City, 1974

Davis, Brody & Associates' successful attempt to break down the mass or straight upward bulk of the tower was clearly the aesthetic intent in the modest, yet elegant Waterside Housing on Manhattan's East River in New York. The slender towers, pinwheel in form and minimally obstructing river views for their neighbors, themselves composing into an interesting overlay of changing urban form relationships, have larger apartments at their top section within an overall rectangular profile, with corners cantilevering over 45-degree chamfered planes in their midsection, and the lower part of their shafts cut back to

form reentrant corners. Although the shaping of the shaft is aesthetically form making in intent, in that the tower's bulk is less bulky and obtrusive, its aim is also an environmentally sensitive response and a more gentle and refined form presence.

The more playful treatment of breaking down a building's basic rectangular mass by the insertion and projection of strikingly distinctive geometric elements is the idea dramatically executed by Arquitectonica in their design for the Atlantis apartment building in Miami. The building's reflective glass mass is topped by a red triangle at its corner; four yellow triangular balconies are cantilevered from its north facade into which an overscaled square hole is also punched, a "skycourt" which is echoed as a "pushed-out" and displaced 27-foot cubic volume lying where it "fell" to the ground housing a squash court

■ Johnson & Burgee, Pennzoil Plaza, Houston, Texas, 1974–1976 (Photos: Richard W. Payne)

and exercise room. The building's narrow end is rounded as a nautical-like gesture to Biscayne Bay, and the south facade is overlaid with a 3-story, overscaled blue-stuccoed square grid. From the skycourt, a red spiral stair, cantilevered out beyond the building's flat plane, affords access to four apartments as well as panoramic views to the bay.

In comparison to Arquitectonica's somewhat flamboyant, whimsical, and nostalgically romantic modernism, Pennzoil Plaza in Houston by Johnson & Burgee is, similar to Waterside, a geometrically manipulative, modernist approach. Here a simple geometric idea, prompted also by not wanting to design a straight-up and unbroken tower, affords total visual clarity to the design. Twin 36-story towers, mirror images of each other and trapezoidal in plan, are related at the ground level by triangular shaped plazas that are 8-story spaces enclosed by a 45-degree glass slope. This slope repeats at the top of the towers where executive suites are housed when, rising straight upward to the twenty-ninth floor, they are then similarly angled-off to repeat the 45-degree theme. The "twins" are in dramatic tension since they are separated only by a narrow 10-foot vertical slot, making them a changing visual presence in the urban landscape. The geometry of the idea is absolutely clear, especially since the towers are unbroken, neutral masses clad in bronze-tinted glass and a dark brown anodized aluminum curtain wall. This in the interior contrasts with the white painted steel trusses that roof the courtyards in more animating filigree patterns of lines and shadows.

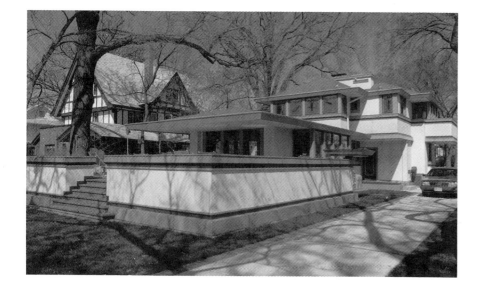

Since it is a visual manifestation, the manipulation of an idea derived directly from geometry invariably presents its origin with a degree of clarity. Geometry implied in an idea or method of building can in itself impose a strong visual presence and be a persuasive form determinant of how a building is consequently organized in response to function as evidenced by the Pennzoil towers. It is even more essentially a form generating device in the idea of "house" as shelter, which has often led to the roof, symbolically the sheltering element, to be designed as a universal type of umbrella beneath which space can be generatively organized, occasionally independent of but usually in relation to the roof form. The anonymity of the modern flat roof freed architects from any such constraint. The nineteenth century Shingle Houses clearly had rooms located and arranged with respect to complicated systems of roof pitches. The idea of home was further reinforced with the symbolism of the hearth, used invariably as a focus in the pinwheel type plans of Wright, as the notion of warmth and security, the eternal symbols of "home," and also used as a visual anchor for the interlock of pitched roofs. The layering of interlocking pitches, as seen in his turn-of-the-century houses in the Chicago suburb of Oak Park, was an aesthetic that Wright was a master at freely handling: an overall discipline in form from the roof above, a skillful and free-flowing organization of interpenetrating spaces below.

The roof as a singular and clear structural idea can liberate functional arrangements below and also exterior form configurations especially when, as a flat plane, it can be cut away purely in response to spaces below without any geometric imperative of its own form. Each attitude toward the roof plane has its implication in space organization and disposition of structural systems to carry the roof, which in turn imposes a strong discipline upon the flexibility of functional arrangements beneath. The important point is that initially in design there is primary importance in the recognition of the strong geometric implications and often limitations on form flexibility that systems of roofs imply. In turn, this in itself can become an organizing aesthetic, another type of cogent idea of assembly and consequently a very potent form generator.

■ *Left:* Paul Heyer, Knoedler Gallery, New York City, 1976 *(Photo: © Norman McGrath).* *Right:* Paul Heyer, Hammer Gallery, New York City, 1980 *(Photo: © Norman McGrath)*

Interpretation of the idea of purpose as a refined sense of function can also be the vehicle to form derivation and treatment of space as illustrated in my design of the Knoedler and Hammer galleries. Located in comparable Manhattan townhouses they have in common the function of showing paintings, but each with a different emphasis that stems directly from the difference in the art they represent. Knoedler, with its contemporary artists producing very large and variable proportion color field painting needed a flexible, fairly open, and neutral environment. Hammer, displaying smaller in scale Impressionist, early American and other forms of easel-art of the realist persuasion implied a more classic, yet intimate and scaled down sense of space, and even different yet related types of backgrounds for the art. The more minimally treated Knoedler volume preserved a monolithic flow of space but one still punctuated into connected yet separately defined volumes—the barnlike lack of intimacy and scale of many galleries in Manhattan's Soho art section was considered anathema. With Hammer Gallery, the overall space sequence has echoes of the salon in the grander arcadelike effect of its column-articulated, neutral pale beige space, contrasting with the richness of red and green velvet on the upholstered walls of its main exhibit "rooms." Since high ceilings were not so critical, these were lowered in central areas to form light coffers and space for air-conditioning ducts and to also articulate the flow of interior space. Although the play of form, detail, and color is appropriately stronger at Hammer, both galleries respect and derive their character from function, expressed in the sequential display of art in a space of presence where architecture becomes a framework for the exhibition of another art form.

■ Ulrich Franzen & Assoc., Veterinary College, Cornell University, Ithaca, New York, 1975 *(Photos: Norman McGrath)*

■ Ulrich Franzen & Assoc., Boyce Thompson Institute, Cornell University, Ithaca, New York, 1979 *(Photos: Peter Aaron/Esto)*

■ Hammond Beeby & Babka, Tri State Center, Northbrook, Illinois, 1977 *(Photos: Howard N. Kaplan)*

The interpretation of function as the impetus to organize a building within certain desired parameters is also fundamental to the final aesthetic of two buildings at Cornell University by Ulrich Franzen, in what he refers to as a "combine" idea of architecture. In the Veterinary College building, office, public, and social areas are behind a standard glass curtain wall, whose "tautness" is visually reinforced as part of the facade and breaks outward at an angle from the main form. On the opposite and southern exposure, laboratory and support spaces are behind a heavily modeled brick facade. The contrast between the treatment of the two facades, one protected against the sun and the other receiving northern light, and the different textures and materials is fused aesthetically through the transition device at either end of heavily expressive, brick-clad stair towers. The expressing of elements remains a building theme, carried also into the three red air intake pipes in front of the glass facade and exhaust ducts punctuating the top levels of the solid brick facade. This type of tension through a disciplined spirit of "collaging" a building, finds different impetus in the Boyce Thompson Institute for Plant Research. The south facade, facing a highway and parking areas, is deliberately expansive in scale and contains laboratory areas, where the building's primary function of growing and testing is conducted behind an unbroken wall, topped by a continuous greenhouse. Behind this is a continuous 1-story service area for the preparatory work for growing specimens. The north side of the building, facing toward the more intimate scale of the campus, contains research offices and is scaled down by horizontal bands of windows to offices and the projection of an administrative and entrance wing. The strong sculptural expression of mechanical devices again further articulates the overall form as they become the sculptural expression of the vertical rise of the solid south facade of the upper levels of the office section.

The employ of the "collage" idea in the more functionally anonymous speculative office building, here located on a major tollway curve approaching an airport, is the device used by Hammond, Beeby & Babka in the Tri-State Center in the search, in an undistinguished context, for a more distinctive structure with presence. The east and west facades of the 5-story building are precast concrete panels detailed to express their fenestration patterns of round pilasters and square windows, while the north and south facades, cut away and attached to emphasize their nonstructural character, are of reflective glass. The porte cochere entrance is designed to reinforce the collage theme at a more personal scale. In contrast to Franzen's clearly crisp and modernist aesthetic, this building alludes to a more suggestively neoclassic imagery.

The assimilation and direct expression of visual dissimilarities as they derive from a concern to incorporate into a coherent whole a more independent and multiple building expression is fundamental, but in an entirely different sensibility in the Mt. Healthy School by Hardy Holzman Pfeiffer Associates. The building is protected against its northern exposure by a giant right angle of masonry, which Hugh Hardy cites as reminiscent of old Indiana buildings of severe, stark masonry walls and rusticated stone lintels. To the

■ Hardy Holzman Pfeiffer Assoc., Mt. Healthy School, Columbus, Indiana, 1972
(Photos: Norman McGrath)

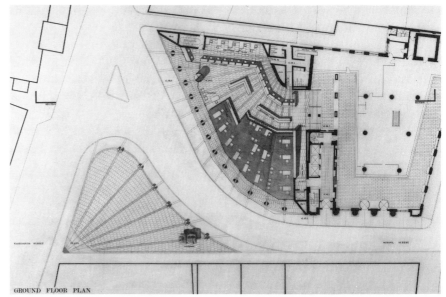

■ Kallmann & McKinnell, Boston Five Cents Savings Bank, Boston, 1971–1972 (Photos: Ezra Stoller)

GROUND FLOOR PLAN

south three clusters of classrooms visually break open to views over fields. Hence in the exterior the animated and variable is juxtaposed with the quiet and somewhat deliberately boring. The interior organization, conceived of open and closed, flowing and defined spaces, is at opposing angles to the rectangular, repetitive structural grid, which again is at an angle to the pattern of mechanical ducts, service pipes, and lighting grid layouts. The overall volume, composed of elements each seemingly responding to its own law of derivation and organizing geometry, is a conscious attempt to make parts of a building respective of different generating forces, the whole becoming an overlay where various geometries intersect creating a richness born of complexity and predictable accident but, because geometry is the overlay catalyst, one devoid of confusion. It is a building quite typical of the modernist concerns of the late sixties—at least stylistically—and early seventies, before the more eclectic priorities of the Post-Modern drive of the mid-seventies drastically shifted design attitudes.

Where the giant right angle wall quietly and modestly defined the hard edge of a form and became the foil for the more faceted teaching cluster elements of the "third" facade at Columbus, it becomes the "backdrop" for a sophisticated urban play in ideas of penetration and the layering back of urban space at the Boston Five Cents Savings Bank by Kallmann & McKinnell. The awkward, wedge-shaped site that the banking space occupies opens outward to visually embrace a small triangular plaza onto which it fronts and within which for continuity the granite and concrete finishes of the bank repeat. The building's curved exterior perimeter is gracefully delineated by an arc of eight 65-foot-high columns, set back from which and thereby forming a colonnade, is the glass facade of the banking hall. From these poured-in-place concrete columns, posttensioned and tapered concrete beams clear span to the concrete core at the apex of the triangular space. The columns are also split apart down their middle to allow the radial configuration of beams to penetrate them thereby inviting the eye to carry through any defining line of structure. The airiness and penetration of the structure backlit from the bank is especially dramatic at night, and interestingly frames vistas of the adjacent structures across the plaza seen from within the bank. A glazed skylight above the colonnade is a further reiteration of the idea of light and sight penetrating the density of any notion of the traditional "wall" as the building's exterior boundary, as the eye is led inward, or conversely outward, through a sequence of inferred planes. The column arcade somewhat resembles a proscenium—without the sense of mystery of the theatre—where the eye is deliberately engaged and drawn both in and out. Elemental also is the strong expression of construction and structure, characteristic of the firm's work as seen in their earlier and adjacent Boston City Hall, which reinforces the overall clarity of the idea with a rigor reminiscent of the Gothic era of the column and buttress.

The Illinois Regional Library for the Blind and Physically Handicapped also draws heavily on the idea of wall as a motif whose form is appreciated aesthetically and not presumed to derive directly from function, in a manner

■ Stanley Tigerman, Illinois Regional Library, Chicago, 1978

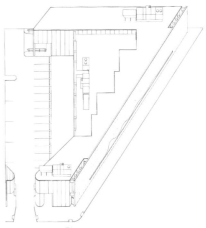

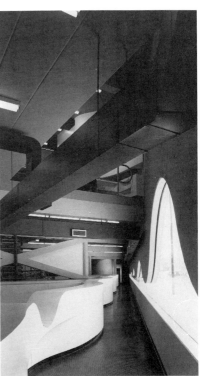

that its architect, Stanley Tigerman, refers to as a study in reversals and inversions. The triangular-shaped building is a wall in front and a machined object in the back. The building's hypotenuse is a relentlessly long wall of concrete construction, the denseness and impenetrability of which is belied by a continuous 165-foot-long wave of a window. Since there are no supporting columns the wall above acts as a giant beam. The unbroken run of the low window allows people in wheelchairs and seated staff a view to the exterior and reflects the circulation pattern immediately adjacent to it. As if to reiterate the wall as a planar frontispiece element against which the building is encrusted, the mass of building is detached from it by the device of large scale slots at both ends—a mannerism reminiscent of Kahn, Giurgola, and other architects of the Philadelphia School of the 1960s. The design effort to dematerialize and penetrate the visually dense is exactly opposed by the bulk of the building, clad in lightweight baked enameled panels made to appear as solid and opaque. The circulation is organized in a linear pattern for memorability to

■ Stanley Tigerman, Daisy House, Indiana, 1975–1978 *(Photos: Howard Kaplan)*

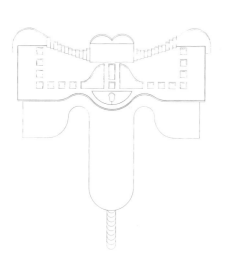

the blind and all public areas used by them are round cornered and built in for predictability. Since many legally blind people have some minimal degree of vision, and the building's urban context has a grayish lack of distinction, the building juxtaposes against its gray wall a lively and bright color scheme of a structure painted yellow, perimeter panels baked enamel red, and all exposed mechanical and electrical elements painted blue. It is a project that denies institutional dreariness, and there is humor in its whimsy.

A private residence in Indiana is also idea in derivation in terms of wall symbolism and again an injection of whimsy that takes itself even less seriously. The frontispiece approach wall of the house is finished in white stucco inside and out, is also again detached and bannerlike treated and, in contrast to the rest of the house which is a windowless and unbroken curve, finished both sides in cedar. The central bell, a Spanish mission touch, was a request of the owner. All the windows of the house are in the planar white wall, whose curves in elevation, ingeneously and symbolically derive from an inversion of the plan curve of the house form. The obviously suggestive genital form configuration is intentionally apparent. In a subsequent house in Illinois, the "wall" becomes a series of small 16-foot wide gable-roof volumes, intended as a remembrance of the vernacular idea of house as a "village." Against this metaphor, in a project again exploring notions of opposing thoughts, is an "entrance" concept employing the classical sweep of an "embracing" colonnade in the sense, for Tigerman, of the Roman sixteenth century Villa Giulia by Vignola. Such juxtaposed contradictions and preoccupation with dualistic thoughts has been somewhat endemic to some architecture of the eighties, especially of the Post Modern genre, and has been an increasing motivation behind Tigerman's basic approach to design.

The wall as an enclosing skin, as the boundary of form and definer of volume, the referential plane that might give suggestions about interior function, the wall as neoclassic facade that as frontal face to the public was the value announcer of importance and purpose, or the wall as the Gothic luminous membrane and structural web of colored glass and lattice of stone all were an historic attitude from which the former buildings have to various degrees departed in search of new, built meaning. John Hejduk, to whom Tigerman acknowledges a debt in the inferential attitude to the wall, has pushed this notion to a distilled level of communication where wall as transition device becomes far removed from ideas of the barrier between exterior and interior, both physically and symbolically. In his design for a Wall House, functions are totally separated, reduced to elements each seeking to directly express its essential property, then reassembled as parts into a relational whole which, while it is abstract, is not an abstraction. Abutting the wall and on one side would be a ramp and a stair tower combined with an elevator—or all the vertical movement systems—and on the other side the four stories of the house, which are designed to project from the tower element as they penetrate the wall in the passage openings but do not physically touch the wall. The wall thereby becomes a threshold or transition and a referential relationship is continually made to it as it is traversed every time in the movement from one room to another. The wall is a vertical plane which, as a conceptual tool, is neither pictorial nor picturesque, does not enclose volume but is an opaque plane that as an idea draws a firm distinction between private interior volume

■ Stanley Tigerman, Barrington Hills Residence, Illinois, 1981

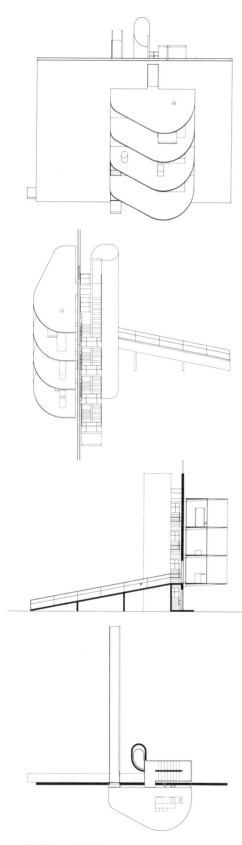

■ John Hejduk, Wall House, 1972

and systems of circulation and entrance. Hejduk sees color as an important tool in the composition. The wall would be a white plane, against which the precise circulation volumes would be seen in perspective, banded gray at its edges and with a reflective, chrome treatment on the side exposed to the metal and glass private space volume, which, in itself, is an internalized condition within its curving grand-piano-shaped form but simultaneously external in its expression of anonymous use. Form is not an expression of purpose but rather a sense of presumption that function will inevitably happen. Building becomes a collage of physical motifs, its origins in De Stijl and Cubist art, but with clarification more purely expressed than the architects of the modern movement in Europe of the twenties were able to achieve with their stronger emphasis on the logic of construction method and more literal thoughts about function.

In the architecture of Peter Eisenman the notion of wall is completely destroyed and replaced by an attitude idea based upon a sequence of shifts between the relationship of solid, plane, and underlying grid. The spirit emanates from a layering attitude toward the idea of structure where generatively the structure of form affects, even infers meaning. Like Hejduk there is a departure from traditional meanings and an absence of reference to notions of symbols of predetermined images. Where in Hejduk's house elements are intentionally apart, in Eisenman's work components are inextricably interlocked as they become collapsed inward, almost slid onto organizing and regulating lines and entwined as they reemerge outward as layered exterior form. Such is the Miller House documented by Eisenman as House III. (The Roman numeral at once declares a commitment to the idea of House as an episode of evolving explorations, of variations in the pursuit of spatial consequence through the medium of abstract organization.) The anoxometric drawing shows the evolutionary transformations: A cube is divided by planes (walls), by a grid (columns), the solid is rotated, planes sheared, the solid split and rotated, the process repeats in its entirety in the relationship between solid and grid, and finally the two processes, solid-plane and solid-grid unite to become volume-wall-column of the house. Spaces are delineated within the fractured complexity; functions are orchestrated, they do not formulatively originate. Whereas in the Hejduk Wall House elements are intrinsic, in House III they are entwined, layered assembly. Emphasis is on the generation of form as an order that architecture can subscribe to and derive from, from within. It is intrinsic. The dialogue between architecture and context is incidental, it becomes a part of architecture solely as extrinsic presence. The idea is ultimately that the object exists and has meaning as it provokes the onlooker to respond to it interpretatively. The product, or building, of intent strives to reveal the process of its origination. Since the process is a response to abstract manipulation, the object, of consequence, embodies and manifests this as a more abstract presence.

The project for House X designed a decade later shows exactly the same introspective concern for how architecture goes together independent of external or extrinsic conditions, where the process of design itself is above notions of program, site, construction method, and client. Even so, the end result, because of the attitude toward space and its definition or lack of, emanates from the more subjective compositional and stylistic concerns of the modern-

■ Peter Eisenman, Miller House, Lakeville, Connecticut, 1970 (Photos: Dick Frank)

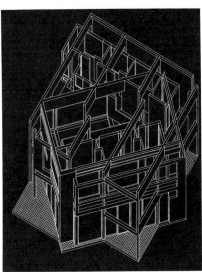

ist idiom. House X is likewise antiobject, its parts, skeptical of perfectability, are not suggestive elements of or to a whole, but of separateness, here within the generalized regularity of four quadrants, yet still in a state of decomposition. Planes are edges of volumes, windows are not present as scale referentials, "wall" here is purposefully detached as glass bonds elements. The only seemingly natural touch is the landscape slope, which runs through the house to split it into the four quadrants.

Seeking to reconcile these notions of intrinsically private abstraction in a public situation is the significance of Eisenman's first comprehensive built project, the Wexner Center for the Visual Arts at Ohio State University. Here the town and campus grids are interlocked employing their rotation not to reiterate but as a device to establish their own distinctive and relative coherence within the site. It becomes the method to clarify the site. The curved entrance forms fronting the campus, still abstractly yet pertinently, are an urban memory reference to an armory demolished in 1959, used as an ironic

device and a way of astutely resolving the dilemma of how one might preserve an abstraction while also using it as a particular and topical, if idiosyncratic, reference. In a time of interest in historic reference in the eighties, Eisenman has achieved this with a symbolic rather than visual gesture, demonstrating his critical ability to provoke and encourage dialogue, redefinition, and interpretation.

Geometry as regulator is after the fact in Eisenman's work, especially as he has become more preoccupied with deconstructivist notions of design in the latter half of the eighties. It is a convenient and relative organizer. In the architecture of Charles Gwathmey and Robert Siegel geometry in a pure and more literal sense is fundamental in buildings that, unlike Eisenman's, intentionally are more responsive to function, site, and method of construction and hence derive more immediately from the spiritual foundations of the modern movement in architecture. The reductive simplicity, planar authority and solid to void clarity allows the geometric idea to visually prevail unequivocally in

■ Eisenman Robertson/Trott & Bean, Wexner Center for the Visual Arts, Ohio State University, Columbus, Ohio, 1985–1989 *(Photos: Jeff Goldberg/Esto)*

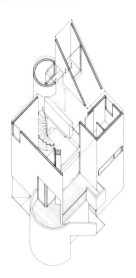

■ Charles Gwathmey, Gwathmey Residence and Studio, Amagansett, Long Island, New York, 1967

the Gwathmey Residence and Studio on Long Island. The design for his father is typical of the architect's early work in that its volumetric and elemental form is composed of curves and angles juxtaposed against a basic rectangular volume. Changing and varying ceiling heights and overlooks afford a verticality to the interior that is fundamental to the space concept in that it creates a sense of bigger size, as does the opening outward to the site through simple rectangles of glass. The volumetric sense of the exterior (here of 1-inch by 4-inch tongue-and-groove vertical cedar siding) is emphasized by the overall sense of tautness of the exterior skin.

In contrast to the dynamic flow of space in Gwathmey/Siegel's architecture, in the interiors of Gamal El Zoghby sets of simple geometric forms, derived from the idea where each is rigorously responsive to an almost compulsive—and aesthetically directed—singularity of function, are organized in a complex pattern of an almost one-after-the-other connected flow, where there is a sense of the defined rather than contained, within interpenetrating yet still clear demarcations. Such a resolution of individual parts related into a total harmonic order is basic to the Trettin Apartment in New York. Self-contained modules of designated function, with precise and delineating geometry, are juxtaposed to amplify space in both their separations and functional dependence. While the spaces are without furniture and objects, they are not minimalist because the attitude to function in its specificity leads to high degrees of complexity in form and plane, nor are they in any way hi-tech, since construction method is most elemental—invariably plywood planes having formica, carpet or paint applied as a finish—again, for a nonengaging object presence. The idea for El Zoghby is to expand the consciousness of receiving and perceiving environment as a context of highly select content, a liberation devoid of contents that might constitute a secondary level of engagement for the viewer. While the idea of selectivity is of essence reductive in philosophical intent it is complicated and inclusive within its own language of architectural conclusion.

The late sixties and early seventies' buildings of Michael Graves somewhat summarize these many attitudes toward wall as building envelope, geometry as a visual relator, the penetration of plane and structure, function as a declarent of purpose, especially as form might itself serve to promote function, and color

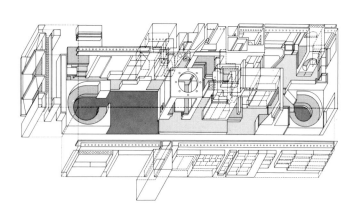

■ Gamal El Zoghby, Trettin Apartment, New York City, 1975 *(Photo: Robert Perron)*

as a referential tool. Graves's interest in the history of architecture and painting as *idea* source differentiates his architecture from the likes of Eisenman whose work is intentionally abstractly removed from culturally connective meaning. Graves strives to make visible the relationship between architectural form and the complex notions and ideas from which it derives, and the oppositions that bring meaning to architecture: architectural rules as a form generator opposed to the users requirements; the idea of a horizontal plane read as romantic or perceptual, opposed against a vertical plane as abstract or conceptual; the real use of the building opposed to the symbolic use or interpretation by the viewer; the plan as designed, to the elevation as perceived; the solid volume of the private, real use world to the negative open volume of the public and symbolic world; the emphasis upon primary aspects without excluding the incorporation of secondary meanings; the structuring of built systems and subsystems, layered with images and notions of ideas drawn from architecture, history, painting, and so forth, history and painting being the source to derive inspiration that will bring a sense of meaning to architecture. Because of the complexity of these oppositions the architecture of Graves appears often as groupings of unrelated components without cohesion, for example, in the Snyderman House in Indiana. Here, the guest suite angles obliquely outward from the facade in a surface of curvilinear forms, whereas family areas recede behind the exposed orthogonal frame and grid of the building's skeletally defined periphery. From the basic rectangular mass, elements also extend outward to embrace the landscape and symbolically almost balance the build-

■ Michael Graves, Snyderman Residence, Fort Wayne, Indiana, 1972

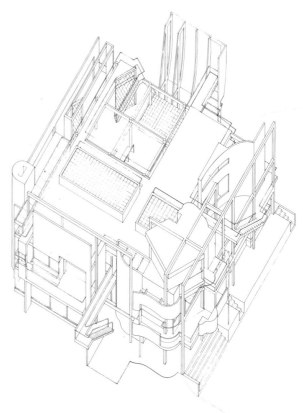

ing mass on its site. For Graves the natural is important in that he seeks a dialogue with nature where lyricism, movement, and irregularity are seen as attributes of nature; and stasis, regularity of form, and geometry is synonymous with the constructed. Color is used to reinforce design theme and to mute the ideality and perfection of the white frame. It is employed for figurative associations, blue for sky, brown for earth, green for vegetation. It is an architecture where the force of meaning derives from configurations themselves rather than organization; this is in comparison to the work of Gwathmey and Siegel where the manipulation of space results in configurations that are built directly upon a building's organization as it derives from purpose. The facades of Graves's buildings are assertive in a manner that forces visual associations through echoes of associative metaphors. They say everything and nothing about what they veil, or conversely within their intricate theme pattern, little about what is inside. Whereas Mies van der Rohe's facades, derived from an entirely opposite philosophy, also declared nothing and conversely everything through elemental anonymity, Graves's layering of themes says little through the complexity that requires deciphering, and everything in that nothing is ignored as it might become built presence and meaning.

Another and different sense of history, in the spirit of the neo-classic tradition of the French visionaries of the later eighteenth century, is fundamental idea to the whimsical, controlled clarity and geometrically derived authority of The Orangerie by Roche, Dinkeloo & Associates. A poured concrete pavilion conceived as a small, hollow cube, it was designed to terminate the axis of an allée of trees in the grounds of a private house. It was to be a play of light on form as, through a window slot opening and skylight defined by an inward sloping plane, sunlight would beam downward into a colonnade space with a central, apsidal wall focus.

The College Life Insurance Company of America, by the same architects, is also an idea based on an abstract, geometrically disciplined concept, but here for a monumental composition consisting of three identically designed 11-story sloping office towers (eventually planned to become a cluster of nine towers). The truncated reflecting glass pyramids, placed against an L-shaped

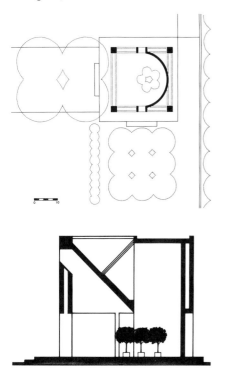

■ Roche Dinkeloo & Assoc., The Orangerie, 1968

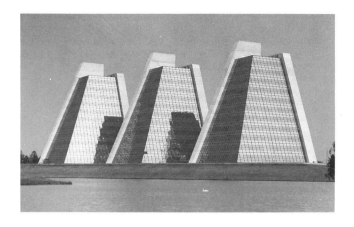

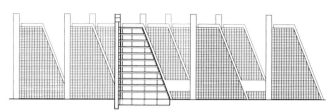

vertical concrete core space in each of the structures, is a vision of awesome detachment from a distance, scaleless and remote from human identification. It is a truly withdrawn monument to the architectural form abstraction potentially inherent in twentieth century technology and a precise demonstration that idea in architecture can also powerfully derive from technique and new means, which in turn, in application has opened the horizon to new forms and ideas about our world; not technique for its own sake, but as it derives within the language and frontal development of an art form.

Just as steel and reinforced concrete in architecture initiated the potential for a whole new scale of space, new techniques in the art world opened the door to expansive environmental painting rather than object imagery. When Jackson Pollock moved his canvas off the easel with its limitation of size onto the floor of his studio and dripped paint onto the canvas rather than apply it with a brush, new imagery immediately came from new technique. Then, instead of painting within a contained framework, the picture of predetermined size as in easel painting days, a further new idea was born, that of cutting the picture out from the larger canvas by essentially visual editing. It was feasible, in effect, to select a picture, or pictures, from one huge canvas. The development of idea and imagery was sequential and grew out of the artist imaginatively pursuing the nature of art, of belief inspired by command of technique. A new way of doing things in turn opened the door to new ideas about the nature of art.

Dripping paint then immediately led into the idea of staining raw canvas with the "new" acrylic paints of the art world with their brilliant, vibrating panorama of color. This produced the intense hued canvasses of Morris Louis, Helen Frankenthaler, and Kenneth Noland and his "target" pictures with their "flailing" edges. Having established the creditability beyond applying paint with a brush to dripping and staining canvas, new ways of applying paint called for new, more sophisticated and tightly controlled techniques. Idea pushed and challenged for a more subtle means of applying paint, which, in the hindsight of history, inevitably led to the spray gun in the sixties and a new avenue of imagery through the flat and subtly shifting mists of color of Jules Olitski. In the world of sculpture, David Smith in the United States and Anthony Caro later in England, opened a whole new vision of assembled form through

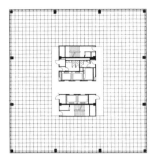

■ Daniel, Mann, Johnson & Mendenhall,
One Park Plaza, Los Angeles, 1972

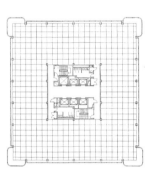

■ Daniel, Mann, Johnson & Mendenhall,
Century City Medical Offices, Los Angeles,
1969

■ Daniel, Mann, Johnson & Mendenhall,
Century Bank Plaza, Los Angeles, 1973
(Photo: Lang)

the use of available industrial steel elements. Form, and in turn image, grew out of the nature of materials, technique was derived, and technique plus imagination led to a new idea about sculpture.

Technique and a systems attitude in the work of the Los Angeles firm of Daniel, Mann, Johnson & Mendenhall, starting in the mid sixties under the design leadership of Cesar Pelli and Anthony Lumsden—both of whom had worked for Eero Saarinen and later Roche, Dinkeloo & Associates—led to an

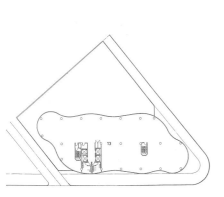

architectural expression referred to by Lumsden as "non-directional, non-gravitational enclosure." It was an idea of the skin of a building as a membrane, quite different from the curtain wall with its expressed mullions somewhat echoing and reminiscent of a column-beam facade division. An idea of the building also removed from an expression of the mass of a building as comprising a top, middle, and base, a contemporary extension of a classic tradition. In their designs the skin does not express the organization or disposition of interior functions neither is it expressively a structural system, but a flexible veil with which to wrap a volume potentially divorced from any rectangular or directional and proportional notions. The idea was for an aesthetic system without the intrinsic implication of form that would suggest a logical and functional relationship of the program. The evolution of their search into lightweight skin enclosures led in a series of Los Angeles buildings from the wrapping of the conventional rectangular volume in the Century City Medical Plaza building, to the curving of corners at One Park Plaza, to the more sculptured yet still basically rectilinear total volume of the Century Bank Plaza, to the totally undulating, curving facade of the Manufacturer's Bank.

The development of this theme coalesced in the more monumental design by Lumsden for the Bank Bumi Daya in Indonesia. The curved membrane of the upper tower, rising upward out of an expanded floor area at the base, gives the building's glass surface a sense of mass, while the ends are indented to emphasize verticality. Both the elegance and complication of the tower derive from the 6-story parabolic curve, generated by the curved upper section, intersecting the inclined angle of the straight plane of the lower floors.

The intersection of straight and curved planes, but in the horizontal direction, became the aesthetic of two subsequent projects by Daniel, Mann, Johnson & Mendenhall in the mid 1970s. In the Lugano Convention Center, the skin became a rolling, undulating linear membrane cut off bluntly in section so that the silhouette or end elevations of the building became a literal representation of the section. The end of a building as an idea in traditionally turning a corner was ignored as it was seemingly simply sheared off visually for the concept of an extruded form implying extension or future growth. In Lumsden's projected Beverly Hills Hotel for Los Angeles, the undulating

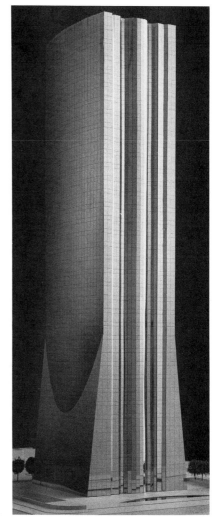

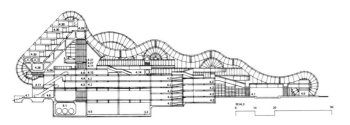

■ Daniel, Mann, Johnson & Mendenhall, Lugano Convention Center, 1975

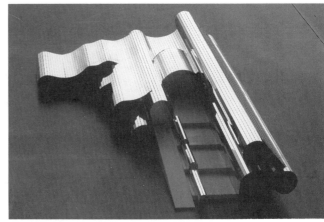

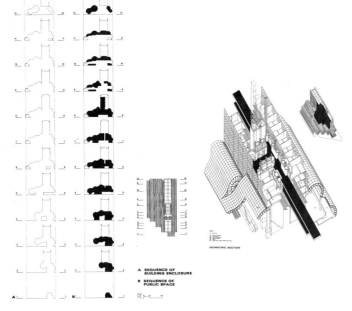

A SEQUENCE OF
BUILDING ENCLOSURE

B SEQUENCE OF
PUBLIC SPACE

■ Daniel, Mann, Johnson & Mendenhall, Beverly Hills Hotel, 1976

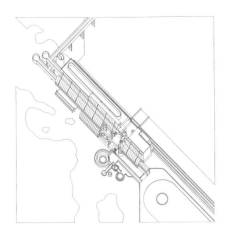

■ Daniel, Mann, Johnson & Mendenhall, Tillman Water Reclamation Plant, Los Angeles, 1973–1983 (Photo: Anthony P. Verebes)

■ Cesar Pelli, U.S. Embassy, Tokyo, 1972
(Photo: facade, Masao Arai; detail of entrance, Mitsuo Matsuoka)

curved glass and aluminum plane was to have enclosed public space, from which would have risen a more conventional slab block of hotel rooms, for a more tightly geometrically developed sequence of the rolling and sheared off idea. Architecture almost as a linear diagram was again employed by Lumsden in the administration building servicing a sewage treatment and water reclamation plant for Los Angeles. Here the building's low profile is enhanced by gardens and a lake juxtaposed against the expansive and mechanical organization of the 88-acre treatment facility.

In his design of the Pacific Design Center in Los Angeles by Cesar Pelli, then of the Victor Gruen office, the approach was similar; to wrap the entire volume of the simple, blunt geometric forms of characteristically linear development of space, in a continuous, monolithic and scaleless surface (see page 52). However, in the United States Embassy office building in Tokyo, the building is again linear but here the simple form is clad in a modular abstract grid of mirror glass and anodized aluminum, a thin and hard membrane with minimum reveals again without structural expression, where the entrance is given emphasis by "cutting-away" the membrane to let the beam and column structure emerge as a colonnade. Likewise the ends of the building again reveal the concrete structural frame which, as if to reinforce a synthetic presence, is treated with a shiny epoxy paint. With the idea of the exterior so abstract, monolithic, and intellectually removed, small cuts and projections as at the entrance and the gently curved ends, cause the smallest shadow line to become a strong highlight. The play, if more articulated, is still subtle and abstract, the building's skin against the surfacing of structure; the clean, simple expression of an idea brought directly forth from contemporary technique and a brave new world attitude.

The development of a new spirit toward volume in a building and how to appropriately enclose that volume has been an elemental idea in the work of Lumsden and Pelli, and posits the importance of progressional evolution in the design process as an idea is worked at, evolves, and matures. In the process of refining an idea, one gropes for a new one, hence the notion of episodes in the creative process where a theme is pursued through a series of works, which in architecture certainly makes sense where a designer is confronted by similar type commissions in one area of the country, with a constant method and technology of building. Clearly, there is no virtue in change for its own sake,

■ *Top:* SITE, Indeterminate Facade
Showroom, Houston, Texas, 1975.
Bottom: Tilt Showroom, Towson,
Maryland, 1978

but there is obviously great merit in the cumulative, continuity of effort that
grows out of sureness and confidence. Idea can therefore also be an evolving
notion emerging from an attitude toward search within an art form or, collectively, a mood that is almost prevalent in the air. Given the thought of designing
a chair with three legs instead of the conventional four, the obvious move then
becomes the eventual design of a one-legged chair. Eero Saarinen's concept for
the pedestal chair came out of this climate: He simply was the first designer to
arrive at the conclusion with great design authority. The whole need for legs
idea in the design of a chair had earlier been under scrutiny in the furniture
world following the design of Breuer's cantilever Cesna chair.

The sense of challenging our own capability to resolve problems that
seem to suddenly surface in the design community can also result in design
statements about our intellectual climate, especially as they tongue-in-cheek
make light of our propensity to take ourselves too seriously. Such is the Indeterminate Facade Showroom in Texas and the Tilt Showroom in Maryland,
both designed for Best Products by the group called SITE, under the leadership of sculptor turned environmental "documentor," James Wines. Both
designs become a vehicle to expand even our understanding of architecture, as

idea becomes a total commitment to the witty and visual denial of reality and reason in architecture. The first building is realized in what appears as a stage of crumbling self-destruction. Architecture becomes social and psychological commentary rather than an exploration of form, structure, and material. The latter detaches, precariously raises up and tilts outward its exterior block wall, denying absolutely the equilibrium and logic of masonry construction. It is also a commentary on function because function is not expressed but simply revealed by the lift of a corner. Both buildings are about and reactions to the most mundane imagery of the suburban shopping center. They are rhetorical statement rather than the resolving of design problems in the manner that the American flag paintings of Jasper Johns became more appropriate and pertinent because of their dependence upon familiar imagery. Architecture here is subject matter and not the objective of design. As Marcel Duchamp's work as a Dadaist was a stinging critique of modern life that in its selection of common-

■ Prentice & Chan, Ohlhausen, Henry
Street Settlement, New York City, 1975
(Photo: Elliot Fine)

■ Paul Heyer, New Life Child
Development Center, Brooklyn, New York,
1971 *(Photo: John Veltri; drawing: Paul Heyer)*

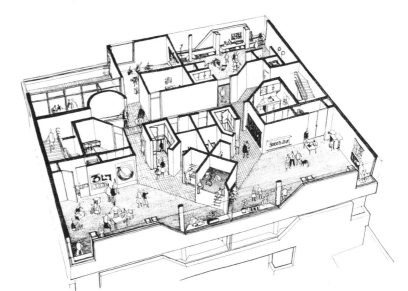

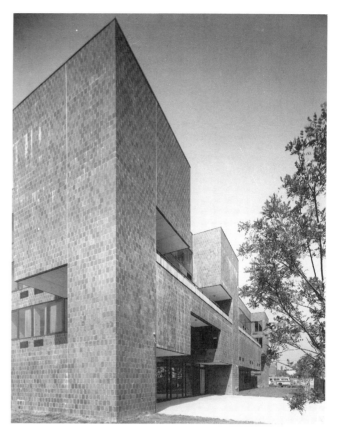

place objects as the creative vehicle permissively mocked the seriousness of artistic intent, so Wines, an arch-idea-man, raises originality of image to total conclusion.

Ideas grow out of a cultural climate, but they can also reflect a societal imperative. Einstein split the atom when our technology and the economic base for our standard of living could not practically advance without its power. Our ambitions in space and the development of computer technology were nurtured in the womb of our technological capabilities. Techniques and aspirations, ideas and how they are implemented are firm companions in our culture and the advance of new possibilities.

Albert Speer designing for the Third Reich demonstrated well that architecture can be used deliberately and intentionally to signify power and authority. Hence we have idea as social persuasion. Fortunately, government in America actively seeks a more accessible relationship with the electorate. This was the intent behind the Boston City Hall of Kallmann, McKinnell and Knowles, a building whose philosophy is directly attributed to the desire for dialogue, physically, historically and socially. A monumental structure in size, it is still in the spirit of social meaning and relevance, which was one of the cornerstones of the modern movement—the promise of a new vision of quality of life not for the elite but for everybody. This idea was fundamental to the advocacy movement of the late sixties where local communities organized to sponsor modest community-oriented structures financed with the aid of government programs.

■ *Left:* Le Corbusier, Monument of the Open Hand, Chandigarh, 1952. *Right:* Marcel Breuer, St. Johns Abbey Church, Collegeville, Minnesota, 1963 *(Photo: Paul Heyer)*

The objective was to increase the options for the people availed of the least number of alternatives in life, going beyond purely user-oriented criteria and bureaucratic strictures to seek an architecture of social benefit and environmental consequence, demonstrating that good design is not reserved for an exclusive segment of the population, nor is quality solely commensurate with infusions of money. Design and idea begin with theory, thought, and commitment. Improving the quality of life and bringing a sense of faith, hope, and community spirit is basic to any aspirations of people living in areas of urban poverty.

The advocacy movement produced some modest but quality public buildings in poorer areas of New York City, for example, the Henry Street Settlement, a center for the performing and visual arts by Prentice & Chan, Ohlhausen. Located on Manhattan's Lower East Side, once a focus for poor and aspiring Jewish immigrants it has now, symptomatic of our urban times, also become a mix of Black, Puerto Rican, Italian, and Chinese. The building invites people into its socially important arcing forecourt and hence inward

■ Venturi & Rauch, Franklin Court, Philadelphia, Pennsylvania, 1976 *(Photos: Mark Cohn)*

into its flexible and exposed concrete and block interior. The New Life Child Development Center in Brooklyn's Bushwick section, designed by myself, also has a forecourt entry leading to a sequence of related social spaces where a sense that the community purpose prevails is basic. Likewise, for the C.A.B.S. Nursing Home in Brooklyn's Bedford-Stuyvesant area by William Breger Associates. The 4-story building focuses inward to a central, open atrium which is protected by a glazed space frame canopy. Patient rooms ring the building's exterior, with circulation areas and social dayrooms overlooking the court. The space is a bright and cheerful social heart for the community it serves, reminiscent of the southern patio, an oasis in an area of physical and social desolation. Appropriately all three buildings have core spaces as the stage for social contact and interaction.

While idea in architecture derives from many sources and influences, it is finally the force used and shaped by the architect's imagination. It is the seed in the earth, the life source that will nourish, develop, and bring forth the fruit. It is almost transcendental. Idea has even become as symbol to cultures historically.

But idea in architecture, although it will often manifest symbolism, is itself beyond symbol, it touches the spirit. Le Corbusier's open hand gesture of brotherhood at Chandigarh or Marcel Breuer's sculptural "banner" visually announcing St. John's Abbey Church in Minnesota, are powerful elements of a design, but such adjuncts should never themselves be confused with idea behind design. They stop at idea embodied as sculpture and do not make the transition to encompassing form and hence architecture, as in the work of Wines. Symbol as object is surpassed to become symbolism as a recall of time past, in Venturi & Rauch's Franklin Court in Philadelphia. Here a 1-foot square steel frame outlines a suggestion of Benjamin Franklin's house and print shop, situated above a new underground museum and in a landscaped court behind five reconstructed eighteenth century street-facing houses originally designed by Franklin. The architectural elements and the symbolism of the design significantly evoke the past as a living, functioning memorial to Franklin and a center for today's visitors. It is a project where symbolism itself has been devised as an idea that touches the mind and imagination. This is one of the reasons that old buildings have a special appeal: The fact that there has been prior use, life and meaning within a structure moves our mind beyond the physical limitations of space to a sense and symbolism of life. This is a strong reason, beyond pure economics, for the interest in adapting or adding to existing buildings. The transference of an idea and its rephrasing in a new context can bring an air of richness and history that is hard to capture in an entirely new building. In bridging or incorporating time it can bring tissue and roots.

Idea in architecture is a complex yet fundamental set of rationales that come together at many conceptual and physical levels. But even as concept it is the coherent idea of function, structure, environment, social responsiveness, culture, symbolism, and memory, all expressed as form, where the experience of space and ambience of feeling predominate. Idea then becomes concept and content, concept the strength that carries architectural statements and content the presence that endures.

6

Order as Context

■ Although the natural landscape has its own generative design parameters relative to the compatibility of elements to it, of the appropriateness and complement between it and architecture, the compatibility of elements one to another requires a whole different level of design sensibility and attitude of conditioned relationship. The relationship between elements implies the exercise of implicit priorities and the following of determined rules, of a dialogue with precedent. Thus, the question of Order, the notion of regulators.

There is an attitude of thought that appears to represent that art simply pours out of the inspired creator as true poetry and that any orderly structured context is just a barrier that makes creative effort rigid and dull. Certainly intuition is fundamental to the creative process, but a good artist, while depending on intuition, is always challenging it intellectually. The command in a work comes not from a febrile frenzy but from the artist's seemingly effortless control of a medium—style evolving from a heightened awareness, of understanding precisely the nature of a problem and what needs and wants to be said. It is a fallacy to believe that feeling or passion might be precluded by prior thought and sensitive structuring or by the boundaries of a discipline and theory.

Although the artist is working between tensions, the creative process is in fact a struggle to resolve or direct disordered elements. The charm and romance of chaos lies in chance and happenstance, the excitement of the unexpected. These are important in the creative process yet when they become the initial impetus or goal and the design act the product of an absence of aims and intentions, everything then becomes an isolated event without validity except within its own terms of reference. The danger of this nonapproach to design is that without a comprehensive understanding of problems within a context, small and at the time seemingly reasonable steps are made to answer immediate, specific problems. These steps, often at first imperceptibly, can direct us away from broader objectives.

Order is the exercise of reason to unify action toward determined objectives and to establish an appropriate hierarchy of relationships. It is the artist's sensitivity that ensures that concepts of order are not contrived and do not force uniformity or rigidly prescribe responses that would be a design restraint. Variety is inherent in the complexity of our life and only awaits compatible and appropriate expression. Flexibility and growth must also be logical coefficients of order.

The notion of order is that of a framework of probability against which we can project our surprises; the rational, complex framework that environmental and technological decision making demands. This can certainly be conceived to accommodate diversity and the variety of disparate elements. At this level the architect can then make the important distinction between general ideas and the way they can be phrased to accommodate the particular ideas of context and design. For example, when discussing construction methods there are constants that have a universal tenability; these in turn are modified by the personal and specific. The constants are guides and measures of intrinsic nature and characteristic; modifiers are the personal interpretation and response to the nature of the characteristic. By the nature of its properties wood has implicit, inherent characteristics. Whether the architect chooses a conventional two-by-four framing system or a framed beam and panel system, such selection becomes the personal modifier to the universal constants inherent in wood. Each choice is equally true to the nature of the material but is very different in application and resultant appearance. Choice is both selectivity and how the individual interacts within an overall system of order. Nature is universal, choice is personal. And, creativity is the synthesis of sensitive selections made from universal constants. Reason and objective then become one with imagination and action, conformity of feeling without uniformity of response.

The landscape, too, has its own dominant characteristics as a universal determinant within which we build, as buildings as finished objects are our personal modifiers or choices that interact in this system. The landscape, in terms of a universal determinant, virtually demands some restraint and respect from architects. This is precisely the reason that the grand, shingled houses of the turn of this century were so effective architecturally. Generally rambling and eclectic in their exterior form, their imposing grandeur was environmentally respectful, while their interior spatial organizations were subtle and sophisticated and not at all simple to discern in the overall exterior volume. They were also statements deriving from the skillful manipulation of a learned vocabulary. They had a sense of order in the general, and a sense of variability in the particular. An order of the parts and a manipulation of composition went in tandem to produce a homogeneous vernacular architecture that seemed to appropriately defer to and coexist with the landscape. Such is in contrast to the exhibitionistic edifices, that genre of expensive summer homes that have been somewhat rudely implanted on eastern Long Island's South Shore. As social to our senses as the red tide, they in no way defer individual preferences to a broad respect for a hierarchy of order.

The whole order-disorder dialogue between architects has been spotlighted by the fact that many planned areas supposedly synonymous with order, have been the most monotonous stretches of regimented abstract planning. Such are many of our public housing schemes with an insistent repeat of mundane slab apartment blocks. These unreal worlds, lacking in life, richness, and variety, have actually derived more from expressions of expediency rather than a lack of responding to urban complexity. Sterile geometric patterns have been imposed that have simply not been generated by human activity.

That abstract composition in the classic manner, of grand scale with a strong repetition of image and simple forms, need not result in a stultifying monotony is evidenced in the expansive Christian Science Church Center in Boston, designed by I. M. Pei & Partners and Araldo Cossutta. A Sunday school, church colonnade and administration buildings, built of precision-formed concrete matching in color the limestone of the existing domed Mother Church, combine to form a cohesive composition related to a 670-foot-long by 110-foot-wide reflective axis of water terminating in an 80-foot diameter fountain. The scheme's horizontality, visually punctuated only by the vertical 28-story Administration Building, is further reinforced by the 525-foot-long, 5-story Colonnade Building, which inevitably leads the eye through a repetitive rhythm toward the Romanesque style Mother Church. In a series of compelling and panoramic vistas, the parts are always in deference to the

■ New England Style, Shingle House, Falmouth, Massachusetts *(Photo: Paul Heyer)*

■ I. M. Pei & Partners, design architect
Aldo Cossutta, Christian Science Church
Center, Boston, Massachusetts, 1969–1972

whole. The structure pulled forward, wall and glass planes pushed back, the ceiling canopy of an exposed wafflelike grid of concrete beams, the classic element of the colonnade, all combine in sun and shadow to reiterate that the timeless elements of a classic attitude can find an ongoing pertinence and relevance.

The same is true for the more intricate and complex spatial sequences and multiple building forms of the Indian Institute of Management in Ahmadabad, designed by Louis Kahn. The education and dormitory buildings, which

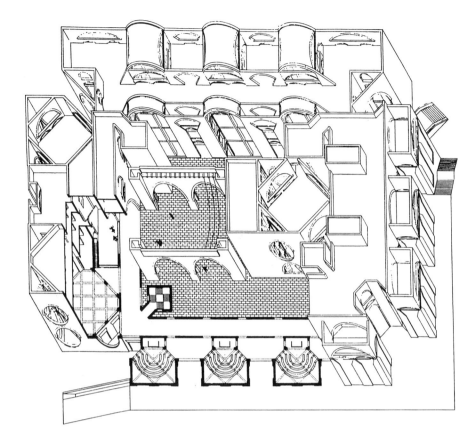

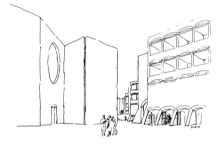

form the core of the college, have a sense of timelessness deriving from their repetition of form, brick, and beam, wall, and column facades accented with almost delicate structural concrete elements used as restraining members for arched openings, forming a "composite order" of construction method. Says Kahn, "a stricter geometry lends itself to direct calculation and puts aside the willful particular, favoring simplicity of structure and space, good for its continuing use in time." Geometry, in a highly articulated set of repetitive relationships often based on the square ("I use the square to begin my solutions because the square is a non-choice, really. In the course of development, I search for the forces that would disprove the square.") is the connective organization. Combined with a simplicity of form, penetrated by spaces to receive the prevailing, cooling southwest breezes, it manifests a rigorously sophisticated and poetic design sensibility, to emerge as an ordered and subtle totality of richness and presence. Again, an ordered composition, vastly different in feeling from the Christian Science Center yet subscribing to the same search for timeless harmony and order, it persuasively demonstrates that richness and order can be concomitant. In that they are strongly disciplined, respect an organizing axis, are responsive to geometry in their shaping, and develop harmony of their parts, both schemes are pertinent contemporary extensions of a classical spirit.

Historically, of course, the thrust of architecture seemed to be more in a common direction, leading to a more unified design effort, a sense of unity in effect stemming from a sense of order. This was obviously easier to achieve in homogeneous periods where there was agreement on attitudes and approaches;

where there was an understanding of the language of the parts and how they would be assembled. In our period, random forces have been the outgrowth of changes and opportunities wrought by the Industrial Revolution, prompting our architectural leaders to point to and explore different directions. This, too, has given aspects of strength to our period because as in pluralistic societies, we have in our search found vitality, stimulation, and growth. We have experienced a time of maximum change with a minimum of predetermination, producing an architecture sometimes of individual clarity but rarely of collective meaning. For architects there is an understandable dilemma; design and conceptual problems are so broad that they necessitate a varied penetration and so new that old formulae and experience is little guide. Correspondingly, there remains a clear need to solidify our efforts. A certain consistency or unity might result from respecting existing patterns, but these are often, and in many instances rightly, being challenged. Order is fundamentally the extension of what exists, but again, we are rejecting almost as much as we are accepting in the world around. Yet, as historical precedent has shown, the ability to plan, order, and discipline energies comprehensively is the mark of a mature society.

What has changed over the past century is our concept of order. Modern thought and behavior, spurred by modern science's studies into such fields as relativity and quantum physics, has led us away from equating judgments based upon absolutes such as good and bad, or beauty opposed to ugliness. To question the premise of ideal or perfect states, to challenge the Greek idea of idealism with our own antihero hero, was to shift our attitude from one of determinism to the idea of indeterminism. There is no such fragile and purely identifiable entity as national interest. Instead there are numerous and often conflicting interests, both collective and individual, which must somehow be reconciled, more or less imperfectly, by political process and the multitude of differing forces that this implies. Life itself is not standardized and static, but personal, fluctuating, often irrational, and invariably perturbing. It is an

■ Roche Dinkeloo & Assoc., Metropolitan Museum of Art, New York City, 1967

assault, not a tidy law brief and we respond to life from within that process. In architecture, conditioned by this climate, we inevitably question the logic of absolute objects brought into existence with the idea that they can have an absolute and durable effect. The finite design process, design for unified or predictable and, therefore, commensurately static functions leading to exclusive and insular design concepts, is totally suspect for its inadequacies. Cause and effect is not so simple to define or react to, nor is it any longer simplistic ritual, nor inevitably complicitory.

Growth and change factors are the strongest assault on the ongoing viability of the exclusive object. Roche, Dinkeloo & Associates' extending the classically insular form of Richard Morris Hunt and McKim, Mead & White's Metropolitan Museum of Art in New York, "clip-on" large scale, sheer glass and slab limestone wall additions; the new a stark contrast that seeks to complement the Roman style filtered through Beaux Arts intricacy of the old. Or Venturi & Rauch in the Allen Memorial Art Museum at Oberlin College, connect a new wing that they pull back to let the classic arched facade of the Cass Gilbert structure stand free, treating the new facade in a checkerboard of pink granite and rose color sandstone to be more analogous to the existing structure. Both

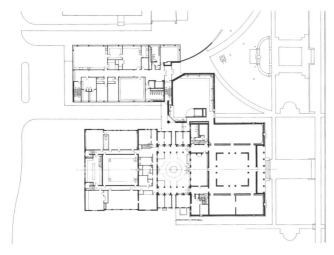

■ Venturi & Rauch, Allen Memorial Art Museum, Oberlin College, Ohio, 1973

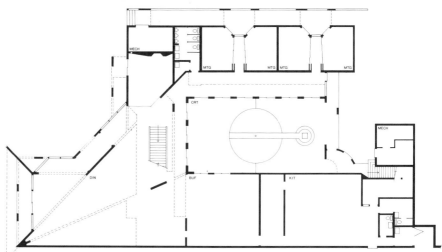

■ MLTW/Moore-Turnbull with Lyndon, Buchanan and B. Beebe, Faculty Club, University of California at Santa Barbara, 1966–1968 *(Photos: Charles W. Moore)*

architects' approaches are forced to deal with the completeness and resolve of an existing structure by a more variable connective idea.

The architecture of Robert Venturi is by philosophy antiabsolute, loosely but thoughtfully assembled, variable, and of philosophical choice inclusive. With certain historic and popular culture predilections, his work looks more toward order as participatory, contextural, and especially referential, rather than intrinsic and of a composition through reductive idea and such classical devices as repetition and balanced harmony. Venturi describes his philosophy as "non-straight forward"; it is hybrid and equivocal rather than pristine and pure. Venturi says, "I am for messy vitality over obvious unity, richness of meaning rather than clarity of meaning." The ordinary, familiar, and associative is elemental. The house designed for the architect's mother in the Chestnut Hill section of Philadelphia in 1965 (see page 38) is a major early statement in this belief. References to house, the sloping roofs, the central fireplace, the

nestled-in homey scale, the application of moldings, the chair rail, smaller windows, the path to the front door—all make this house seminal as an influence on much subsequent architecture. All are basic to the traditional house and are incorporated in this design in the spirit of the architect's awareness of Italian architecture rather than the traditional American house.

With Charles Moore, similarly referential ideas are incorporated also not because they might comprise a totality, but simply because they *add*. His themes are more indigenously American in derivation and overtly playful as elements. His accents of color and graphic devices are freely and eclectically assembled. The incorporating symbolism seeks relativity through an expressive, vernacular contexturalism as evidenced by the Faculty Club at the University of California at Santa Barbara by Charles Moore and William Turnbull. It has a red tile roof and white wall exterior in the Santa Barbara tradition, the desire for a visual liaison dictated by the university, and a stage-set type interior incorporating historic elements including pieces of a fourteenth century Spanish ceiling obtained from the Hearst estate. Reuse, especially of historic elements, is a direction that has appealed strongly to Moore, as is also seen, for example, in the four "sort-of" classic style columns of his own weekend pavilion house in California, built in 1962. It is ideas as ordering principles as they are relevant to our time and especially *a* place. While Moore and Venturi are obviously disinterested in order through convention, they are searching for it within their own oeuvre. They seek a more personal architectural vitality that also does not sacrifice relativity in any muscle-flexing type of exhibitionistic mode.

From Joyce and Baudelaire to Pinter and Beckett, contemporary literature has also abandoned ideas of simplicity to grasp at complexity beneath and beyond appearance. Order in unity, order against disorder, the old measures are no longer one against another. The modern theologian, psychologist, and psychiatrist no longer confronts a world of good and bad, but a world of behavior based upon a standard of morality, responsibility, and accountability.

Now order accommodates variability, order is achieved through tension, even beyond harmonious equilibrium, and reality is inclusive of change. Equilibrium in spans of time is seen as varying in degree. Order and disorder are viewed as conditioning one another. Processes of the natural and constructed world are viewed as closed systems with feedback establishing equilibrium in the system. An architectural corollary: Louis Kahn's notation comes to mind of a problem telling you what it wants to be, or, Sullivan's statement that the problem contains the seeds of its own solutions. Consequently, for the architect the consideration is no longer a passive analysis of cause and effect, but effects within a total process, the process itself becoming suggestive. Complex interactions that themselves become effects within whose parameters the architect in this frame of reference seeks to create an inclusive order.

Writers like Pinter and Beckett manifest this beautifully. Plots are oblique and implied rather than frontal. Situations develop and evolve within the staged situation. Such theater demonstrates that the thrust of the abstract, external and logical should not—and need not—exclude the questioning and mysterious. The possible does not initially predetermine what is possible, the creative effort is more adventurous. The shifts from select to reject attempt to penetrate deeper to the invisible. The design problem informs the architect in the struggle to resolve its inner demands.

Beyond surface aesthetics to inner meaning, it now becomes clear that our abhorence to many planned communities is actually not their order (or really superficial organization) but the fact that their order is phony, arbitrary, and excruciatingly limited. All acts of design must for reasons of practicality be based upon assumption and exclusion, but we feel betrayed when the omission takes too much from the human. Where an operative force to the minimization or exclusion of other equally important forces—in the case of many planned communities the naive delusionary aesthetic—becomes an imposition on or dominates human needs, we seek to apply correctives, much as nature works to correct imbalances in the functioning of its own systems in the effort to sustain itself. We simply find such orders stultifying. We disagree and rebel against them. In a residential interior, total visual order to the extent that it precludes usual domestic activity, for example leaving a newspaper on a table, is another level of imposition which again is entirely unnatural.

However, true order is beyond this, as is evidenced for example in the architecture of Richard Meier. In a contemporary idiom within a framework of formal notions about architecture, he endeavors to be responsive to functional and technical ideas while also subscribing to the idea that buildings can make a larger symbolic statement about their role in our culture. Here, order is neither arbitrary nor stultifying. While his architecture is intrinsically insular and explicitly detailed in the somewhat classical sense of the search for perfection, its spirit is purist modern, with all the healthy and heroic optimistic overtones of the twenties l'Esprit Nouveau. In a sequence of houses in the later sixties and seventies, commencing with the Smith House in Connecticut, and culminating in the Douglas House in Michigan, variations on the cube as an organizing form were sequentially explored through containment, diagonal rotation, linear extension, simplification, elaboration, and a stepped layering. The effort was cumulative in exploration. Diagrammatic rationale illustrating response to site, program, entrance, circulation, enclosure, and structure

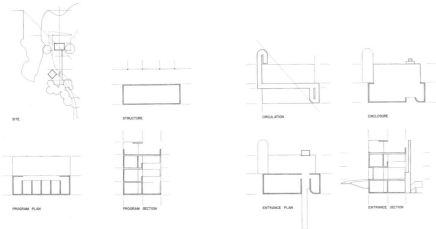

SITE   STRUCTURE   CIRCULATION   ENCLOSURE

PROGRAM PLAN   PROGRAM SECTION   ENTRANCE PLAN   ENTRANCE SECTION

accompanied these houses as the predication and explanation of design configurations, whose logic was codified within axonometics, designed to depict the sophistication of analysis and its crisp resolution into formative options. The Bronx Development Center, a residential complex for 384 mentally retarded patients also exhibits a similar discipline of form and consistency of attitude at a large scale. Rather than orienting toward the surroundings of the desolate urban site the solution is a contained object, a 4-story building organized around a central court. Elements are pushed into this and pulled outward at the building's edges to break down the overall mass in scale. The repetition of the 5-foot 9-inch grid in both plan and elevation, the strong form echo in the four similar residential components, the repetitive treatment of the rounded corners of gasketed windows and the shimmering sheet aluminum

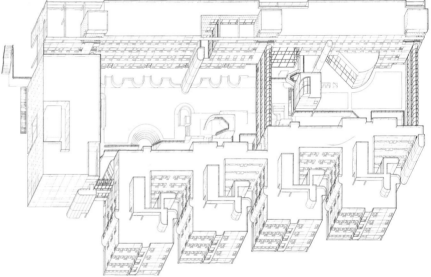

paneled facade is a consummate resolution designed to pose hope that we can confront confusion and inconsistency through formal reasoning. Although the building has been criticized for not being "homelike" and since its design the state has developed new criteria for housing the retarded in smaller, more family-structured contexts, the building remains an example of architecture of control subscribing to the idea of a higher, intellectual order, based upon theme variations of systems and elements that comprise its formative possibilities.

The new Administrative Headquarters Building for Renault, in Paris, again by Meier, is a further exploration in this direction. It is organized on an orthogonal grid system derived from the plan dimensions of the existing building, against which is juxtaposed a rotated 24-degree grid to align with the

■ Richard Meier, Renault Headquarters,
Paris, France, 1982 *(Photo: Ezra Stoller)*

banks of the river Seine and hence, while establishing the potential for a more
dynamic spatial order, emphasizes a new orientation toward the city. Its effort
to link old and new and develop an order out of the existing while also
responding to broader, relative urban organizing patterns, make this proposal
pertinent today and more urbanely sensitized than Le Corbusier's proposed
insular clean sweep that would have destroyed rather than absorbed existing
patterns in several successive proposals for parts of Paris more than a half
century earlier. The rigorous and complex organization of the Renault addition seeks a unison through a plied, rational manipulation of existing facts, yet,
as with all art of such classic intent, its raison d'etre is also to transcend.

In 1984, being awarded undoubtedly the decade's most prestigious commission to design the new $360 million J. Paul Getty Center on a spectacular
110-acre site atop the Santa Monica Mountains, Meier again, as shown in his
published design in 1991, returned to an organizing, layered, shifted and
intersecting grid. Here the 22.5-degree shift interlocks the center's major
buildings and aligns them with the angle of the site's two ridges, which also
follow the bend of the San Diego Freeway at the site's eastern edge. The
complex is fractured into a series of pavilions, the main museum itself comprising five, each to be connected by covered or glass bridges. The museum's
central plaza opens to a series of landscaped terraces which in turn open to and
between the two ridges on which the major buildings sit. Overall the complex
explores more than any of his previous, says Meier, the relationship of building
to landscape—here on the grandest of scales. The galleries are to be a sequence
of classically proportioned rooms with traditional details, connecting Meier
with such disciplined influences as Soane and Schinkel says the museum's
director reverentially. Rules anchor, the imagination manipulates, as these two
neoclassical giants of the nineteenth century persuasively showed.

■ Richard Meier, Getty Center, Los Angeles,
California, 1984–1996 *(Photo of model:*
Tom Bonner)

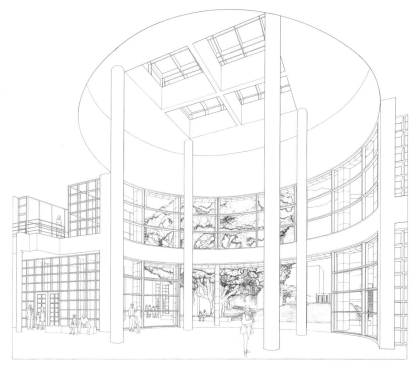

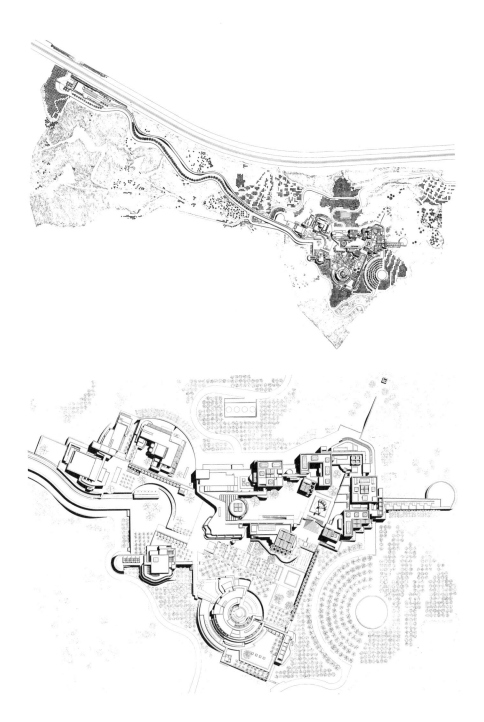

As evidenced by Meier, the architect does not begin to approach a design problem via imposed formulas, arbitrary aesthetics, or some emotional palliative like a love of happenstance. He or she begins with fundamentals. Aesthetics is the skill at manipulation after the diagnosis and definition of the objective. Manipulations of design follow conceptualizations of appropriate form. The creative process begins and can only begin, if it is to have validity, after the correct formulation of the problem. Colored interpretations lead to distortions. Likewise, it is dangerous to accord specific attributes to what initially are only broad generalizations. To short-circuit the correct problem

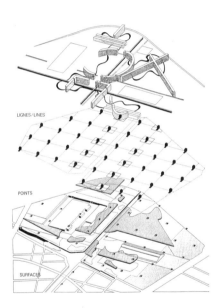

LIGNES / LINES

POINTS

SURFACES

■ Bernard Tschumi, Urban Park for the
Twenty-First Century, La Villette, Paris,
1985 *(Photos: J-M. Monthiers)*

definition, or to ignore any of the forces operable upon a problem is to immediately place limits on the creative end. Generating functions themselves
even suggest highly sophisticated, complex systems of organization where
geometry is at base incidental, in other words not necessarily aesthetic in
derivation or not an imposed order.

Geometry, in this instance in a fractured and provocative sense, is very
much the precept for regulator and order, and one that is methodically and
relentlessly imposed, in the approach of Bernard Tschumi as evidenced by his
La Villette, a 125-acre cultural and recreational park for Paris, which he won in
competition in 1982. Whereas Meier overlays and shifts grids in a totally controlled and aesthetically calculated manner, Tschumi intentionally collides
variable organizing geometric systems. Whereas Meier has scholarly aspira-

tions and his manipulations have their origins in well-mannered classicism, Tschumi's references are Constructivist in architectural terms or what became more generally popularized in the latter half of the eighties as Deconstructionist—an attitude positive and affirmative and not of necessity, as it is sometimes presented, about dismantling or the disturbances of collision, nor certainly yet another reaction intrinsically developed contra to Post Modernism.

Seen historically, Deconstructionism seems inevitable. The sixties evidenced a persuasive questioning of absolutes. Kallmann and McKinnell had referred to the dangers of the absolute dominion of the singular and self-enclosed form raised to universal significance. Their intent was to imbed a building both culturally and contexturally. Invitation as receiving was likewise basic to Venturi's position summed up in his ideas of inclusivity and non-straightforwardness. His position was soon to be apparent as one of cultural references and familiar associations. Tschumi, with certain philosophical but not aesthetic similarities, has pushed to very different ground, related to decentralization, sequence, and the dispersion of subject executed within a persuasive, nonstylistically referential architectonic idea of concept. His parameters of a disjunctive architecture embody the methodological plan, fragmentation, the strength of disassociation and superposition—the relationship of different concerns that can be independently and equally applied to the same analysis—and the elemental reliance upon disjunctive analysis. These ideas present themselves in La Villette as programmatic components distributed via a regular 120-meter grid, marked by "follies," brilliant fire-engine red constructs housing the park's social facilities: conservatory, community building, restaurant, nursery, video cafe, theater, and so forth. This clear and emphatic point grid is in turn overlaid with a system of vehicular and pedestrian, often waving and sweeping lines of movement referred to as a "promenade cinematique," and yet a further overlay of open spaces used for the likes of playing fields and markets.

The basic and highly complex variations in the "follies" occur within the generalities of a 10-meter cube of space, where forms are seemingly often inspired by the imagery of the Russian Constructivists. Back to the modest, simple, structural realities of manipulating the elemental square is, in a totally different vocabulary, the interplay of organizing squares in a less formal sense and more vernacular spirit in the Community Center at the Atrium in Illinois

■ Booth & Nagle, Community Center, Elmhurst, Illinois, 1972

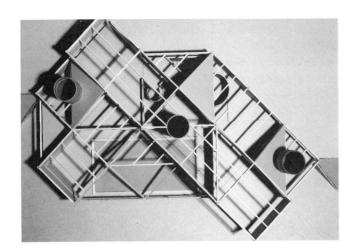

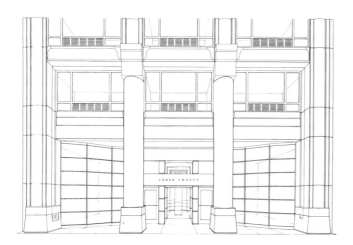

■ Booth/Hansen & Assoc., 320 North Michigan Avenue, Chicago, 1982 *(Photo: Timothy Hursley)*

by Booth & Nagle. Here the example is of an architecture deriving its aesthetic from ideas which generate simpler notions of function and structure sensitively interpreted within an overall discipline. In the Atrium, a structural organizing theme as the response to open space requirements and the accommodation of service spaces in cylinders centrally placed within these square modules is expressed in the exterior and the interior to become integrated form through the linear expression of structural elements read against planar forms.

In a subsequent design by Laurence Booth, a 26-story apartment building on Chicago's North Michigan Avenue, the search for a sense of order through the expression of structure remains, but here in a more decorative sense and with appropriate expressions of urbanity. The base of large entry columns capped with ogee curved moldings and suggested capitals, leads upward into a shaft strongly reminiscent of the Louis Sullivan era of the three-part "Chicago window," culminating in a series of setbacks and a peaked penthouse roof line. The main rise of the shaft and its ornamented molded facade is of concrete, poured against fiberglass forms to ensure their smoothed, curved profile, all monolithically painted a light pink color. Side flanking walls are of unadorned pink stucco panels between the expressed structural framework. Hence, structure employed as decoration and texture, again strongly in the Chicago tradition, leads to a use of structure as more visually engaging.

Structure again employed as the device to organize component functions, similar in spirit to the Community Center rather than the adorned North Michigan tower, is the vehicle toward order as presence in the physical education building at Phillips Exeter Academy. Where larger athletic facilities tend to "package" functions within expansive and undifferentiated surfaces, the

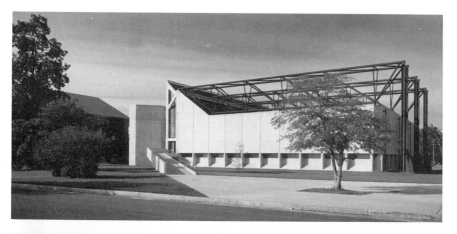

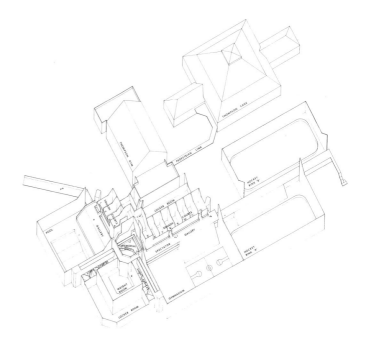

expression of functional elements makes processes legible as large-scale volumetric form in Kallmann & McKinnell's Exeter building. To leave interior
spaces free and clear of obstructions both visual and literal, the structure is
repetitively expressed as a visually detached reference system accenting the
overall exterior mass. This in turn is complemented by the linear expression of
a powerful and organizing circulation system. The effort is to find a harmony of
expressed parts with structure and circulation paths as the ordering ingredient.

Also generated by a circulation spine system but with a simpler steel
structure subordinate to the overall neutral skin of glass and aluminum, is the
very different in spirit Comsat Laboratories by Cesar Pelli and Philo Jacobsen
for the firm of Daniel, Mann, Johnson & Mendenhall. Here a primary circulation corridor is connected to a secondary and parallel all-glass-enclosed spine,
which serves to shelter courtyard spaces while affording outward views from it
and through it across these courts from the main spine. Its simpler organiza-

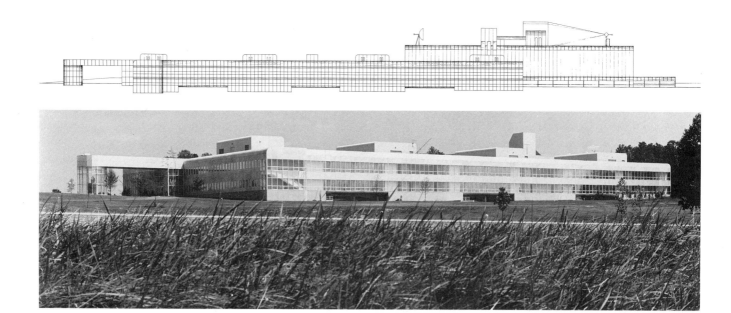

■ Daniel, Mann, Johnson & Mendenhall, designers Cesar Pelli and Philo Jacobsen, Comsat Laboratories, Clarksburg, Maryland, 1967 *(Photo: Stephen Hill)*

tion and expression shows a different aesthetic than the Exeter building, achieved through a more reductive as opposed to a more robust and expressive use of architectural elements. Both, however, subscribe to the desire to organize architecture in a manner that looks for order within attitudes toward skin, structure, and circulation.

In the natural landscape order embraces the total process of origination, development, and disintegration. The ecological process is one of relationships changing, growing, and self-generating where there is a unity, even an ambiguity. In an often outward chaos of forms one senses an underlying order. In this context we have to consider questions of scale. Although a specific purview may not appear to have order since it lacks immediate clarity, this may be because it is an integral relationship of an order beyond the scope of immediately visible comprehension. What at first appears as imperfections in matter, for example crystals, are discovered to be suggestive of arrangements and combinations on a larger scale. In a Jackson Pollock painting the canvas can mean different experiences depending on the distance from it. From afar, color, structure, and texture remain a murky interlock. Approaching the canvas the viewer becomes aware of overall pattern and suggestions of structuring emerging. Finally, close to, the stimulation of flecks and sweeps of the intricate weaving of color that fights for attention is a small personal world of visual excitement. Questions of order and disorder are hence relative to scale. Human scale is, in turn, relative to a sense of visual order. As observers we love to discover the known amidst the unknown. Discovery is one of our greatest delights, especially when it is unexpected.

Detail, discovery, and the relationship of elements to a whole is fundamental to Harvard University's Science Center by Sert, Jackson & Associates. The component parts of the building, almost a functional microcosm of urbanity in itself, relate to circulation patterns and the massing and scale of its surroundings. A park on top of a vehicular underpass is designed to link the Center with the sequence of campus spaces comprising Harvard Yard. The

■ Sert, Jackson & Assoc., Harvard University Science Center, Cambridge, Massachusetts, 1973 (Photos: © Steve Rosenthal)

building's mass also steps down to a low profile facing this park to draw its scale into that of the Yard. The scaling-down of the large and bulky elements of the Center's 291,000 square feet is visually achieved by the facade projections, which reflect the placement and division of interior functions. Its composition, intelligently fractured in its overall form, still derives from the expression of functions and a straightforward employment of simple methods of construction assembly, executed in the uncompromised spirit of a modern, vernacular architecture. The embracing of the exterior urban circulation system of the campus inspired a complementary circulation system for the building's interior of two, skylit arcades forming the basic T pedestrian-organizing system, another variation on the Exeter Academy and Comsat Buildings. It is intensely urban in spirit, posing implications of what the organization of circulation systems, directly relative to pedestrian scale and the animation of visual experience along such paths might be. The personal coexisting with and enhancing the collective.

In an insular context, for example a weekend house secreted in the woods, the limits upon an architect's freedom are purely personal, between architect and client. In a transient setting such as an exposition, where the whole architectural game is one of "visible cleverness," stimulation can reasonably be prioritized above polite juxtaposition. Here, often the selection of the architect is frequently the selection of the design: What else would Buckminster Fuller do other than a geodesic dome at Montreal for the World's Fair in 1968? If personal expression does not disrupt collective order it is not, collectively, of importance; if it does it is invariably environmentally detrimental. When an architect flexes design "muscles" in a serene context by placing an aggressive design in a historically harmonious setting, the personal impinges on the collective. It does not respect or continue existing order. The Portals, a fifty town house scheme on a site of less than 1 acre in Chicago by Booth Nagle & Hartray, is 4 stories in height for scale compatability with surrounding turn-of-the-century houses. It shows that high-density solutions can be achieved without resorting to the seemingly inevitable high-rise solution. The exterior brick envelope, with thematic projections and corner windows for views up and down the street reminiscent of the traditional bay window, is an elegant, modest example of appropriate, quiet urban vernacular. Although it presents a somewhat formal side to the street, toward its internal mews exposure it is more informally rambling. The scheme achieves its variations by employing only two house types. Here, the "house" is organized as functionally inner response, the envelope predominantly for urban continuity and compatability.

In a subsequent design for the 26-unit Lehmann Court town houses in Chicago, James Nagle, again with a central interior garden and a sparingly articulated facade, but here with a repeated gable roof form, tried to recall the front house to carriage house relationship typical of much of historic Chicago housing. The again simple vocabulary of form provides a link with the restraint of the historic prototype while also seeking to create a cohesive new neighborhood. With their direct and basic approach, both projects seek a quiet and uncompromised sense of urbanity drawing their presence precisely from this sensitivity at a manageable scale.

These ideas were further developed by Nagle, Hartray & Associates in their subsequent design on Schiller Street for a row of five 3-story town houses.

■ Booth, Nagle & Hartray, The Portals, Chicago, 1972 (Photo: Philip Turner)

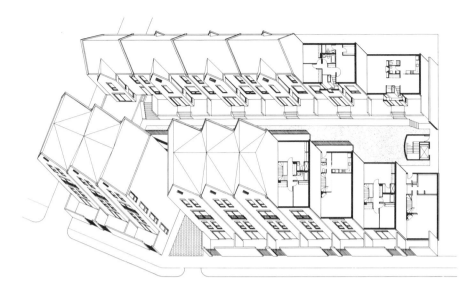

The impetus for the curved fronts derived from the earlier design for a residence in Lincoln Park on Chicago's North Side that had employed an expressed joint stuccoed facade, curved jambs, and glass block openings with cut stone headers and sills. The design sensitivity followed a scale and attention to detail typical of the area. The repetition of the curved bay front in five houses, in this instance of a gray brick veneer trimmed in limestone with expansive gridded glass bay fronts, shows how ideas can carry over to an appropriate, larger-scale application and, in addition to repetition, also the value of masonry as a durable, urban facade expression.

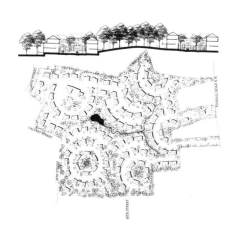

■ Arthur Cotton Moore Assoc., Foxhall Crescents, Washington, D.C., 1983 *(Photo: Maxwell Mackenzie)*

The linear flow and connectibility of elements is essential to such urban inspired housing and is precisely the component missing in the house "floating" on a lot concept, intrinsic to the disconnectibility of suburbia. In the design of Foxhall Crescents, Washington, D.C., Arthur Cotton Moore sought visual connectibility by designing shallow houses whose tan brick and limestone veneered facades are stretched out to the minimal 8-foot side yards required by zoning, linked by fences and curved to simulate crescents that follow the hill contours of the site. The imagery of the eighteenth century English concave and convex sweep of crescents, in addition to historical allusions to motifs by architects such as Serlio and Palladio, is present in such devices as the turreted corner houses at the ends of the crescents, the 2-story arched window and entrance door with sidelights, and the classic tripartite organization of rusticated base, piano nobile, and attic cornice. The desire for order and historical continuity underlies both the planning concept and its execution in architectural detail, all striving for an environment of harmony and accord. This example, the first twenty-six houses of a projected 120-unit development, again has the advantage of manageability of scale, but, with common principles at their origin as their foundation.

Classical principles are again fundamental to a small but comprehensively planned resort development of 80 acres, to eventually total some 350 private structures, by Andres Duany and Elizabeth Plater-Zyberk at Seaside, on Florida's Gulf Coast. Its spirit of "community" emanates from a different yet equally comfortable and familiar set of values: tree-lined streets, sidewalks, pedestrian and bicycle routes, and a well laid out overall plan visually reinforced by carefully prescribed design guidelines that govern height limitations, setbacks, distance between buildings, and materials. The social, grass roots urbanity of Jane Jacob's sixties lament, presented in her book *Death and Life of Great American Cities,* here becomes a positively conceived, picturesque, and homey vision rooted in the 1980s renewed interest in classicism, a sense of place, and the basic values inspired by American vernacular architecture. With over forty communities at various stages of planning and execution to their

■ Andres Duany and Elizabeth Plater-Zyberk, Seaside, Florida, 1984–1991

credit, Duany and Plater-Zyberk's accomplishments have even attracted the attention of Prince Charles (who favorably refers to Seaside in his *A Vision of Britain*) with his known predilection for the timeless canons of classical taste.

The "urban code," the rules for development at Seaside, permit a wide range of design solutions, from Leon Krier's classically inspired house for himself, to a less conforming and more regionally characterized, modernist style house also for himself by Walter Chatham, even to the houses that flank the wider streets opening to the water and the narrower streets paralleling it. A further example of harmony without narrow uniformity is Steven Holl's more aesthetically controversial to the residents, "Hybrid Building" (as he still likes to refer to it), the town's first central, dominant urban structure. Housing shops and offices, with above "boisterous" (with an arc shaped curved metal roof) and "melancholic" (with sculptured awning frameworks atop) residences. Conceived in a more minimal modernist style, it shows another "way" and within its own parameters further demonstrates the viability of the town's aesthetic

premise and commitment. It is to its planners credit that having conceived the town's structure and its guiding rules they then stepped back and have not designed a single building at Seaside to date, validating themselves the belief that diversity and varity are elemental to the urban construct. Examples of the orderly manipulation of a language of design elements at the likes of Seaside, the folksy and familiar conditioned by a vernacular classic vision, move the traditional American townscape away from the suburban laissez-faire sprawl mentality toward a reexamination of how the environments of eighteenth century England and nineteenth century Beaux Arts Paris were able to carry the elements of such architectural packages into an elevated achievement of total environmental persuasion.

Order is a question of magnitude and content. The environment is a totality, which we dissect into parcels of varying scale that have a stability that we work within. In this sense the collective image is a further urban fact that negates an absolute aesthetic. At an urban scale lower Manhattan is collective imagery, not the result of a finite design process or an exclusive design concept, but the product of many random forces—an open-ended and additive process. Like a Pollock painting, from a distance to within we perceive and respond to it in differing ways. Here, order is the harmonious interaction of elements within systems, and this we comprehend as an abstraction. Consequently, at an urban scale, the important thing is not so much the object itself as the relationship between objects, that buildings are not isolated events but elements in a chain of events. At a participatory scale from within the urban fabric the factor of order becomes the relative functioning and aesthetic delight of the totality of parts in view. Within a specific building the inner world becomes the factor of harmony. Again, scale and participation are interlocking and cumulative acts toward order. Such interaction makes us aware of order not as autonomous, but relative as it underlines interdependence.

Sert's Science Center achieves this relative order within essentially the envelope of a single building, in the Boston State Service Center, with Paul

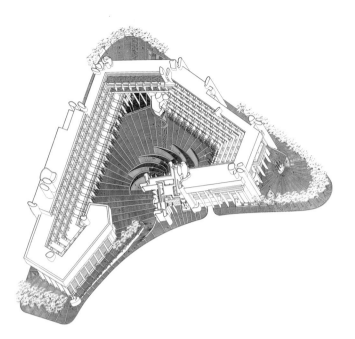

Rudolph as coordinating architect, three separate buildings are conceived as a monolithic totality. They encircle a central, angular, and irregularly shaped pedestrian plaza that evokes remembrances of the ambience and scale of the historic Piazza del Campo in Siena, Italy. Covering an extensive parking facility, the pedestrian sweep of space punctuated with cascading stairs, is defined at its perimeter by the raking profile and stepped-back facade of a 6-story office building. In the grand Italian urban tradition, a tower, in this instance a 28-story office structure, was to have been the vertical pivot for the space. Economics have mitigated this final element in the composition from being constructed. Carefully scaled to its historic environs, the perimeter building is punctuated by vertical cylinders that house elevators, stairs and toilets, bringing a sense of urban monumentality to the composition. This triangular-shaped building is also cut back at its three exterior corners to form small public approach piazzas facing the surrounding streets. In comparison to the more tightly disciplined, structured, and linearly repetitive nature of the Science Center, Rudolph's is an exhuberant, plastic, and epic Baroque flow of building and space. It also posits what a cohesive and distilled presence executed with a sophisticated sense of urbanity might become as urban sense. Where many present-day office structures are monotonous boxes that stand in isolation with urban relativity, Rudolph's Center stands for unison, richness, and harmony; where many center city complexes are developing central atrium core spaces that must eventually siphon off and secrete inward the vitality and street life of cities, it continues as a direct descendent in the grand tradition of the shaping of urban space. It makes its gesture to continuity and seeks to make the individual act responsive to a higher order.

The enlarged sense of urban scale at the perimeter facades and the more intimate pedestrian scale of the stepped-down profile to a 1-story element to the interior piazza in the Boston State Service Center, has a parallel, but different aesthetic pertinence in Rudolph's multiuse project for Singapore. Here a U-shaped shopping area is covered by a glass-roofed atrium to another

stepped-back bowl of space, which is further complemented by an open piazza related to the surroundings in the opposite direction, again with shops to the adjacent streets. Astride these two spaces defined by plaza level shops with three floors of small office spaces above, is an office tower combined with apartments above that spiral upward and are fractured in profile to emphasize the residential scale of this component of the project. In a multiuse singular cluster of building it seeks, again through the relationship of scales, to become both a relative element in and to its environment, and one that, in turn, invites a new dialogue by virtue of its own presence. It responds to the idea of a more encompassing order to which all elements of the urban context might subscribe and indeed reinforce.

Today there are finally signs of the recognition of the importance of this idea in the fact that architects, in a profession that for so many decades has been primarily building conscious, are again in the tradition of all great architecture, becoming conscious of urban space; aware that the spaces between buildings are as important as the buildings themselves. After all, or above all, they become the spatial network of definition and participation where order is not imposed but is a loose framework, allowing particular forms to be accommodated as they are suggested by specific problems, which, in turn, becomes the context of order itself, where variety and activity is a further derivative factor that makes the environment come alive.

At this broad environmental scale, just as the Renaissance developed its set of criteria, we can move toward an accomodating order or norms of organization when we begin to study the systematic structuring we can derive from science and technology as the means, with social forces indicating ends. Since the options are greater today the order is by necessity more complex. Such forces become cohesive when we recognize various modes of communications as generating organizing systems creating an integrating urban matrix. Communication suggests methods of structuring the elements of our environment into an appropriate relationship of parts, thereby suggesting even further refinements in such generating organizing systems, even new derivative systems. For example, what role is appropriate for the central business core in our cities given our movement toward decentralization? Transportation is a good illustration to consider because its only near rival is economics as a city-shaping force today, and it is apparent by now that it is an environmental as well as technological problem. Mobility, the rhythm and speed of movement, suggests cohesive design systems on a comprehensible scale for the city. Architects have flirted with this idea, from Sant'Elia with his 1914 Citta Futurista with its layered and expressionistic image of concretized movement patterns, through to Le Corbusier in the Algiers Plan of 1930, where a ribbon of an apartment building was to have been built following the curve of an expressway whisping through the countryside, to his studies for "Une Ville Contemporaine," a grid city of three million in a park, structured strongly around circulation systems, to his plan for Chandigarh based on the hierarchy of the 7 Vs of circulation, from the expressway to the pedestrian path. Louis Kahn explored it in his Philadelphia Plan of 1952 where visually defined "canals" of movement were intended to

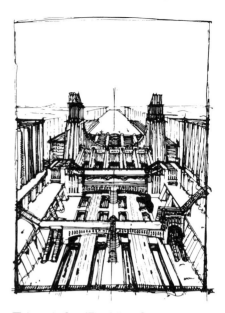

■ Antonio Sant'Elia, Milan Central Station project, 1914

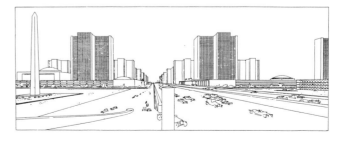

■ Le Corbusier, "Une Ville Contemporaine," 1921–1922

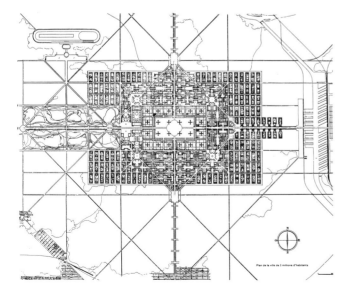

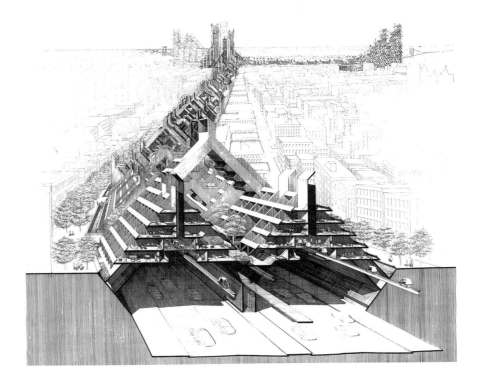

restructure the dynamics of traffic flow, with huge circular towers, the "cathedrals" for parking, monumentally demarcating the periphery of downtown. It was a scheme based on the acceptance of the reality of traffic flow and not a visionary exercise. Even the Beaux Arts architect Eugene Henard, creating classical images for an urban Paris at the beginning of this century, designed his Rue Future, a virtual web of organized and interlocking movement systems, contained within the framework of traditional architectural imagery.

The urban matrix by its nature implies large scale systems within which human "pads" of organization can be developed, neither compromising the other, each with their own integrity. This was the impetus for Paul Rudolph's visionary proposal for the Lower Manhattan Expressway in New York. The large megastructure, to contain most of the functional elements of a city was to have bridged the island with variety, happenstance and more meandering patterns, disciplined within a powerful linear image of order at a new and aggressively persuasive scale. The factors of ownership and land assemblage, the large economic commitment implicit in such a scale of development, questions of social dislocation, all acted to negate such developments. This is further companioned today by our cultural concern for preservation, continuity, and an interest in a more intimate and idiosyncratic sense of scale. If such proposals appear, like the dinosaur, somewhat antiquated today, they still raise fundamental questions that require addressing in the future, about the nature and scope of comprehensive development in the search for new urban attitudes.

The airplane with its range and speed extended our concept of mobility, and the electronic age further dramatically changed our communication patterns. It gave us the sophisticated means to communicate directly between points, implying less travel for the purpose of work, although we will no doubt still travel for pleasure, but along different routes. The implication is that mental and manipulative skills might work from anywhere, pointing to the possibility of new and autonomous closely knit communities with more self-contained households in the future. Struggling to find a point of sanity on the five o'clock expressway may be a fallacy in the electronic age. These developments will not mean the end of physical contact; the umbilical cord is stronger than a world of nonfood food, and nonsex sex. It does mean though we have to give a new positive determination as environmentalists to our understanding of community and conviviality. We have to develop systems of social interaction where people can profitably mingle as they did along the routes of communication, the mesh of walks and defined urban spaces in historic communal life.

The philosophy behind the ideas of Paolo Soleri for example, aim at integrating a more efficient and effective habitat, one responsive to societal needs with greater environmental sensitivity both in terms of ecology and energy. His effort is the making of a human universe where the individual can flourish intellectually and where, from designing in concert with the statistical procedures that nature offers, harmony can supercede disharmony. His design for a community of 12,000 people in Canada, proposes a climatically integrated microcosm of city functions where proximity and concentration mean an economic response to the severe climate and a saving in energy consumption. In austere winters with a mean temperature of 0 degrees Fahrenheit, its enclosed central space would afford a temperate climate for residences as well as the entire city, and cultivated with flower gardens and vegetable beds it proposes an intermediate environment, designed to passively catch and trap the maximum amounts of sunshine. In colder and wind blown northern cities laid out in the typical grid pattern, such garden-type focal environments can move toward efficient developments that offer both physical protection and mental relief from the climate and even cool retreats from the summer suns.

The Commons and Courthouse Center in Columbus, by Gruen Associates with Cesar Pelli as the design partner, is a more standard center city focus

■ Paolo Soleri, Regina, Canada, 1976
(Model photo: Ivan Pintar)

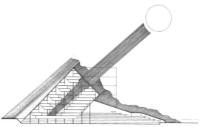

■ Gruen Assoc., Cesar Pelli Partner for Design, The Commons and Courthouse Center, Columbus, Indiana, 1970
(Photo: Balthazar Korab)

of a shopping center with community and parking facilities constructed in a northern city. Where the typical suburban shopping center has drawn people away from downtown, the Commons is a lively magnet to revitalize the old core area. Sheathed in glass, to be transparent to the street and physically an extension of the sidewalk life, its size and shape are derived from interior functions while trying to relate to the diverse scale of surrounding buildings. It is a building of transparency and reflectivity that becomes alive as it interacts with its users. The glass-enclosing skin gives the impression of a volume of space rather than a mass of building, where visual penetration starts to break down feelings of isolation. Although more matter-of-factly conventional than the Soleri proposal, it shows an awareness of a new urban scale and a sense of resolution through order that derives from a more encompassing sense of urbanism. It also tries to come to terms with implanting a much enlarged scope and scale of activity within an existing and at times outmoded urban matrix. The scale is changed but not at the expense of compatability in both extending the context and recognizing the accommodation of future growth as a basic factor of urban design.

Both of these schemes, the former more visionary and the latter pragmatic, conceived in quite different spirits and attitudes toward architecture, demonstrate that concepts of organization and movement inevitably suggest a sectoring of the environment related to functions and activities. This 'pad' idea is even reinforced by the practicalities of politics and economics of land ownership, use, and development. Historically, the unified complex, the grand sweeps of the Renaissance and the Georgian and Regency terraces, gained their cogency from a comprehensible image. They were like sectors of order with qualitative values built in to the concept, for example the row house facing the park or square. While they were not too big to sustain interest, repetition expanded impact. There were subtle changes and repeats within the whole, enough diversity of related detail accommodated within the geometry of parts of the architectural order that there was variety within harmony. Although the order had clarity and discipline this did not mean sameness. At first glance they appear as similar, but one can soon perceive that they possess very individual characteristics. They were a cumulative effort within an order, essentially following but slightly varying a pattern. The repeat house, the repeat elements all through subtle nuances and shift of detail, reinforcing a total vision.

Sometimes grand as at Bath, England, more variable, as in Georgetown, Washington, D.C., or more random as in Santorini, Greece, such architecture was essentially background building, providing a wonderfully rich foil for the civic and religious buildings set against its backdrop and gaining in presence from a relationship to it and the urban spaces it defined. The relationship too was based upon a hierarchy of building types, the more important as dominant and focal, the more universal, as textural, unifying context and space, structuring matrix. The role was clear; object defining space, object in space, or the relationship each to the other.

Throughout the history of architecture it has been important to define the role of a building in the landscape, be it focal, repeat, flanking, turning a corner, even how it meets the ground, what happens through the middle section, and finally how it terminates against the sky; to consider buildings as they visually relate one to another, the old to the new, and how transitions are made from one scale to another. History has found discipline and surety of response to such questions and developed an order where style has not had to dictate the function and function has not of necessity needed to fit the style; where principles have been wisely followed and given creative and sensitive response, and the principles themselves have proved to be pertinent for their generality.

The search for a norm is fundamental to all larger accretions of buildings and the college campus has been typical of this as illustrated by two complexes for the State University of New York, the six-college complex at Buffalo by David Brody and Associates, and the Student Union Facility at Purchase, by Gwathmey Siegel & Associates. Both seek to create harmony in a more pastoral setting through a repetition of form, elements of scale such as window openings, and a reliance on a unifying brown brick as the facade material. The Buffalo scheme, or Ellicott complex, for 6,000 students with 3,300 of them resident, comprises three pinwheel-type groupings, each of two colleges. These are

■ Davis Brody & Assoc., Ellicott Complex, SUNY, Buffalo/Amherst 1974

■ Gwathmey Siegel & Assoc., Dormitory, Dining and Student Union Facility, SUNY, Purchase, 1969 *(Photo: Bill Maris)*

identified by 10-story towers serving as gateways from and connected to a continuous podium of brick-paved plazas and walks affording entrances to all the buildings, which in turn "leaks" visually outward to the surrounding landscape. Concerns of community and privacy with spaces juxtaposed with soft green areas, the separation of vehicular traffic, the attention to the pedestrian both along protected walks and as they are visually stimulated by changing silhouettes, distinguish this example of good urban design principles.

While the Ellicott complex raises itself above a landscape, disengaged but visually related to it, with the Purchase facility, a U-shaped configuration opening to a south-facing view down a grassy meadow is embedded into the green landscape. The space, the transition between the strong axiality of the campus and the meadow, has a triangular shaped dining hall in one corner which becomes a more open and hence, although constructed in the same brown brick, accented element read against the backdrop of the 800-student dormitory building. Semicircular cylinders housing stairs and larger-scale spaces such as academic facilities, in conjunction with some pulled-outward room clusters, give a repetitive vertical accent to the facade, "read" against the strip horizontal bands of the windows of the residential units. Both projects strive, from different design vantage points, to create cohesive environments of compatibility and presence at a broad scale. They manipulate familiar themes with surety and conviction. They show that architecture can have the necessary dual qualities of collective meaning with individual clarity, that a sense of unity can be achieved while preserving diversity.

The elegant sweep of a crescent, the beauty of a natural site to make the norm extraordinary, the campus enclave backdropped against a pastoral meadow, all are equally persuasive as totality. Often today the architectural challenge is to create presence and place in a situation that brings little or nothing as a context. Building a 74-unit low- and middle-income apartment complex on a narrow site squeezed between a country club and the honky-tonk reality of

Highway 66, Antoine Predock followed the indigenous sensibility of his native New Mexico exampled by the Taos Pueblo, a native American communal dwelling continuously inhabited since it was built in the thirteenth century. Ironically adobe or "earthen architecture" is both the fashionable material for the rich in the American Southwest and the promise of a home for the poor of the Third World. In his Albuquerque development Predock's aesthetic is that of the monolithic presence of the adobe gracefully emerging from the earth, here executed in bands of integrally colored stucco on frame construction. The overall form is compactly organized into four "houses" with, drawing from the motel prototype, integral parking courts. A long landscaped earth berm seeks to buffer traffic noise. The scheme's strength architecturally is that through a simple palette, it establishes a directness of architectural form manipulation that results in an uncontrived modern presence, empathetically connected to regional origins.

Where Predock, in the "Beach" apartments, creates colored and cubistically modulated "blocks" as both architecture and landscape, hard-stepped edges backdropped by rugged mountain profiles, the Rio Grande Nature Center is at a profound level an introduction to site and its ecological system of animals, plants and soils, especially water and the rediscovery of the threatened wetlands—here those of the rolling valley of the Rio Grande River at the foothills of the Sandia Mountains. The building itself, a bare concrete and sparse yet powerful presence, is also gently dignified. It unites with nature, never trying to command it. A curved wall of the main exhibit space is penetrated by windows carefully positioned to focus across the water upon featured landscape views, to trees, wetlands, and distant mountains. The landside is bermed to bed the barely visible structure into its water-edge site. The building is entered through this grassed berm via a corrugated, 8-foot-in-diameter galvanized metal tube. The engineered sense of retaining walls, culverts, and water lapping concrete is a landscape presence that expands beyond Predock's more customary

■ Antoine Predock, Rio Grande Nature Center, Albuquerque, New Mexico, 1984
(Photo: Timothy Hursley)

■ Louis Kahn, The Salk Institute for
Biological Studies, La Jolla, California,
1959–1965 (Photos: Jim A. Cox)

adobelike cluster forms. It is an excellent example of the validity of collective meaning; of building, landscape, and ecological systems fused; of unity, inclusion, and order as intrinsic. Both the Beach apartments and the Nature Center demonstrate that the architect responds to the divided and complex as a whole, avoiding formula-type answers and convenient oversimplification. The responsibility is not to an atomistic world of fragmented objectives, but, as we confront nature's inventiveness, to a world of heightened involvement and responsibility at an inclusive scale. Nature creates within order. Through our creativity we aspire to order.

Louis Kahn's Salk Institute for Biological Studies on the Pacific coast near La Jolla aspires within its own spirit to an order achieved through clarity, definition, and consistency of application. It stands as a testament to Kahn's word, "Order *is.*" Two parallel laboratories, each an uninterrupted 65 foot wide and 245 feet long and encircled by a perimeter corridor, flank a central court. The support elements to these totally flexible spaces are placed in a peripheral relationship to this corridor. They are the studies and offices for scientists, fractured in profile and vertical in rhythm, which line this central court,

■ Louis Kahn, Richards Medical Research
Building, University of Pennsylvania,
Philadelphia, 1957–1961 *(Photo: Paul
Heyer)*

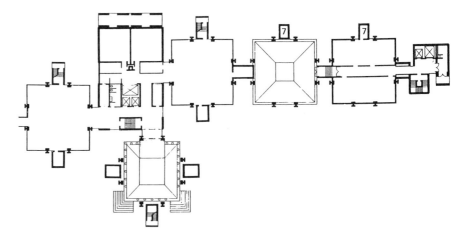

connected by bridges to the perimeter corridor and receiving views of the
ocean by virtue of exterior walls angled toward it. The idea is simple and
strong; the served space of laboratories where research is performed, the
serving space of offices where thought initiates. In a more meaningful and
intrinsically philosophical way, Kahn had returned to a theme he explored in
the Richards Medical Center at the University of Pennsylvania, a building that
was a landmark in the architecture of the late 1950s. There, Kahn for the first
time at an accomplished level explored the theme idea of "servant" spaces,
ducts and stairs expressed as vertical and solid brick elements on the exterior,
in contrast to "served" spaces, open floors for the researchers expressed via the
openness of glassed spaces. Clearly, in the institute at La Jolla, a new level of
realization and accomplishment is evident for this idea. Kahn also resolved the
disadvantages of the earlier Richards Medical towers with their small and
inflexible laboratory spaces, and unprotected glass areas resulting in glare and

thermal problems. The institute manifests beauty of mind and act; of the resolution and articulation of the major elements of the building, each, to put it into Kahnsian language, being what it wants to and needs to be, to the precise detail and execution of beautiful concrete surfaces. Even the component of structure derives from the need to enclose specific spaces, specifically and pertinently, rather than offer a general envelope within which specific space might then be designated. The central court, as a typical Kahn-like space of detached quiet, has a symbol of his gentle and poetic mind: an axial sliver of shimmering blue water, a band pointing toward the ocean epitomizing what human endeavor can accomplish at one scale with geometric clarity and authoritative but modest deliberation, to give to the scaleless sweep of the ocean, here the Pacific, a poignant gesture.

Whereas Kahn's sense of order confronting the ocean derives from a classic spirit that is both measured and controlled, Frank Lloyd Wright's, in the presence of the desert, is a more organic feeling of a building as a manipulative dialogue of its realities, as is evidenced by his complex of school, office, and home at Taliesin West in Arizona. Battered walls of poured concrete with large desert boulders as aggregate, form a base for a superstructure of redwood trusses with canvas screens suspended between them. A rich sequence of shaded spaces interlocked with terraces, gardens, and pools, an originally dramatic oasis at the edge of a plain and the foot of a mountain, it is now encroached upon by suburbia. The architecture and landscape treatment holds within it the color and warmth of desert hues, as furnishings and all applied elements were also carefully selected and combined to reinforce presence as a totality, as total related order. Both complexes confront nature in a majestic sweep, standing proudly in its path of demand for the surety of control and the power of poetic authority. As such both stand as high art. They

■ Frank Lloyd Wright, Taliesin West, Scottsdale, Arizona, 1938 *(Photo: Paul Heyer)*

succeed as creative art through the embodiment of order both intellectual and aesthetic.

From the swirling, eruptive, and turbulent seascapes of Turner to the lyrical, pastoral, and contemplative fields of the Impressionists half a century later, aesthetic order was the avenue to aesthetic success. The orders were different, personalized, and there is delight in this discovery. Their presence is in that they both touch at the nature of art through order. They say that the larger order must be recognized and considered. Given just a minimum of care and thought in their selection, both can perfectly coexist on the same gallery wall, different yet compatible.

7

Coherence and/or Inclusivity

COHERENCE IN THE form of elemental idea has invariably underscored great architecture. The buildings of history that endure in our memory are primarily those based on control, principle, and aesthetic command, those with clarity of concept and execution. They manifest an attitude toward design that seeks the clear idea, the singular uncompromised statement, ignoring in the process what was relegated to not so consequential or of lesser importance. Such demonstrations of fluency and control inevitably come from a clear fix on notions of essential selection. From Phidias to Palladio to Paxton, this idea has endured.

In the early period of the modern movement the idea of coherence was elevated to all encompassing canon, as even the execution of a basic idea was ideally to be in a reductive aesthetic. The architecture of Mies van der Rohe most clearly personifies this attitude in architecture. "Less is more," one of his most famous edicts, typifies the movement in Europe at the beginning of this century to "clean-up" (or down) architecture. The desire was to eliminate the decorative elements from buildings, especially those associated with the Beaux Arts style. This trend was companioned by a growing intellectual excitement for the simple, functional products of American industry. Realizing the clarity and expressiveness of industry and its close connection with aesthetics, Adolf Loos, a Viennese architect, saw America as the land of technology and opportunity, an attitude shared by many of the other pioneers of modern architecture, as evidenced by their subsequent residence in America. Reacting against the decorative exuberance of the Art Nouveau and taking the view that ornament is a crime, Loos wrote: "The evolution of cultures marches with the elimination of ornament from useful objects." In the same year of 1908 the painter, Henri Matisse, wrote: "All that is not useful in a picture is detrimental. A work of art must be harmonious in its entirety, for superfluous details would, in the mind of the spectator, encroach upon the essential elements." A mood was in the air. Eliminate decoration, concentrate on function, seek to express forthrightly a building's integrity and, what in the twenties became hypothesized as the heart of the De Stijl movement in art, expand the understanding of creating more flowing and intricate configuration of space. In contrast to the refined, decora-

■ Skidmore, Owings & Merrill, Marine Midland Building, New York City, 1967
(Photos: Building, Cervin Robinson; detail, Ezra Stoller)

tive vocabulary of classical architecture, the crystalline simplicy of what historically became known as the International Style was persuasively elemental. The economy of means idea for the early pioneers of modern design seemed to parallel the spirit of the timeless idea that beauty could derive from the basic framework of truth; decoration hence was viewed as passé.

The striving for coherence embodied restraint, elimination, and more importantly as we look for a perspective on the architecture of today, exclusion. Mies van der Rohe's example of reductivity was an idea that was to inspire many other architects to design similarly rigorous buildings, for example the Marine Midland Building in Manhattan's financial district designed by Gordon Bunshaft of Skidmore, Owings & Merrill. It is a matte-finished, black anodized aluminum clad shaft that rises straight upward, serenely and cleanly from its plaza, as a minimal and virtually unbroken volume. Its quiet smoothness is elegantly accomplished with only two minor deviations from its sheer plane: the ⅜-inch projection of the window trim that holds the bronze-tinted glass precisely in the main plane of the building's frame and the 2-inch deep grooves for the window washing rig at each column. A single spandrel panel between columns, eliminating even the visual interruption of the continuous vertical mullions of most curtain walls, further emphasizes the sheerness of the exterior plane. Its

■ Edward Larrabee Barnes, IBM World Trade Americas Far East Headquarters, Mount Pleasant, New York, 1974 *(Photos: Bernard Askienazy)*

quiet authority is a perfect foil to the red-painted, elongated cube-shaped rhombohedron sculpture by Isamu Noguchi, a further minimalist accent at the building's primary street exposure.

An even more reductive exterior plane elegantly fuses the IBM headquarters in Mount Pleasant by Edward Larrabee Barnes, with its beautiful treed landscape setting. The facade here is a mullion-free, butt-jointed glass window wall, with continuous spandrels of a dark green anodic aluminum, the whole merging with, receding into, and reflecting its estate setting. The glass appears as an almost nonexistent membrane from interior spaces, where view and a sense of openness are further dramatically achieved by floor to ceiling partitions of glass, clear where only a sound separation is required, reflective for partial visual separations, and mirrored where opaque walls for privacy were desired, further reflecting the surrounding landscape. Both structures reflect the single-mindedness of their solution, one supported by impeccably authorative, minimalist detailing.

Craig Ellwood's Joy Manufacturing Company in Los Angeles is by comparison more articulated in that it breaks its three functions into connected volumes: a 2-story glass walled administration building, a brick enclosed 1-story connected volume for a warehouse, and a high-ceilinged testing laboratory space. The sepia-colored steel and bronze tinted glass office volume expresses in its entirety its skeletal welded frame structure, which contrasts with the infilled brown brick and framed warehouse building which, in turn, is seen against the frameless high brick mass of the laboratory volume. As is customary in Ellwood's work, structure is articulated as the architectural expression and as is to be expected by one so close in spirit to Mies, detailed with an uncompromising visual elegance. All three volumes show the command of synthesis, of clarity in thought and implementation that can result from a focused logic of design where essentials prevail.

The effort parallels in spirit that of artists like Josef Albers, Barnett Newman, and of more recent vintage Carl Andre, Donald Judd, and Dan Flavin, who aim in their art to strip away visual rhetoric and easy appeal to the

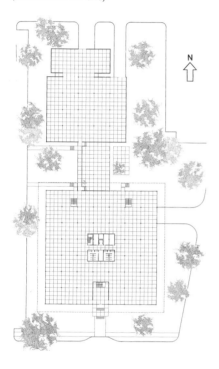

■ Craig Ellwood, Joy Manufacturing Company, Los Angeles, 1972–1973
(Photos: Marvin Rand)

eye. The intent, especially with the latter three artists, is beyond the classical distillation, where to simplify and reduce is to focus on the essential and elemental. Here, fixations can become singular in the extreme, but pertinent if the work has a level of profundity. Fundamentally in all creative endeavor the artist selects, or has already philosophically embraced a thrust of approach or overview that casts aside diversions and impediments to the progressively developing realization of an idea. Of necessity, the search for the relevant excludes the gratuitous and irrelevant. Intrinsic to any creative endeavor is selection and in the creation of any art it is in reality obligatory.

We have stumbled a little around this idea in recent years, reassessing what might have been omitted or overlooked in art and architecture. When the Olympian ideas of modern architecture swept aside the past with all its "encumberances," elements of tradition and the comfortable and familiar in scale were lost to many sterile and visually uninteresting facades and spaces. The idea that contexts are historically incremental was also lost in the move to build a "better" (in reality a more economically profitable) world. As we reassess some of the tired formulas of modernism, the rise in interest in the more eclectic aspects of the arts in the seventies and eighties is not coincidental. The thrust in a single direction has been questioned as *too* singular an impulse. If something seems too well made, too controlled, too easy, is this coherence achieved through too simplistic a notion of order? Since we recognize all ideas of order as accommodating the diverse, random, and even arbitrary, omissions can also be viewed with suspicion.

Simplicity is the purest and most difficult condition to achieve and is not synonymous with easy. In film, Ingmar Bergman's deep concentration achieves the sophisticated simplicity that embraces the complexity of combining reality and fantasy, tortured nightmare with lyrical dreamlike sequence. With the elimination of the extraneous, what remains is the power of emotion and truth: art that transcends the commonplace as it sweeps away distraction to spotlight beauty made visible through aesthetic decisiveness and eloquent truth. The sureness of sensibility is bared through an inclusive attitude. To quote Alberti's definition of beauty at the beginning of the Renaissance in Florence, "a harmony of all parts in whatsoever subject it appears, fitted together with such proportion and connection that nothing could be added, diminished or altered, but for the worse."

A fully worked-through idea remains a consummate theme in the arts. The artist seeks not to tamper with its urgency and elemental quality. While simplicity can bring surety to the creative act it need not preclude the search to express the complex natural patterns of human activity. Sir Joshua Reynolds eloquently said, "when simplicity, instead of being a corrector seems to set up for herself, that is when the artist seems to set up for himself solely upon this quality, such an ostentatious display of simplicity becomes then as disagreeable and as nauseous as any other kind of affectation."

To see and react to the fundamental forces acting in a time is also a move toward significance. It is quite apparent that our age has produced a variety of new ideas and technical images which the creative person cannot ignore if a work is to be valid in the twentieth century. One of the most forceful ideas is that of *the economy of means,* which derives from the spirit of technology and mechanization. The elimination of the superfluous, the no-more-no-less-

■ Mies van der Rohe, Project for Glass Skyscraper, 1920–1921 *(Photo: Courtesy Museum of Modern Art)*

than-is-correct-and-appropriate has to a large extent become a canon of our time. Of course, this principle is not pursued for simplicy sake per se, but because, as in all great art, one focuses on fundamentals in endeavoring to make the important statement.

A concern for the precise employ of new techniques and materials that express a natural involvement with our life styles is elemental to a wide body of sculpture and painting, where art is seen as an environmental coefficient rather than a precious museum piece. In paring down to the essence of things, there is an obvious parallel to our own human organism where everything is basically relevant and serves a purpose. Technology may have been the initial impetus, but much that is most creative today from the spaceship, to the building, to the modest kitchen appliance, seems to be an expression of real including symbolic purpose, committed to the idea of the totality of life within a unified environment. This is *our* comprehensive awareness of our world and is the historical shift of our focus.

Literally born of our technological capability, no building type epitomizes our new attitude toward design more clearly than the skyscraper. From the early towers in the late nineteenth century with their delicate ornament, articulation at their base, emphasis on the entrance, and broken profiles, all gentle echoes of historic styles, the tower at its best had "evolved" by mid-twentieth century to an elegant box of which the Marine Midland building is

■ Cesar Pelli & Assoc., Museum of Modern Art, New York City, 1984 *(Photos: General view, Museum of Modern Art; garden detail, Kenneth Champlin)*

a classic example, to the "cheaper" type of minimal box of which there are unfortunately too many examples. In the 1980s there were fortunately numerous interesting buildings breaking away from that mold, and some of the dynamic promise of Mies's visionary Berlin skyscraper proposal found realization, except with more aesthetic, historic recall.

Designing the facade to the residential condominium above the Museum of Modern Art in New York, in conjunction with an expansion of the Museum's exhibit spaces, Cesar Pelli has conceived of a tower sheathed in multicolored glass, where the patchwork quilt of pale colors contained within a complex patterning of mullions expresses the interior by giving clues to the use of spaces. In contrast to the facade of the office tower, the intent is to show the variable and differentiated space of a private use building in the form of a varied but all-over pattern, where pattern is clearly different from decoration. The effort is to develop a more complex language of design within stringent economic controls. As it rises, the tower has symmetrical setbacks recalling the slenderness of many archetypal skyscrapers designed in the 1930s in the United States.

Setbacks become the aggressively dominant form design theme in Pelli's four office towers ranging in height from 33 to 50 stories and built as part of the World Financial Center in Lower Manhattan. Here four reflective glass and granite towers rise from continuous granite-sheathed bases. The proportion of

■ Cesar Pelli & Assoc., World Financial Center, Battery Park City, New York, 1982–1987
(Photos: View from Hudson River, Peter Aaron/ESTO; winter garden, Jeff Perkell)

granite to glass is greater at the base of each tower, gradually lightening up the
height to become completely reflective glass skins. At various intervals the
towers are set back and ascend visually toward distinctively shaped, copper-
clad tops. The base deals with the reality of street life and urban form; the
shaft derives from the spirit of the dominant modernist tradition of equivalent
facades based on the concept of a repetitive Cartesian grid; the top deals with
the crowning element as essentially part of a skyscraper collage, an element
of the building but one with also a broader, urban skyline role. The more
elaborate setbacks and stepped, angled profiles of the towers are an effort to
reduce their bulk, as is their shiny sheathing of granite and glass. Both of these
projects by Pelli are in the modernist tradition of employing available technology rather than high technology. While they are sleek, they are brought
together with an unfussy, assembled feeling of ordinary catalog elements, that
is they are not highly refined in their detail nor thought of as polished pre-
cisionlike artifacts.

The desire to make the "tower" more contextural became the motivation
for Pelli's subsequent design of the 60-story office building at Carnegie Hall.
Respectful of the contiguous 1891 Italianate in style Concert hall, a building of
character and presence and one steeped in New York's cultural history, the
tower's slenderness, only 50 feet wide facing 57th street, and its multicolored
brick facade—11 colors ranging from dark green to vibrant red—distinguish it

from new, adjacent glass high rises. The base of the tower is a 6-story street facade, aligned with Carnegie Hall's heavy cornice and carefully banded and configured with windows to dialogue with the hall. Set back 31 feet from this city-scaled "base," the tower rises as a slender volume, with clustered setbacks reminiscent of Carnegie Hall itself. The shaft terminates dramatically against the sky in an array of 10-foot I-beams, cantilevered from the building's top floor and forming a visually penetrable cornice. The three Pelli projects provide a

■ Murphy/Jahn, State of Illinois Center, Chicago, 1979

■ Murphy/Jahn, Xerox Center, Chicago, 1977

■ Murphy/Jahn, One South Wacker, Chicago, 1980

■ Murphy/Jahn, North Western Terminal, Chicago, 1987

useful, generalized comparison; they evidence the shift in design emphasis and aesthetic preoccupations from the simpler to the more complex, from the transparent, reflective and hard-edged, to the more modulated, textural and ornamentally patterned, from a more reductive modernism to a sensibility more inclusive and historically associative. They conveniently encapsulate the short sweep of the history and shift of attitudes of the late 70s to the late 80s.

The characteristic repetition of grid in various forms, similar to Pelli's buildings, is also present in four very different Chicago towers designed by Helmut Jahn of Murphy/Jahn. The Xerox Center has a sleek skin of aluminum and reflective, insulating glass, here gently curving around the street corner with rolled, flat, grill-like authority. In the State of Illinois Center the curve becomes a dramatic raking arc, with office space encircling a monumental-in-scale public space in the form of a circular central atrium, thrusting through the roof line as a grand, truncated cylinder. Three setbacks in the facade produce smaller, 5-story subatriums up the building's height and the exterior is a combination of alternate strips of reflective vision panels and opaque, colored spandrel glass.

Less vigorous in its concept and looking more determinedly back over the shoulder to the thirties is the One South Wacker, 40-story office tower. Here, the articulation of the facades is created by filling in the abstract grid with silver and gray reflective glass. The programmatic requirement of three large and different floor areas has resulted in a modeled, three-setback form, where the entry corner of the building is also stepped back to create an intimate entry court with 3-story atriums above and below each setback. The vertical atrium idea of both the State of Illinois Center and One South Wacker has the functional advantage of producing U-shaped office floors, increasing the building perimeter exposure to natural light without, for energy conservation considerations, increasing the exterior wall area.

The North Western Terminal, combining an existing commuter terminal with an office facility above, also has an atrium concept used to similar advantage but here appropriately recalling the grand railroad concourse of an industrialized era. A continuous street level arcade leads inward to a sequence of multistory atriums that generate a sense of expectancy in the commuter traffic flow, culminating in an 80-foot-high and naturally lit, central space. The varying floor bulk and the symmetry of its distribution reflect in the tower's exterior form, a three "extruded" shape idea shifting against each other, coming together at the base and top. The smooth, streamlined curves have an obvious intentional affinity to the image of trains, movement, and the symbolism of machine-made objects.

Symbolism, a concern to creatively use modern materials and technology in a modernist spirit, and a sense of continuity drawn from the historical allusions of skyscrapers of the twenties and thirties distinguishes two other towers by Jahn. The first, an office building in South Africa, is intricately faceted like a diamond conforming to the sloping height restrictions of that city's zoning, while also symbolizing the business involvement of its developer. Here the atrium notion as an energy idea is totally transformed into a double-skinned facade: the inner skin of butt-jointed, silicone-sealed, mullionless glass allowing complete flexibility in locating interior partitions against the exterior plane; the exterior skin, a panelized curtain wall of three colors of

■ Murphy/Jahn, 11 Diagonal Street, Johannesburg, South Africa, 1983

■ Murphy/Jahn, Television City Proposal, New York City, 1985 *(Photo: James R. Steinkamp)*

reflective glass acting as a drapedlike, giant sunshade, with the space between these skins providing a naturally ventilated, environmental buffer. The second, the 82-story Bank of the Southwest tower for Houston, returns to a more tradition-in-spirit obelisk form where the corners of the tapered shaft are gradually stepped back to terminate in a sloped roof with a spire and beacon reminiscent of New York's Chrysler Building. The heavily, rhythmically faceted facade comprises combinations of granite, aluminum, and glass, emphasizing the slenderness, verticality, and shape of the shaft. Echoing the configurations of the distinctive gabled top, the towers monumental base is rotated at 45 degrees so that the four 100-foot-high entrance porticoes face the corners of the city block. It is a gesture to establish an appropriate, transitional civic scale to the street.

The stepped obelisk form has increasingly preoccupied Jahn and it reappears in the monolithically insular and urbanistically simplistic proposal for a central 150-story tower, flanked by six 76-story residential towers supported by other retail, commercial and parking areas, the first proposal for a vacant 100-acre site on Manhattan's West Side. It appears again in Philadelphia in a commanding, elegantly graceful and that city's largest tower, one finally able to entrepreneurally break the city's height limit of not exceeding the until now city-wide dominant statue of William Penn atop City Hall. Whereas the growing public sentiment at the end of the eighties against the excesses of economically motivated developments of tremendous urban consequence, because of their deleterious scale impact upon qualitative factors of urban life,

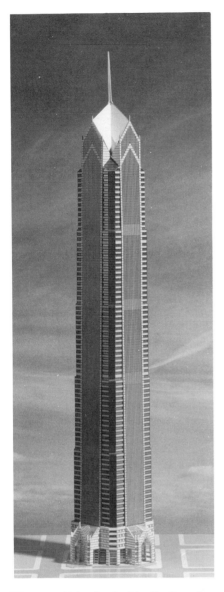

■ Murphy/Jahn, Bank of the Southwest, Houston, Texas, 1982

■ Murphy/Jahn, One Liberty Place Tower, Philadelphia, Pennsylvania, 1987

■ Murphy/Jahn, Messeturm, Frankfurt, Germany, 1990

seems to have effectively stymied the progress of the West Side proposal, Philadelphia's One Liberty Place might well prove to have just slipped in under the wire of public resentment and antagonism against large-scale development that might compromise long-held sacrosanct ideas.

Jahn has brought ideas and scales explored in the United States also to Europe and its contextural traditions and smaller, more intimate scale. In Frankfurt, a 70-story tower composed of a square to circle plan form, terminates in another variant on the stepped pyramid top. Stone at the ground level, to harmonize with the adjacent turn-of-the-century historic Festhalle, and

■ Kohn Pedersen Fox, 333 Wacker Drive, Chicago, 1984 (Photos: Overall, Barbara Karant; detail, Gregory Murphey)

glass against the skyline, it stands companilelike as a visual anchor to an exhibition complex. This tower likewise draws its inspiration from American skyscrapers of the twenties and their aesthetic dependence upon symbolism, stylization of setbacks and formal and ornamental expression. The towers of all three projects also continue the Murphy/Jahn interest in the stylized marriage

■ Kohn Pedersen Fox, 383 Madison Avenue, New York City, 1984–1988 *(Aerial photo montage: Jack Horner; photo of model: Jock Pottle/Esto)*

of technology with the aesthetics of historic tower forms. Rising 825 feet as Europe's tallest tower, the Frankfurt building also probably charts a course for architecture in Europe, away from the minimal, lifeless boxes of the sixties toward a stronger union of a new awareness of historic form, reinterpreted and rerationalized, but with a dependence upon modern systems and technology at a whole new scale with which America has become accustomed.

Responding more inherently to its urban context, although again a large building, is the formally powerful and elegantly assured tower at 333 South Wacker Drive by the New York firm of Kohn Pedersen Fox. It is a luminous glass-clad form rising from a carefully proportioned granite base, the sweeping curve of its primary facade elegantly following the broad scale bend of the Chicago River, with its other rectangular-in-configuration facade facing Chicago's downtown Loop area. In its detail it also looks back to early modernist and Art Deco themes, which it employs with contemporary élan.

As the Jahn towers have evolved from an interest in more modernist to referentially historic themes, so too has the architecture of Kohn Pederson Fox as is seen in their later proposal for 383 Madison Avenue. In seeking to manipulate air rights transferred from Grand Central Station to permit excessive bulk and hence a more economically attractive development, it too was halted in 1987 amid the growing sentiment of public concern for restraint. In this instance the tower would have been an accomplished design, one with an affinity to its neighbor the Chrysler Building and the distant Empire State Building. The shaft, although monolithic is a composite of scaled-down and basically vertically expressed elements, in turn broken down into the classical

■ Kohn Pedersen Fox, 70 East 55th Street, New York City,
1984–1986 *(Photo: Cervin Robinson)*

■ Kohn Pedersen Fox, The St. Paul Companies Headquarters,
St. Paul, Minnesota, 1991 *(Photo: Don F. Wong)*

formula of base, shaft, and capital. The 25-story office building at 70 East 55th Street completed just prior to this proposal consummately accomplishes this tripartite division, reinforcing the lower section as the street wall, above which and set back rises the shaft and a twin-towered, cruciform top. This "small" tower results in an urbane and regularly classical exterior at once complementary and discreet, an accomplished example of urban sensitivity and responsibility. It seeks, as did the Bank of England in its Classic style, to respond to and follow street lines and, with subtle variations and shifts inherent to form and surface and the surroundings, like the Manet paintings of Rouen Cathedral, to be in relative, subtle, and complementary change.

The nature of the tower is inherently that of a more isolated epic. In their St. Paul Headquarters, Kohn Pedersen Fox seek to overcome this isolation by developing, instead of a composition of expressed parts, a continuity of buildings, each individual component conceived as a discreet and geometrically clear form responding to its context yet assembled to produce a complex

■ Edward Larrabee Barnes, John M. Y. Lee Architects, IBM, 590
Madison Avenue, New York City, 1983 *(Photos: Cervin Robinson)*

■ Der Scutt, design architect, Trump Tower, New York City, 1983
(Photo: Norman McGrath)

■ Johnson/Burgee, AT&T Building, New York City, 1979–
1983 (Photos: Richard Payne)

and asymmetrical whole. The scheme is entered through a small basilicalike form, a transitional element between existing and new. A cylindrical glass tower is the composition's pivot and terminates pedestrian approach vistas. A low rectangular block defines the street edge while serving as a building base. The main tower with its pyramidal metal roof relates to the collection of roof forms in the area, seeking to complement, like a village seen at a distance, the effect of a collage of steeples. Local stone, used in a planar way to emphasize its often non-load-bearing nature in contemporary construction, is employed as a grid with punched window openings against which the more figural elements are

■ *Above and facing page:* Johnson/Burgee, Republic Bank, Houston, Texas, 1983
(Photos: Richard Payne)

■ Johnson/Burgee, Transco Tower,
Houston, Texas, 1983

developed, using reflective glass and metal cladding. With its "composite" philosophy it strives for a harmonious presence not through formal, aesthetic rules as for example Manhattan's Rockefeller Center of the thirties, but via the notion of accretion—if an instant one—where elements enjoy individuality but with collective consequence.

Three skyscrapers also illustrating changed attitudes in design thinking, again toward the skyscraper, are encountered within a one city block radius in Manhattan. The IBM building by Edward Larrabee Barnes, the Trump Tower by Der Scutt, then of Swanke Hayden Connell, and the AT&T building by Johnson/Burgee. The 43-story IBM building is an extension of the minimal, no-texture, tight skin facade tradition, its dark green polished granite slabs instead of glass, aesthetically treated like a metal curtain wall, bringing a slightly stronger sense of visual durability to the architecture. Breaking away from the conventional rectangular box comes in its more soaring and angled, five-sided shape and its dramatic, cantilevered street level corner. The 60-story reflective glass tower designed by Der Scutt, gains its variability and slenderness from an intricate progression of zig-zag cut backs that maximizes prestigious "corner" offices and apartments. The basic derivation of the tower's mass originated with the desire to provide a minimum of two exposures to as many rooms as possible.

By contrast the 37-story AT&T headquarters is a rough-textured granite, historically inspired, eclectic tower. Paralleling the Louis Sullivan sense of the skyscraper's three elements: the base is a 131-foot-high plinth with a 110-foot central arch flanked by six arcade openings, which in turn are flanked by lower

arcades with oculus apertures above, and the shaft is a vertical ribbon of ribs that terminate in the crown, a broken sloping pediment, split at its apex by a concave circular hollow, glibly dubbed the "Chippendale" top. The inspiration of the Roman and Baroque where the broken pediment is a familiar motif, to the Early Renaissance base in the manner of Brunelleschi and Alberti, is a vigorous revisiting and reinterpretation of history rather than a reiteration of historic elements. Johnson, with one of the most topically sensitized intelligences in architecture, astutely codified the emerging post-modernist priorities in the late seventies with this preeminent landmark structure of a new referential genre.

Whereas the former buildings seek to define new parameters as they might pertain to the shape and treatment of towers, the 780 Third Avenue, 50-story tower by Skidmore, Owings & Merrill with Raul de Armas in charge of

■ *Above right:* Johnson/Burgee,
33 Maiden Lane, New York City, 1984
(Photo: Nathaniel Lieberman)

■ Roche Dinkeloo & Assoc., Denver Towers, Denver, Colorado, 1981

design is rather a refinement of a central theme in that firm's oeuvre: the unbroken, upward thrust of a singular and slender, flat shaft to which one cannot add or subtract. The slenderness of the concrete "tube" is made possible here by diagonal concrete bracing within the exterior wall, which distributes the wind loads equally among the perimeter columns, an idea first developed in the late sixties by the late Fazlur Khan, an engineer from the Chicago office of Skidmore, Owings & Merrill. The structure is the visible architectural expression of its diagonal bracing, identified by the stepped path of blanked-off windows at each floor level in the red polished-granite facade. The elegance and finiteness of the idea are embodied in the tower's dimensions which are of themselves complete and contained by virtue of the diagonal geometry: The shaft is four squares in height, one in width, and one half in depth—*Q.E.D.*

The former skyscrapers are clearly indicative of a spirit of natural evolution, rather than an indictment of or an expression of a sense of failure of modern architecture; the AT&T tower embodying the most prevalent historical references and in many ways being the more romantic and seminal of the solutions. A quest to synthesize forms and elements that might become a more overt embellishment of the modernist high-rise tradition is with varying emphasis obviously the underlying inspiration in three other skyscrapers by Johnson/ Burgee: the 64-story Transco Tower of gray reflective glass progressively set back from the corners, its central section capped by a double-pitched roof entered through a 90-foot-high granite archway; the Republic Bank consisting of two distinct yet form-related and connected elements, a 56-story red granite tower stepping down in a sequence of three vertical segments, the building approached through a grand banking hall also with a myriad stepped profile and likewise entered through a grand, in this instance 75-foot-high arched doorway; and finally the even more historically inspired design for 33 Maiden Lane in Lower Manhattan, a circular turretlike columned and crenelated corniced tower in a somewhat neo-Gothic spirit.

Philip Johnson's attitude toward design has basically always had strong classical affinities, even while his buildings have been executed with deference to the "bauen" modernist tradition. A similar sympatico has been the approach of Kevin Roche. In the projected, two 55-story towers for Denver, stronger historical references are also basic to the design in a project whose imagery appears as a cross between a rocket on the launching pad and a medieval campanile. The minimal manipulation in the exterior form, where indents create corner offices, provides the upward sense of thrust, which is reinforced by the pointed top, creating an entirely usable space due to a clever square plan shape achieved by a diagonal rotation of the square. The granite base is conceived to use the expensive material for the maximum effect at the ground level. The pinking-shear decorative motif of the grand entrance emphasizes the archway in a familiar Romanesque pattern, one also favored by the nineteenth century architect, H. H. Richardson.

Michael Graves's prize-winning design for the Portland Building is even more historically associative and less modernist as it employs the elements of history, as did the Romanesque-inspired revivalism of Richardson, to become an imaginatively vigorous development of historic principles applied to the solid and robust tradition of the classic authoritative, bureaucratic government headquarters. Rather than denied by aesthetic device, its frankly squat form becomes the building's celebration as accented by subtle, pastel colors. It is embellished by archetypal forms, intended as validated and referential historic symbols of our participatory democracy. The building's decorative aspects, considerably reduced and compromised from the winning proposal to the executed building, are allegorical with an aesthetic predilection toward the classical formalization of elements filtered through a classicist and art nouveau sensibility. Elements in the main facade, in addition to serving a decorative role are also intended to convey the interior functions of the building with a relative symbolism. A small pavilion atop the main facade, projected outward and supported on a giant sconce, was conceived as a look-out point to spectacular views of the Columbia River over parklands. Its hutlike form "emerging from the mountain" is a theme common in classical architecture, a favorite of Graves, and was intended to declaratively evoke the relationship between man, nature and building. Other rooftop pavilions reiterate this theme and combine to

■ Michael Graves, The Portland Building,
Portland, Oregon, 1980 *(Photo: Paschall/
Taylor)*

create a miniature cityscape to the surrounding buildings looking down upon it, a specific requirement of the building's program. Through such referential metaphors, these archetypal elements are intended to become philosophically pertinent to the architectural effort rather than gratuitously decorative.

The Humana Building in Louisville, also by Graves, further develops these themes. Fully occupying its riverfront site, offices are generally expressed on the exterior by 4½-foot-square windows "scaled to the human body and able to particularize the outside context." As a gesture to the river, an outward bowing porch is a terrace roof garden in a tower that is symbolically crowned by a health club. Says Graves: "The formal gestures and activities of our building are, we believe, natural and intrinsic to urban structure in general and a river city in particular. In their figurative and thematic aspect they attempt to reaffirm and reestablish humanist aspirations for the city which have been too long neglected by modern architecture."

The Portland and Louisville buildings are obviously based on a reassessment of Modernist fundamentals, which because of their pristine thrust and freshness, received more critical attention as the Modern movement swung into the 1920s, than what appeared as a less innovative evolution and an outgrowth from more eclectic and traditional attitudes. But many of the admired early Modern structures relied strongly upon appropriate embellishment for their architectural impact, and Graves's work endeavors to expand on this tradition. The compact massing of Richardson's late nineteenth century buildings, for example, had restrained and delicate embellishment, as did such landmark structures as Chicago's Monadnock building of 1892—at 17 stories high the tallest load-bearing wall building—by Burnham and Root. Louis Sullivan's last major commission, the Carson Pirie Scott department store in 1900, also in Chicago, gained its expression from a basically unadorned structural framework but with a delicate intricacy of ornament appropriately at the street level display windows and as an emphasis to the entrance. Such buildings embodied the robustness of the best of the American tradition as they avoided affectation, mannerism, and involvement with fashion. Wright's architecture continued this interest in related decorative elements as enriching the theme of a building into the first half of the twentieth century as he used detail to accentuate surface continuity shaping space. Such decorative predilections earned for Wright among some of the modernist critics the somewhat facetious title of the greatest modern architect of the nineteenth century. Importantly, all of these architects did not ignore the point that in a building, whatever its instigating philosophy, the eye needs delight, and that if ornament was not applied then it must be substituted for by notions of decoration that themselves become integral to the architecture.

This has been the thrust in the desire to broaden the language of the early modern structures as architects have explored the richness of solid to void contrasts, structure as plane and line suggesting space, the interplay of light and shadow, texture of material and detail of its connection, the use of color and various furnishings, the incorporation of mechanical services and interraction of environmental protections, all collectively eventually leading to the enrichment of architectural form. Where coherence remains a measure of architecture today, it is clear that it must be accomplished now through an inclusive attitude of response to and beyond such concerns. The work of many of the architects practicing in a more modernist derivative vein today, also clearly recognize in their architecure that simplicity no longer has absolute value as a goal per se, unless it can derive from the imaginative distillation of a broad range of architectural fact.

The work of Gwathmey/Siegel and Richard Meier is indicative of a vigorous continuation of the spirit of Le Corbusier and similar modernist architects, indeed an evolution into a new vocabulary of formal expression as it derives from interpreted function. For both firms the exterior form gains its sculptural impact as it directly reveals and dramatizes the interior organization of volumetric space and elements as they manifest themselves as the architectural expression. Space is variable in plan and section and hence expresses itself hierarchically in the simultaneity of interior-exterior form. Form derives from the inside outward. No decoration is applied. The intrinsic form of parts as they are juxtaposed to other forms to combine a whole becomes the archi-

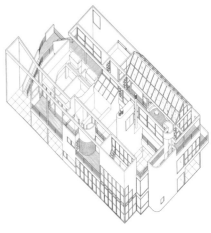

■ Gwathmey/Siegel, de Menil Residence,
East Hampton, New York, 1983 (Photos:
© Norman McGrath)

■ Gwathmey/Siegel, Steinberg Residence, East Hampton, New York, 1987–1989

tecture. The impact of their buildings is almost more appreciable at night when the illuminated facade is read as a negative. The de Menil House by Charles Gwathmey and Robert Siegel, for example, is a multifaceted though composite environment comprising strongly expressed and interlocking elements that are combined and comprehended as a singular structure. Space is more elaborate and concomitantly traditionally compartmentalized in comparison to their earlier houses in this vein, and there is a stronger reliance on traditional materials and color used to "code" the various elements. Whereas their early houses presented the *prism pur* of the early modernist cube or rectangle, gouged away but still retaining the lines that defined the edge of the form, here the erosion of the *prism pur* has been taken another step towards complexity.

The idea of the modern villa comprising main house, caretaker's house, pool facilities, tennis court, guest wings, auto court and garage pavilions, and structured landscape gardens and treed allées are again the genesis for the Steinberg "composition," another asymmetrically organized oceanfront East Hampton residence. Here the language of the facade departs from the "almost" white, (actually palest of silver gray vertical wood siding) of the former residence to "retreat" to the weathered nineteenth century shingled estate architecture so familiar to the traditional Hamptons in general. The geometry remains absolutely crisp and the ocean front *brise-soleil* facade again frames ocean views and protects from the powerful, fabric-fading sun. As the exterior seeks a softer presence, so too the interior moves in the direction of a gentler, meaning less relentlessly white, modernism.

The Atheneum Center in New Harmony and the Hartford Seminary by Richard Meier, reflect also themes that are organized and refined for aesthetic effect, not as applied or false components, but the relationship of built volume synthesized through structure, of movement made visible. The Atheneum, the more visually complicated of the buildings, is an arrival, reception, and

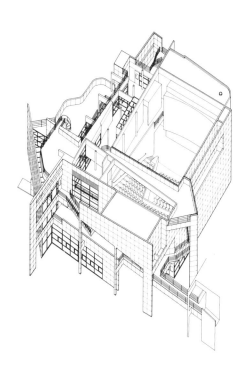

orientation center for visitors to this historic town. The facade is white porcelain enamel panels on a steel frame. The building is essentially a dynamic circulation system where the main 180-seat theater and four exhibit galleries are revealed as a changing, staggered, and overlapping pattern of provocatively engaging spaces, seen from processional ramps, stairs, and balconies. The 5-degree shift in geometry of a diagonal grid laid against the building's main

■ Richard Meier, The Atheneum, New Harmony, Indiana, 1975–1979 *(Photos: Ezra Stoller, Esto)*

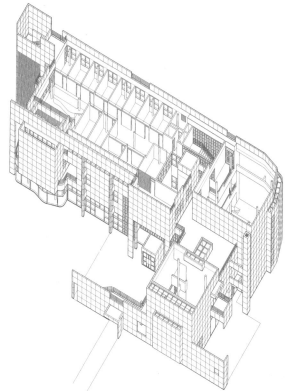

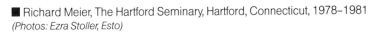 Richard Meier, The Hartford Seminary, Hartford, Connecticut, 1978–1981
(Photos: Ezra Stoller, Esto)

othogonal one, forces the impression of spaces narrowing then opening up, and of the gentle, visually engaging and dynamic transition from one geometric system to another. The Seminary, an interdenominational research center, is also a pristine white-panel-clad structure, although here more compactly organized into an L-shaped form. Again, larger public spaces rise vertically through the building's mass with the intent that their sculptural presence is experienced at many levels. Light, both direct and diffused through windows and skylights, makes this presence luminous, even shimmering. The buildings appear as an example to, rather than a contextural response to their surroundings, what Meier terms "reciprocal involvement."

The modernist spirit elaborated upon and redefined is also fundamental to the "Rigged House" by John Johansen for himself. Clearly in the modernist

■ John Johansen, "Rigged House," Stanfordville, New York, 1974

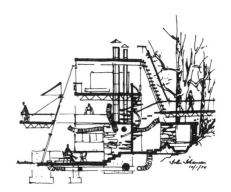

idiom, it is a far cry from the refined and pristine structures of Meier. Johansen's house is a central and generalized space, defined by eight rectangular tubes, two for each side of the 30-foot square of a 3-story-high sloped sided building which is enclosed by lightweight, translucent yellowish fiberglass sheets forming panels with clear styrofoam insulation sandwiched between. From the steel tubes hang 64 red-painted industrial shackles from which cables support suspended platforms or balconylike rooms. Change is the primary aesthetic, its mechanism conceived almost like the rigging of a sailboat. Even heating ducts seem to hang almost temporarily from platforms, inviting the move to another location or the promise of service to an added space. The building is in no way a resolved object, it is rather almost a kit of parts inviting different moves.

These ideas were further developed by Johansen in a prototype Luxury Resort Hotel for a semitropical waterfront location where a structural frame, reminiscent of metal frameworks which might be mass produced for outer space, shelters an open central space to become the organizing accommodator of more aggressively kinetic notions. Draw bridges, exposed inclined elevators, wind turbines, moveable sun shuttering, changeable scenery, room liners as changing stage sets, floating lounge pads, intra-neighborhood people-mover conveyor systems, and a hot air balloon bar are all vividly expressed to comprise a multiple kinetic sculpture of ultimate variable character.

Adhering to the spirit of ad-hocism present in Johansen's more industrial aesthetic but deviating from it in that it is not a system of attachment, Frank Gehry's own house in Los Angeles is rather a collision of parts, built to stay but with a deliberately unfinished, ordinary builderlike sensibility of parts. An existing and very pedestrian two-story gambrel-roofed clapboard residence had much of its interior removed and walls stripped back to their original two-by-four stud frame, beams, and rafters. It was then expanded by wrapping the old house with a metal slipcover creating a new set of spaces around its perimeter. The antirefinement type enclosure is built of the most mundane

■ Frank O. Gehry & Assoc., own house, Los Angeles, 1979 (Photos: Paul Heyer)

materials, corrugated aluminum metal siding, plywood, glass and chain-link fencing, and deliberately has randomly slanted lines and angled protrusions. Although the house retains a certain minimalist sense, the effort here is cluttered expressionistic and the sensibility is freely intended as artistically intuitive, of accident not resolved. The palette is anti high-tech in preference for a visual presence that is off-the-shelf and ordinary "cheap tech." Gehry considers buildings as sculpture with the freedom from restraint that this might imply, hence it is not surprising that his work has an affinity to the collages of Robert Rauschenberg, especially in the artist's ripped cardboard assemblage period of the 1970s. (Gehry himself designed a line of corrugated cardboard furniture.)

With the original house almost intact formwise, Gehry, in effect, lifted back the skin to reveal the building as layers, with new forms breaking out and tilting away from the original, to create a forerunner of the Deconstructionist spirit of the eighties. It is almost an idea of 'wrapping' à la the artist Christo, but where Christo seeks through a veil to transform the original to a new sense of being and meaning, Gehry rather produces a discontinuous juxtaposition where one system collides with another resulting in, to quote Bernard Tschumi, a "super position or disjunctive disassociation." Where Johansen assembles technological-like elements freely seeking dialogue through the combination, Gehry, through collaging, also basically (but with a different aesthetic) derives an approach to design from the methodology and respect for construction and its architectonic potential as a form maker and space generator.

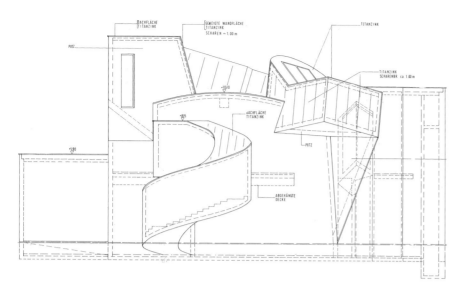

■ Frank O. Gehry & Assoc., Vitra Museum, Weil-am-Rhein, Germany, 1990 *(Photo: Peter Mauss/ESTO)*

■ Frank O. Gehry & Assoc., American Center, Paris, France, 1991 *(Photo: Joshua White)*

■ Peter Eisenman, College of Design, Architecture, Art and Planning, University of Cincinnati, Cincinnati, Ohio, 1990 *(Silk screen roof plan, John Nichols; model photo, Dick Frank Studio; gallery perspective, Eisenman Architects)*

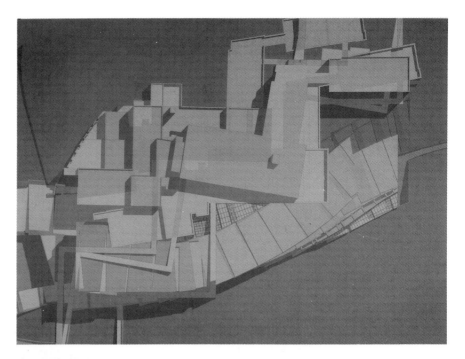

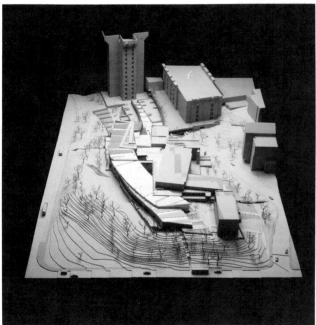

Using a palette of strongly architectonic forms, the formative ideas explored in his own house were further developed at a comprehensive urban scale in his design for the Loyola Law School. Expanding the original campus of essentially one building and a parking garage through an incrementally phased master plan, Gehry designed a compilation of academic facilities, necessitated by a community comprising 1,000 students, housed in individually expressive structures. The result was large-scale disparate elements dexterously juxtaposed—thrust inward or conversely pushing outward—against buildings and urban

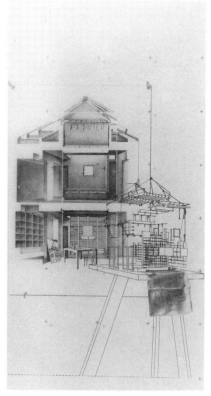

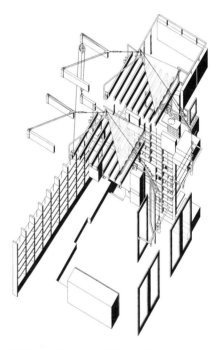

■ Thom Mayne and Michael Rotondi,
Morphosis, House Venice III, Los Angeles,
1985 *(Photo of model: Tom Bonner)*

sculptural elements that themselves were formally not reconciled in a traditional sense. It further evidenced Gehry's interest in the discreet interlock of disparate forms which, through collision and seeming disorder, somehow combine to create a presence in resolution—probably the basic reason why Cubism and Expressionism is so obviously his connection to Modernism.

This is readily apparent in his Vitra Design Museum, a small, 8,000-square-foot building on two floors basically for the exhibit of chairs, design, and educational programs. The building is a continuous changing swirl of white forms on the exterior, each seemingly without apparent relationship to the other, with its interiors a dynamically powerful interplay, in turn directly expressive of the exterior convolutions. As a totality it resolves itself into an entwined coherent display in much the same way that Gehry's 1990 proposal for the American Center in Paris will likewise bring the disparate functional and spatial demands of classrooms, art and dance studios, film, and live experimental theater and apartments into a more centralized though again a visually discordant, volumetric totality, here at least tenuously deriving from the zoning and urban context. While acknowledging its surroundings, it is also obviously intent upon transcending them.

In comparison with Gehry, and indeed Meier, Peter Eisenman is much more theoretical and esoterically and linguistically moved in his derivations. He is closer in spirit to Tschumi—and both are closer to Deconstruction's great philosophical exponent, Jacques Derrida—but again there is a basic difference. Whereas Tschumi's interests are more linear insofar as there are overlays of lines, points, and planes, the essential scheme of Parc La Villette, Eisenman develops organizational geometric forms which are totally transformed by additions and subtractions. In his proposed extension to the College of Design, Architecture, Art and Planning in Cincinnati, the intent is to ambiguously fragment inside and out, new and old, structure and infill. Deriving its origin from the chevron shape of the existing buildings, Eisenman tilts, overlaps, and shifts, where these disjunctions, fuzzy by their movement and displacement, carry the informed memoria of these various formal moves, blurring building both in plan and elevation and ultimately, hopefully, into the undulating site and its apparently not very attractive existing structures.

Other designers in the eighties, pushing and torquing architectural elements and volumes had codified this new departure for modernism, often captured within incredibly complex presentations, beautiful drawings and models, and often tied to the constructivist interest in process. The small 750-square-foot house addition by Thom Mayne and Michael Rotondi of Morphosis in Los Angeles, a sequenced layering of three distinct and articulated volumes resulting in a highly varied spatial epic for this small scale, carries Gehry's house forward into a more apparently stick structural resolution—one rooted in the American tradition of House. In their subsequent Chiba Golf Club project four basic elements are developed: a space for automobile arrival defined by a segment of curved wall; a lineal sequence of volumes accommodating a majority of the program; a second curved wall embracing the larger site and facilitating movement to the grounds; and a pavilion containing space for social events and dining. The two curved walls demark the building's functional spaces, while the pavilion, outside the curved bounding walls, becomes

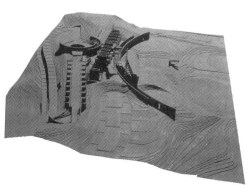

■ Morphosis, Chiba Prefecture Golf Club, Japan, 1988–1991 *(Photo of model, Tom Bonner; photo of sectional model, George Yu)*

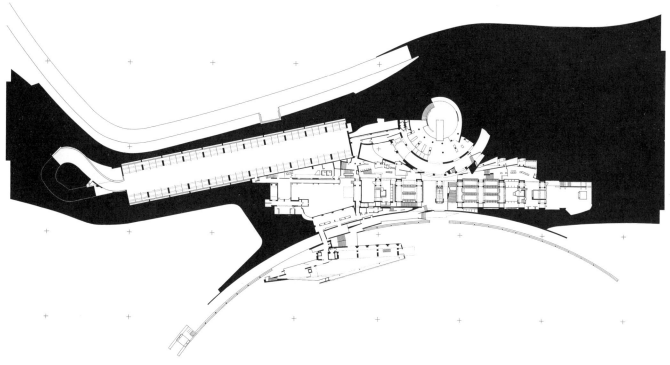

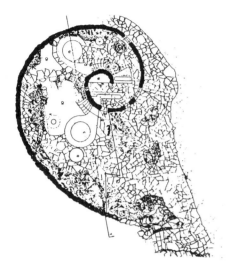

■ Bruce Goff, Bavinger House, Norman, Oklahoma, 1949 *(Photo: Gene Bavinger)*

a raised viewing platform to the course. The Chiba project further develops the fractured language of the Venice III house addition to seek a more complex and blurred demarcation between nature and the constructed. It strives to unite site investigation and architectonic language, exploiting the connective nature of a complex organism while recognizing golf as a game of rhythm, swing, and movement.

As Deconstructionism was a convenient label in the eighties to identify shifts from early modernism, the broader label "Post Modernism" was coined in the 1970s to identify architectural approaches that also sought to deviate from a narrower modernist ideology and aesthetic expression. By the early 1960s however many architects were clearly aware of the need to expand the scope of modern architecture from any restraining, austere, and limited focus. This was quite evident in the composite representation of the diverse philosophies of leading American architects presented in my first book *Architects on Architecture—New Directions in America*. In the early 1950s Le Corbusier had opened the door himself to a freer interpretation of the language of modern architecture, one beyond the disciplining right angle, with his organically flowing and sensual design for the chapel at Ronchamp. Then, and in addition to Frank Lloyd Wright in the United States, there were always architects who had thought of architecture as a more varied vocabulary of expression: The extraordinary imaginative work of Bruce Goff and his colleague and former student Herb Greene, to cite only one example, and Goff's influence emanating from the School of Architecture at the University of Oklahoma in the late forties and early fifties. Goff's Bavinger House in Oklahoma, a continuous open space defined by a stone rubble wall spiraling upward, coiled around a steel mast from which the roof, stairs, and living spaces were suspended, and Greene's own shingle-clad house also in Oklahoma, a conventionalization or abstraction of natural phenomena evoking memories of the prairie, birds, barns, and buffalo, are both tours de force of spirited, organic, and freely associative design. Private and introspective in theme, Goff's architecture depends on allusion and particularity as more fundamental than any sense of visual imagery drawn from tenets be they of modernist or Vitruvian origin, or any effort to establish architectural modes or precedents. It is an ad hocism deriving from context, site, and spirit of client and not one selected to make a philosophical point. It is not Rauchenberg that might inspire this time, but

■ Herb Greene, own house, Norman, Oklahoma, 1960 *(Photos: Julius Shulman)*

■ Venturi and Rauch, Renwick Gallery Exhibit, Washington, D.C., 1976 *(Photos: Stephen Shore)*

Goff's liking for artists such as Klimt, Debussy and Maxfield Parrish. The intent is harmony without conformity or commonality, an architecture of singular spirit born of unique and special need. Such work can demonstrate a cumulative sensibility but not be the type of consolidated episodic evolution to set the example from which movements in art are grounded. This is of course not the intent anyway and is one of the major reasons why Goff remained, while admired for his inventiveness, somewhat isolated as an influence on the mainstream of architecture.

The philosophical digression from the more stringent aspects of modern architecture became dramatized and codified in Robert Venturi's important treatise of the mid-sixties, *Complexity and Contradiction in Architecture*. The thesis was for the hybrid, distorted, compromising, ambiguous, and equivocal, rather than the pure, straightforward, clean, direct, and clear; a messy vitality over obvious unity; richness of meaning, rather than clarity of meaning. Venturi also lauded the ordinary and in so doing pointed a finger toward notions of imagery—even be they ordinary images—as Andy Warhol, Claus Oldenburg and other pop artists were doing in the contemporary art world. Whereas image as the sole idea for deriving form points toward a potentially shallow or decorative eclecticism, with Venturi there is invariably a sophistication of designed "ordinariness" and a transposition of familiar and common elements through a historically aware sensitivity that mitigates this. The simplistic question, for example, of implication—if people like Ionic columns, why not? Even if they clad an engineered, steel frame structure?—does not arise because energies are always directed toward the interpretation of elements and not their literal representation.

The implications and metaphorical reach of a new hybrid language based on the symbols of popular culture were further and visually presented in the

"Signs of Life: Symbols in the American City," an exhibition in Washington, D.C., in 1976 by Robert Venturi, Denise Scott Brown and Steven Izenour. Concentrating on the house, main street, and the commercial strip, its commitment was to the symbolic and familiar. The involvement is not with architecture as high art, and the digression from this idea is more in the realm of the ideological than the formal. The Tucker House, New York, designed by Venturi and Rauch evidences this in that while it is brought together with great architectural manipulative skills, it combines and exaggerates rather than manneristically controls: it is rich in symbolism about the elements that comprise house, but with a shift in context and scale that challenges the viewer to perceive them in a nonorthodox manner. There is an underlying classical symmetry that is subtly pulled out of balance as functions receive their own sense of place, or, the interior as it exerts its own demands breaks down the symmetry of the exterior. Small windows demarcate the minor low spaces and large windows the major second floor spaces. The house is dominated by a broad and widely overhanging gable roof that rises to a central point and is cut into by an oculus, slightly elongated in shape, or optically corrected to appear round from below. Three sides of the main interior space are ringed by a book-lined mezzanine, conceived as a gestural idea, and the overall silhouette of the house is reiterated in the interior fireplace wall. Exaggerations are less evident in the Penn State Faculty Club, a larger shingled structure whose long raking profile hugs the ground line. Blending with and nestled amid a stand of trees, its horizontality is a foil to the verticality of their trunks, evoking memo-

■ Venturi and Rauch, Carll Tucker House, Katonah, New York, 1975 *(Photos: Thomas Bernard)*

ries of the vacation structures in northern areas of the United States. Its form derives from the traditional long and narrow banqueting hall of English universities with their high-arched Gothic windows, but here the clerestory is a horizontal band of windows screened by lattices, and the hall is overlooked by a second floor lounge from a semicircular window.

The historically referential aspects of Venturi's approach to design gained for him the opportunity, after more than eighty architects had previously prepared schemes, the chance in 1987 to design the extension to the National Gallery in Trafalgar Square. Although William Wilkins's 1838 design for the original National Gallery is anything but a tour de force of the neoclassic

■ Venturi, Scott Brown and Assoc.,
Sainsbury Wing, National Gallery, London,
1991 (Photos: Matt Wargo)

period in England—his work does not humble one, qualified in all fairness following immediately after the genius and originality of John Nash and John Soane—it is a respectable building to which Venturi and Scott Brown have made their complementary addition. Its most evident classicism is in the "ganging" of Corinthian pilasters on the cleverly chamfered corner closest to Wilkins's original, and as these in effect "fall away" visually by increased spacing and diminished level of detail as distanced from the original. Even the English critics, always masters of the biting, in their critiques of the more discordant juxtapositions—the solid to void outside, the treatment of the main stair inside, and the detail in general with its classical molded accoutrements—seem more appreciative of the lofty interior gallery spaces and their effective, natural clerestory lighting. There has obviously been enormous attention placed upon the creation of a suitable sequence of elegant and traditional "rooms" to house the National's small-scaled but extraordinary Early Renaissance treasures. It is difficult to imagine any profound sense of distress over Venturi's sincere effort to be eminently mannered and attentive. It is easy to see, however, why Norman Foster's small and exquisitely detailed infill to connect two older buildings at the Royal Academy, which opened contemporaneously with Venturi's addition, should further incite the classicist-modernist argument, which seems to stir such passions in England's Prince-Charles-inspired climate. Its powerful and calm elegance persuasively sings out like the most crisp and pristine bel canto, lauding the virtues of modernism. Venturi's was undoubtedly a "rougher" and more demanding assignment and he likewise posits a compelling argument in a both assertive and self-effacing design for an approach that is equally serious, though obviously derived from completely different parameters.

The modernist ethic in the United States had already been strongly challenged when Venturi's words from the sixties became like a wind against doors that were opening. Exploring architectural expression as it pertains to metaphor and allegory, to cultural and local context, to the referential—even be it historical—has started to enrich the functional, technological, and formal base for designing buildings. As Roman architecture led somewhat sequentially to the Byzantine, Renaissance, Baroque, and the Classical revivals, and as the Victorian era built more inclusively on the Gothic and Classic, so our evolving modern period is building on its own origins, aware both of a wider heritage, while utilizing the potential of our new technology. This is shown in the American Academy of Arts and Sciences in Cambridge, by Kallmann, McKinnell and Woods. The building's perimeter is irregular, colonnaded, and stepped back, an organization and aesthetic theme quite similar to that of the architect's design for the Boston City Hall. But whereas the latter was a strong example of the so-called New Brutalism, and the exposed concrete and tough imagery of the early 1960s, the academy with its brick walls and arcades, as much a recall of the New England porch as the classical loggia, the broadly overhanging eaves of sloped copper roofs, its visible timber framing and extensive use of mahogany trim, is not a "pure" modern structure but rather one that reflects the academy's more traditional tastes. Its gentle domestic opposed to institutional scale represents an amalgam of the eloquence of the turn of the century Arts and Crafts movement, from Charles Rennie Mackintosh and the Viennese Secessionist in Europe, to the Greene Brothers and Gustav Stickley in the United States, comfortably furnished in areas with the

■ Foster Associates, Sackler Galleries, The Royal Academy, London *(Photo: Paul Heyer)*

feeling of an English country house. The Academy is a solidly built edifice in that firm's tradition of fusing program with framework, or the contained with the nature of the container, but here with a more attentive eye to context, referential recall, and how these might generate actual style. As the great English Victorian eclectic, A.W.N. Pugin, imaginatively recombined Gothic style elements to create fresh interpretations of historic precedent, so Kallmann,

■ Kallmann McKinnell & Wood, American Academy of Arts and Sciences, Cambridge, Massachusetts, 1982 *(Photos: Exterior, © Steve Rosenthal; interior, Ardilles-Arce)*

McKinnell and Wood have sought derivation from the movement that was the
immediate precurser to modern architecture. The effort is not to expand on
our vocabulary of architectural form but to consolidate and interpret the
language we already have. The gap between old and new is narrowed and
without compromising the present day integrity of the new. Typical of their
work, the authority and surety of building with respect to the particular system
of building construction remains.

Michael Graves's office building in Portland was also a significant shift in
emphasis from his earlier work. The Benacerraf House addition of 1969—a
radical contrast to the house it connects to—embodies many of the familiar
international modernist themes à la Le Corbusier: the roof terrace garden and
balconies, the screen walls and layering of visually penetrated planes, the stairs
with exposed risers and treads and the pipe railings, and the disciplining
rectangular geometry with a few gently subtle curves played against it. Ambigu-
ities in a frontal sequence of involvement between the pattern of linear
elements and solid planes related within space as volume, is a type of abstraction that becomes clarified as the volume is entered. As similarly, the abstraction and tension of elements through the process of layering in a Cubist canvas
by Braque, Picasso, or Gris becomes clarified as factors such as time and
fragmentation are understood as components of the synthesis. The use of
color and form is again intended to be referential to aspects of nature, and
complexity a resultant of the introduction of more linguistic and metaphorical
theme ideas as they might bring a sense of symbolism into architecture. The
frenetic intricacy of this period, more animated and colorful and less restrained
than the work of Meier, but with a certain visual affinity to it, subsequently
developed visually into components that are filtered reinterpretations of his-

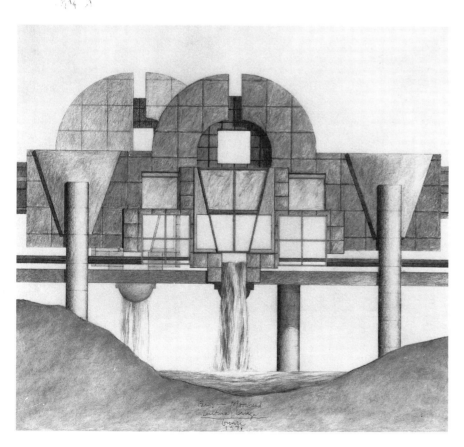

■ Michael Graves, San Juan Capistrano Library, California, 1980 *(Photos: Model, Proto Acme Photo; building, Paschall/Taylor)*

tory combined into almost an abstract collaging of archetypal elements, the column, the pediment, the strong relation to nature as the constant present and what it says to us of the origins of building: "architecture about architecture." Such symbolisms are intensely felt in the Fargo-Moorhead Cultural Center, a structure to span the Red River and linking North Dakota with Minnesota, and connecting a history museum and concert hall on either river bank. The bridge fenestration is in the form of a keystone shape with barrel vault arches and pylonlike columns. Water, pumped from a windmill that is part of the history museum, would pour into the river from a scupper at the base of the keystone. The vocabulary is intended to be a narrative on the agrarian base of these communities, their dependence on the river, the recurrent notion of the dialogue between the built and the natural environment, and the monumental architecture of our western cultural heritage.

The subsequent design for the public library in San Juan Capistrano, conforms with the intent of local ordinances as it endeavors to follow the indigenous Spanish mission style. Generic to this, the building is organized around a courtyard, which allows for thematic subdivisions of the various primary internal uses. As a quiet focus for reading, the courtyard is demarcated by four cypresses centered on a stream of water issuing from the upper level of the site which, in a physical sense, is symbolic of the flow of knowledge from the library itself. The quality and variety of light to the interior through the central courtyard, light monitors, clerestories, and peripheral walls designed to function as filters and reflectors of light, enrich and transform this classic in spirit building, as the entry of light strives to develop the Spanish mission style way beyond its Renaissance origins.

In designing the Walt Disney World Swan (750 guestrooms) and Dolphin (1,510 guestrooms) hotels, facing each other across a crescent-shaped lake and connected by a causeway, Graves's inspiration was not history in a referential way, but a stage-set fantasy world where reality becomes the escape from it. His great talent and sensibility as an architectural muralist and colorist is everywhere evident. As John Nash in 1815 had created a brilliantly original and eclectic retreat for the Prince Regent in Brighton's Royal Pavilion, so Graves has orchestrated a cartoonlike, highly animated and decorated context to challenge Disneyland's cartoon-inspired world. The buildings' simple forms are collaged with overscaled decorative themes, made even more unreal against the blue Florida sky, which extend into the exuberantly decorated and colorful interiors. The gentle arc form of the Swan Hotel, painted with wave patterns, is topped by two 47-feet-high swans and giant clam shell fountains at the roof of two projecting wings. The Dolphin Hotel is dominated by a giant triangulated center, its facade painted with banana leaves and each end adorned with 55-feet-high dolphins. On the water side, four wings are topped with giant urns and flank a dramatic, central entrance beneath a giant clam shell fountain held aloft by happy, cutout dolphins. The interiors are a profusion of themes and playful motifs, always reinforcing the idea of a fantasy world.

History, more literally, culturally, and also more whimsically combined of fragments resembling parts of Renaissance buildings while incorporating the Orders of architecture, is the Piazza d'Italia in New Orleans by Charles Moore. A stage set for the Italian community, it includes a fountain sending water cascading down an 80-foot-long outline map of Italy along cuts resembling

the Po, Arno, and the Tiber, flowing into what might be seen as the Adriatic and Tyrrhenian seas, with Sicily as a rostrum and Sardinia a seating area. The references and their origin are intended to be obvious, if in actuality they are somewhat obscure to the "uninitiated." There is little striving here for esoteric symbolism and meaning, simply a wish to create an engaging and fun experience, no pure Renaissance type fountain with its central cluster of figures but an eclectically contrived experience that almost "pushes" everything together. It is an architecture that strives to mean something to the user, to create a sense of place.

■ Michael Graves, The Walt Disney World
Dolphin Hotel, Lake Buena Vista, Florida,
1990 *(Photos: Steven Brooke)*

A sense of place, continuity and completion of place, is the intent behind
Moore's extensions to the Beverly Hills Civic Center. The 1932 Spanish Colonial style City Hall, with its tower retained as the dominant element and visual
anchor of the new design, becomes in rhythm, expression, and color the
inspiration for the continuity of old and new. The original's overall simplicity,
the repeating of base heights and bay dimensions, the tile patterns and
undulations at the cornice level were all closely followed, even to the two-tone
existing beige color scheme and the Deco-like walls and their appearance of
depth and solidity. The sense of completion comes from the diagonal spatial

■ Charles W. Moore Assoc. and Urban
Innovations Group with A. Perez Assoc.,
Piazza d'Italia, New Orleans, 1975–1978
(Photo: Norman McGrath)

connection of a sequence of elliptical, linked outdoor spaces that now bring a
wholeness to the center. While the new has its own identity it is, says Moore,
"congenial and friendly with the old."

A parallel approach in a different but again historical and eclectic spirit is
the work of Robert A. M. Stern, whose imagery and compositions certainly are
as, if not more, complex and profuse. With Stern the parts from different
cultures and styles are generally more often quite discernible in derivation
despite, again, their transformation from the original context. This does not
mean that they are literal reproductions either, simply that their spirit is closer
to the original. In the Lang House the entrance facade is a long and almost
disconcertingly flat plane, relieved yet at the same time emphasized as a taut
membrane by an applied moulding at chair-rail height which rises up and over
windows, giving a terminal bounce at each end of the facade, and reappearing
as added curved embellishment to emphasize the enlarged scale of the 2-story
height entrance recess. The entrance, deriving from the historic example of
Edwin Lutyens's Folly Farm, is defined within an ovoid shape which in the
Lang House initiates an axis that cuts through the central living space. This axis
terminates in a pair of French doors, centered in a sweeping curved wall with a
high window above, which opens to the grassy slope beyond. The outward
swelling curved wall, flowing as a substantially solid screen element, is almost
detached visually from the main volume of the house, while the clerestory
windows behind bathe the living space in a beautiful light reflected inward
from its curved surface. The building's fractured north facade shows unabashedly the coming together of the buildings two very different skin planes. To the
1929 Georgian style residence which Stern remodeled in New Jersey, he added
at the building's lower level a highly rusticated grotto to create a base to the

■ Charles W. Moore and Urban
Innovations Group in association with
A. C. Martin & Assoc., Beverly Hills Civic
Center, Beverly Hills, California, 1982–1992
(Photos: Timothy Hursley)

house that serves as a pool space. While it has its own landscape presence, it is
in sympathy with the existing house as it is detached from it by a curving glass
greenhouse roof and as it is infilled with broad glass areas between columned
openings. There is a vitality and sense of gentle sophistication and wit in this
addition, where tiled patterned walls further reinforce a subaqueous feeling

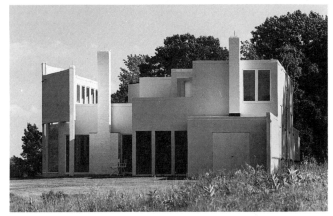

■ Robert A. M. Stern, Lang Residence,
Washington, Connecticut, 1973–1974
(Photos: Edmund Stoecklein)

that make it both derivative yet unique in its grand and monumental handling of elements.

Emphasis in Stern's architecture, as with Graves, is strongly placed on the interior as a frankly decorative late twentieth century presence designed to both relax and delight, an area as important as the too frequently only considered exterior envelope. This concern with the character and ambiance of interior space as it is enhanced by decor is not concern for architectural space per se as volumetric presence, as evidenced in Paul Rudolph's best interiors of the sixties and seventies, but the injection of richness, personalization, coloring, and patterning into interior space which is eclectically furnished, and rearrangeable, a world apart from the built-in look and static arrangements of the mid-twentieth century. In Stern's case it is particular, striving for the tradition of the comfort and casual elegance of the handsome, late nineteenth century country house interiors of England, but with the stylish effects and aesthetic overtones of the art deco. This is the influence for Stern's New York townhouse remodeling, an interior distinguished by a subtle, rich pastel color scheme used to emphasize gently seductive, curving walls.

These earlier themes and interests recur, however in much more extravagant contexts in such as a 1990 New Jersey ocean-front villa. The grandeur of

the Mediterranean or the Tuscan valley is fused here with the Edwardian
country house, again filtered through art deco touches. The classical villa sits,
appropriately, in an idealized and aggressively designed classical garden, while
the rich and highly decorated interiors further establish an umbilical cord to a
European past of detached, elegant aspiration. In such recent projects the
feeling is one of Stern now unabashedly evoking his uncompromised, comfortable vision of the world.

Vision in a sense of recall of the grand, relaxed air of the luxury seaside
resorts of the East Coast is the inspiration for Sterns Yacht and Beach Club
resorts (1,200 rooms on five floors), adjacent to Graves's Swan and Dolphin
hotels, at Disney World. The Yacht Club evokes a sense of the shingled,
salt-sprayed facades of the New England coast—but here a synthetic clapboard
siding of glued sawdust, and columns, railings and cornices of fiberglass

■ Robert A. M. Stern, Villa in New Jersey, 1983–1989 *(Photos: Steven Brooke; courtesy of* Architectural Digest*)*

mouldings—while the Beach Club rather recalls the more festive and casual constructs on the Long Island and Jersey shores. Both seek a marine in character world of the play of light and shadow, a recognizable, real world of escape through association, whereas Graves's escapism is in the form of a less real world of creative fantasy.

However, one of Disney World's most evocative statements, its administrative building designed by the Japanese architect Arata Isosaki, creates its sense of being neither through association nor fantasy. At the center of a long, rectangular 4-story building, collide a grouping of colored cubic forms, gathered around and culminating in a truncated, lopsided cone which, open to the sky, is the world's largest sundial. Because Isosaki brings together a play of variable and almost seemingly unrelated forms, there is the relation to postmodernist interests—only in this instance the references are not historical nor are historic elements used to embellish a structure. While the abstracted Mickey Mouse ears form, used to mark and canopy the entrance to the building, is a beautifully whimsical and obviously playful reference, it is elegant and integral

■ Robert A. M. Stern, Disney's Yacht and Beach Club Resorts, Lake Buena Vista, Florida, 1987–1991 *(Photos: Peter Aaron/ Esto)*

■ Arata Isosaki & Associates, Team Disney, Lake Buena Vista, Florida, 1990 *(Photo: Paul Heyer)*

rather than applique. The collision of sculptural forms in disjunctive connections also draws the parallel to deconstructionism, only here there is a careful functional resolution within the discord. Isosaki, in Disney World's architectural tour de force, eloquently summarizes many architectural attitudes and themes of the past decade with intellect and unselfconscious elegance.

The concern for history and vernacular as a sense of cultural derivation and continuity, as they in turn interact with contemporary technology and its implied imagery, has led to numerous spirited designs that have developed directly from interpretations of these dialogues within a specific situation, for example, building within or in direct relationship to a cultural or historic context. Hardy Holzman Pfeiffer's extremely skilled remodeling of the turn-of-the-century Carnegie mansion, now the Cooper Hewitt Museum, is an interpretative restoration that does not compromise the building's existing character, while enhancing and cleaning up the original's cluttered interior. Teak parquet floors, carved oak ceilings, paneling, and bronze grille work have been essentially preserved as has the mansion's basic axial disposition of rooms. A new elevator and doorways with matching moldings were discreetly installed as were new mechanical services.

In the 1914 Academy building at the Phillips Exeter Academy, a meeting hall to seat 600 on a flat floor was remodeled to accommodate 1,100 persons by sloping the main floor, adding a curved balcony to seat 400, and in areas cutting out and raising the plasterwork ceiling. The old remains a presence in terms of decorative plasterwork and portraits; new elements in exposed steel and chrome piping are visually, emphatically contrasting.

Establishing a dialogue between old and new was achieved in my design for the late painter Sofia Sosnoff's Soho loft by accepting with only cosmetic cleaning up the rectangular space with its central spine structure of cast iron columns, and in a more pristine modern theme suggesting functions within the volume while preserving the openness of the entire space. The volume is

■ Hardy Holzman Pfeiffer, Cooper Hewitt
Museum, New York City, 1976 *(Photos:
Remodeled interior, Norman McGrath; original
interior: Courtesy of Cooper Hewitt, National
Museum of Design, Smithsonian Inst.)*

dramatically and unassumingly lighted from exposed bulbs on continuous
"light beams," which at night provide bounced light upon paintings and in
turn back-lights the white, geometric interior forms. Similarly, the aesthetics of
a pool house addition in Pennsylvania were devised to establish a complementary rapport with the rambling, English Tudor-style house to which it is
connected, while merging with the estate landscape. Hence the new addition

■ Hardy Holzman Pfeiffer, Assembly Hall, Exeter, New Hampshire, 1969 *(Photo: Remodeled interior, Norman McGrath)*

relates to the original building through its pitched roof design and white stucco and brown siding for exterior walls, a palette also expressed internally with interior ceilings of white-painted siding with exposed ceiling beams stained dark brown. Relating to the landscape, used Philadelphia street brick paves around the pool and the length of a gallery connecting to the main house. A skylight bisects the pool area emphasizing the open, penetrated and pavilionlike sense of the structure.

In reconstructing the burned-out interior of Princeton's Whig Hall, Gwathmey Siegel here implanted a streamlined modern volume within the defining perimeter of the 1893 original neoclassic marble shell, a juxtaposition that symbolizes the passage of time as both parts epitomize the spirit of their own technology and culture. Contrast through complement is the basis of compatibility here, the new element having a sense of relativity that comes primarily from its containment within the original buildings periphery.

Starting from the Cooper Hewitt Museum, the previous examples show various typical attitudes toward history in the early seventies: delicately almost restoring an interior; employing new elements to reemphasize the intricacies of an existing space; inserting a completely new and pristine interior within a worn and existing volume; adding a new volume related by color, scale, and the selection of elements to a former; and finally sliding a new and contrasting modern in style volume within a classical, overall exterior skeleton. These sensibilities evolved at the end of the seventies toward an interest in history that was often increasingly more literally historical, as evidenced by Thomas Beeby's design for the North Shore Congregation Israel. Adding a worship space for 300 people and a small social hall to an existing 1,000-seat monumental sanctuary and small school perched on a bluff overlooking Lake Michigan, he

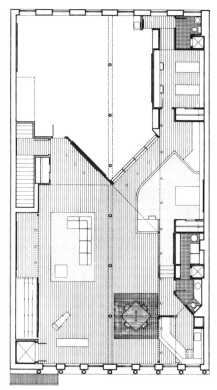

designed a crisply geometric interior enclosed within, in this instance a new and classic in style, even to the incorporation of traditionally proportioned Doric columns, reposeful exterior, which derives directly from the inspiration of classical forms and motifs. The intent is to maintain a sense of monumentality and solitude, while seeking to balance the new volume with that of the existing school wing while also matching its masonry exterior. Where Gwathmey Siegel preserved a classic envelope, the synagogue creates one.

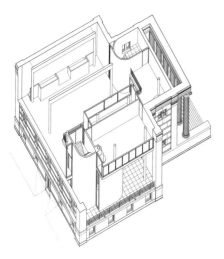

■ Gwathmey Siegel, Whig Hall, Princeton University, Princeton, New Jersey, 1970

Selected from a distinguished field of competitors to design Chicago's new central library in 1987, Beeby looked for precedent in the grand, persuasive urbanity of late nineteenth and early twentieth century civic architecture of the Beaux Arts and the architecture of Richardson and Sullivan. The 10-story classically spirited structure, housing 1.6 million books on open stacks, is richly detailed like its forerunners, from the rusticated stone base, 5-story arched windows to its ornamental pediment of metal and glass. The industrial aesthetics of the turn of the century is also present in the steel and glass winter garden enclosure at the library's top floor. In this tribute to architecture's role as a shaper and symbol of the robust urban fabric, influences are reinterpreted in the spirit of the continuity of the best of our urban heritage as a timeless presence.

The interest in collaging has remained constant, especially where historic elements might add an enriching dimension to essentially new structures. Retaining only the facade of an 1835 Egyptian revival style building to preserve a sense of urban continuity at the street level and as a freestanding "banner" that both announces and defines the entrance plaza to a new 21-story tower addition to the existing Penn Mutual building, is the essential urban idea and salient feature of the building designed by Mitchell/Giurgola Associates. Similar to Whig Hall, the classic element existed, the new was modern in spirit. The new addition, also related in mass to the existing office structure of the corporate headquarters, completes an axial backdrop to the Mall at Independence Hall in Philadelphia. Responding to the architecture of its highly varied and fragmented surroundings, the facades of the tower recall stylistic differences.

Hence, as an assemblage of aesthetic parts, the building attempts to coalesce the fabric of the city with its insertion into its infrastructure. The incorporation of the historic façade affords not only the symbol of urban historic continuity but also, as is invariably customary, the ornamental and enriching element to the more reductive contemporary vocabulary of the new.

The fundamental idea behind such incorporations is the notion of a past, of memory. It is an idea, at least in the work of architects like Giurgola, at base philosophically beyond a concern for image or literal or adapted and stylized use of historic forms and elements, which has been one of the problems with post-modernism at its more historic level of preoccupation. Giurgola cites Marcel Proust's affinity for images and memories and likens it to architecture's cultural tradition, which is beyond the adaption of forms of the past. "We do work with memories," says Giurgola, "but architecture should result not in a representation of images, but rather from a synthesis of images." His design for the Volvo Headquarters discreetly spreads a 3-story complex over its hilltop site, architecturally evoking memories of Josef Hoffmann, Alvar Aalto, Jörn

■ Hammond, Beeby & Babka, The
Harold Washington Library Center,
Chicago, 1987–1991 (Photos: Timothy
Hursley)

Utzon, Gunnar Asplund, to even Aldo Rossi. While the elements compositionally seem casually fragmented in the overall building form, there is also a strong underlying order and powerful restraint typical of these architects. The Scandinavian heritage of these architects is likewise a present spirit; there is also the highly disciplined hard-edged modernism of Rossi's more Mediterranean approach of loggias, terraces, arcades, and courtyards. References and appropriate memory develop from site, program, culture, and context and the history of modern architecture.

Memory can be in incorporation, the entirely new as we see in the Volvo scheme, and in adaption. When the original function of a structure changes, this too can become the impetus for an eclectic aesthetic and hybrid solution for an architect, as with the transformation of a barn from sheltering hay and livestock to a residential use. The original form ideally has preserved its sense of the sheltering structure which comes from the wonderfully forthright and unaffected feeling of the farm artisans' simplicity, with new elements then visually proclaiming different inhabitants and that it is no longer a barn. Such a conversion by Weese Seegers Hickey Weese brings as the signs of new life central openings quietly and regularly disposed in each facade and two pair of skylights. Central rows of struts and cross wind bracing were preserved in the interior, although some vertical struts were eliminated to facilitate circulation, and a new loft floor for sleeping was added. The structural woodsy feel indigenous to this type of building is developed by Cynthia Weese as the overall aesthetic, where "read" against clean white peripheral walls the interior

■ Mitchell/Giurgola with Owe Svard, Volvo Corporate Headquarters, Goteborg, Sweden, 1984 *(Photos: Keld Hlemer-Petersen; drawing, R. Giurgola)*

develops in the spirit of a Japanese house. The exterior, however, conveys the strength of the farming tradition and its companion landscape, the essence of the Shaker tradition where the developed visual sense is of building and its accoutrements reduced to the spare and simple, not only accommodating a more elemental life-style but even suggesting one.

■ Weese Seegers Hickey Weese, Cynthia Weese, partner in charge, Barn Conversion, Illinois, 1977

More radical design modifications and new insertions, while still preserving the stoic and somewhat brooding presence of the barn, can be achieved without too radically compromising a form idea that stands invariably as a symbol to resist the exposure and harshness of the elements and the terrain. While preserving the gambrel roof shape of the Pennsylvania Dutch type barn in south Michigan, Stanley Tigerman clad the entire form in an uninterrupted sweep of black asphalt tiles, into which are cut a new compositional grouping of gray-tinted windows developing an arrowlike pattern. The interior, with a central open well and freestanding spiral stair connecting all levels, is finished in scored plywood siding with all conduit, heating ducts, and plumbing exposed and painted blue, red, and yellow respectively.

Two houses designed by Hugh Jacobsen somewhat summarize primary responses to historicism, vernacular, and its implication as a design attitude. In the Elliott residence in Bethesda, the new left-hand wing, adding a living room and master bedroom, is the twin of the right-hand side which, with its new bay window replacing the old front porch, has been remodeled from an old Victorian house. The profiles, detailing, roof, and clapboard siding of the existing house were replicated in the new wing, which was connected to the old house by a new entrance link with a bridge above for the second floor. A new palette of colors, appropriate to the Victorian era, were selected as a further gesture toward authenticity. However, the new residence designed for south-eastern Pennsylvania is a surrealistic juxtaposition of mixed metaphors, of conventional parts unconventionally combined, of the farmhouse and the

■ Hugh Newell Jacobsen, Elliott
Residence, Bethesda, Maryland, 1977
*(Photos: Original house, Kathleen S. Wood;
new addition, Robert Lautman)*

glass box. From the front the house appears as seven pavilions of diminishing size, each with shingled pitched roofs, wood clapboard siding, and multipaned windows. The reference is directly to the eighteenth century rural farmhouses of the region, where additions of different sizes were frequently made to accommodate growing families. Here, where each section abuts the next, the visible end portion is infilled with reflective glass, dramatizing both the exterior connection and the interior flow of space. Likewise, the entire end of the largest pavilion is an unadorned wall of reflective glass, appearing even more incongruous because of its containment within the detail and profile of a conventional pitched-roof house. At night, with the interior lit, this wall, seen through a screen of twenty-four dogwood trees, becomes transparent with unexpected views to the interior space framed between the vertical grid of framing studs. Such visual illusion, which is emphatically modern, combined with the historical allusion of the frontal experience make this house, with a few degree shifts of vantage from right to left, a totally unexpected collision of the two experiences, and hence, by choice, a protagonist for neither. Or, a truly unique hybrid.

■ Hugh Newell Jacobsen, Residence, Pennsylvania, 1982 *(Photos: Robert Lautman)*

With the design of the Reception rooms at the Department of State in Washington, D.C., (incidentally contained within a spiritless, 1950s late-modern structure), architect Allan Greenberg stayed close to classic themes in concept and details. Rather than collaging old with new expressions, or using the old as a point of departure toward any eccentricities or distortions, Greenberg's example is one of supreme confidence and conviction in classical precedent. Digressions from the classical mode are only in minor variations of details within normative classical themes and their slightly varied yet familiar combi-

nations and shifts of scale, to such 'touches' as the incorporation of the Seal of the United States within the capitals of the Corinthian columns. The whole is intended to tell government that the grand and composed tradition prevails, even endures. In this instance it is the close approximation to and respect for the precedent that results in its consummate presence.

More the norm, however, is that with any degree of historical attitude or contextural approach, its present day interpretation usually is manifest as some degree of transformation—as exampled by the work of both Venturi and Graves—which becomes the final measure of its pertinence toward advancing the status quo, which clearly concerns them both. Many architects in the eighties sought to learn from and expand upon history and our heritage, where the philosophy and aesthetic of modern architecture were likewise not to be decried as they too became a tool and not in themselves a goal. Two corporate headquarters, designed in the late 1970s by Roche Dinkeloo & Associates, sought not to establish any overt or conclusive sense of historicism by the incorporation of traditional elements, nor did they juxtapose disparate elements to create illusions and allusions as with some of the previous examples. They were rather a fusion of the modernist spirit and contemporary technology with a sense of the containment, distillation of idea, and basic composure of the classical attitude. They sought a presence that might be part of a cultural continium, one executed with a sense of elegant, contemporary control and resolve. In other words they were conceived to be more consciously "modern" than the work of either Venturi or Graves.

■ Allan Greenberg, Diplomatic Reception Rooms, U.S. Department of State, Washington, D.C., 1984. View of the George C. Marshall Reception Room from the John Jay Reception Room and the Treaty Room *(Photos: Richard Cheek)*

Roche Dinkeloo & Assoc., John Deere
Insurance Company, Moline, Illinois, 1978

The John Deere building in Moline is as an antibellum mansion, where public areas are in a dominant central section with a colonnaded front porch from which radiate symmetrical wings. The building is clad in ordinary, horizontal aluminum siding and its ribbon windows express a simple and undifferentiated office layout. There are also visual illusions with departures into the unexpected: the central porch has one side solid and the other of mirrored strip windows; the two central columns defining the porch and conversely the landscape view outward, in a manner reminiscent of grand mansions, hover 8 feet above the terrace eliminating any connotation of support, thereby reducing them to a visual, associative, and symbolic role.

The General Foods building in Rye with its dominant central pavilion capped by a rotunda above a huge, carved out portico and colonnaded double wings, has a greater similarity to the Palladian villa (and the White House—"the best known building in the country") whose imagery of grandeur for a producer of consumer products is not entirely coincidental. The building is likewise sheathed in white aluminum siding and its narrow 3-foot strip windows are of reflective glass. Parking, in a 3-story garage, which forms a podium to the 5-story building, is entered across a lake and beneath the central rotunda, from which the visitor ceremoniously approaches the building up a monumental staircase, the inclination of which parallels the sloped grass floor of the portico's exterior.

These attitudes are further elaborated upon in the subsequent headquarters for Bouygues, adjacent to Versailles and an ideal context in which to develop a landscaped epic in the late classical, Baroque spirit, also employing the design devices—axis, pools, planting, courts—of the classical French tradition. Here the approach is more axially formal, between "gateway" wings and into a spatially defined court, similar to the concept of Louis XIV's Palace at Versailles, only in this instance a grand oval in shape. The central component and social core of the building per se is a connected sequence of three domed spaces. The first is a porte cochere for visitor parking, leading to and similar to General Foods, the main circulation area, and finally the third dome forming part of the main dining space. Stairtowers are strategically placed at the building's exterior, employed as vertical elements to embellish the overall form. The buildings are again executed in a palette of industrial materials: reflective glass and aluminum sheets and aluminum muntin bars accented by stainless steel. At the top floor the glass is canted back, forming the typically French mansard roof profile. Where all three of these headquarters designed by Roche look more to history to form generative ideas and concomitantly for the symbolism of presence, their execution is more contemporarily aware in terms of the methodology of realization. Hence, their balance within or deference toward history.

■ Roche Dinkeloo & Assoc., General Foods, Rye, New York, 1977–1982

■ Roche Dinkeloo & Assoc., Bouygues World Headquarters, Paris, France, 1983–1987

History has shown us that detail is also elemental to architecture since it is an important fact of harmonization. Interest in detail obviously parallels an interest in the inclusive attitude. The coherence and unity of a building is dependent upon the extent to which detail is interpreted with and a further expression of support to the basic architectural intent. Ideas of connection are inseparable from motivating concepts. Whereas overrefinement can cloud essentials if there is an overt cleverness and articulation of elements for their own sake or a fussy preoccupation with the small aspects of a building's design, but likewise details will never *make* a building devoid of concept. They might, however, enhance it with the delight of factors that we isolate and discover in the overall. Concern for detail also parallels the architect's technical expertise. In trying to stress what is said, it is important not to neglect *how* it is said. In language the word is isolated and basic, but in combination, through a rich sensitivity to grammar, it can be poetry. Detail also adds depth and richness to our perception of architecture: It was tradition to the eighteenth century French architect and brought clarity to the early nineteenth century. This sense carried through to the admirably refined, classic revival architecture of McKim, Mead and White. The excellence and incisiveness of carving on their turn-of-the-century buildings in New York is an example to *any* period in architecture for its precision and attention to aesthetic resolve. The best examples of our contemporary architecture have continued this attention and it is easy to see why. Through the direct, thoughtful putting together of the precisely detailed elements of a building and the use of quality materials, there is the persuasive impression that, to the smallest detail, the architect has always known what to

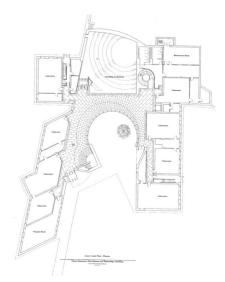

■ *Top and center left:* Pei Cobb Freed & Partners, Science Center, Choate Rosemary Hall, Wallingford, Connecticut, 1989 *(Photos: © Steve Rosenthal). Center right and bottom:* I. M. Pei & Partners, Paul Mellon Arts Center, Choate Rosemary Hall, Wallingford, Connecticut, 1970 *(Photos: Overall view, Nathaniel Lieberman; details, Joseph Molitor)*

do and exactly how to do it. Mies van der Rohe set the pace when he said, "God is in the details." But in actuality, detail transcends aspects of putting elements together: The whole becomes so visible that elements become essence and totality in architecture. We have come the full circle from the French Renaissance to our machined buildings, when the connection can enhance the design as it emphasizes its technicality and is itself actually articulated.

Clarity of concept and its overall support through complementary structure and detail has been and remains a basic theme to architecture. It was underlying fact in the sequence of previously considered historical buildings and it is equally fundamental to many stylistically modern structures. The architecture of Pei Cobb Freed & Partners, for example, while totally committed to the modernist expression, relies heavily on concept through geometry and detail for its impression. The precise execution of a strong unifying idea was basic to the clarity of the Paul Mellon Arts Center, a gateway and campus focal point linking the two prep schools, Choate and Rosemary Hall. Essentially two buildings, one a quarter circular structure containing an 800-seat auditorium, the other a triangular teaching wing with art studios and recital rooms overlooking a glass-roofed student lounge area, the two elements are diagonally bisected by a central tiled walkway onto which their glassed areas front. A strong organizing geometry defined at the roof line as a broad rectangle, yet dramatically transversed and penetrated as a movement path, derives from the simple abstract premise of line, plane, and volume in space, which is manipulated with great sophistication. The monolithic characteristic of concrete is fundamental to the design's realization, as is the coherence of idea deriving from the interlocking of geometry.

In the adjacent Science Center, designed nearly two decades later, Pei again brought two elements together which are also bisected by a pathway across campus and which, approached via a bridge spanning a pond, traverse the building's center. A 3-story L-shaped wing receiving an arced and visually expressed 135-seat auditorium is joined to a slightly angled-away wedge-shaped wing by a layered circulating space behind a raking wall of glass. This inverted conoid introduces a glass plane of converging geometry, a dynamic focus to the otherwise quietly expressed and in this instance, overall brick exterior. The Creative Artists Agency building in Los Angeles yet again develops the concept of two wings, here wrapping a central, 57-foot-high skylit atrium space, itself screened by rows of 1-inch aluminum tubes, a device previously used by Pei in Washington's National Gallery. Here the two wings are curved, employing a geometry of segmented circles with different center points and radii. The atrium is the building's functional and ceremonial core, while the two wings, one glass-walled the other clad in travertine, in this instance respond respectively to the boulevard traffic and the adjacent quieter residential neighborhood, allowing the building to appear almost as different structures.

Developed contemporaneously with the two former designs is the Dallas Symphony Center. Geometry is again, although here more centralized, the resolution to incorporate two elements, the rectangular box of the symmetrical symphony hall, which is dramatically skewed in the encircling lobby space for a total dynamic asymmetry. The concert space is a square seating area flowing into a half square stage for a simple 2:3 rectangle, treated lushly in the interior

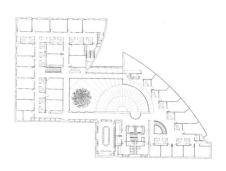

in rich warm colored woods and brass, resembling the richness and patina of a musical instrument. This neutral volume is encircled on three sides—the fourth connects to an administration and musicians' wing—by a wrap-around glass-roofed lobby, tapering inward at the building's less trafficked upper tier levels. The skewing of the segmented glass cone results in a conoid of 211 computer calculated panes, none of similar dimension, supported by an intricate system of trusses each curved on a different radius. The geometry is centralized around the performance volume, overlapping and unfolding from the basic square in a radial system resulting in a continually evolving sequence of views. Again there is the propensity for elegantly expressed, minimalist, geometric forms, against which are juxtaposed meticulously detailed technological elements invariably organized around a multilevel, balconied central space. The message, in a time of diversity, is consistency.

Probably the pièce de résistance of Pei's extraordinary legacy to modernism, his sense of quiet good taste, consummate attention to detail, and clarity of

■ Pei Cobb Freed & Partners, Creative Artists Agency, Beverly Hills, California, 1989 *(Photos: Paul Warchol)*

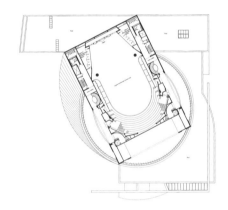

■ Pei Cobb Freed & Partners, The Morton H. Meyerson Symphony Center, Dallas, Texas, 1982–1989 *(Photos: Exterior, Nathaniel Lieberman; lobby, restaurant, Richard Payne; concert hall, Paul Warchol)*

concept is his intervention into the Cour Napoleon at the Louvre. Beneath the new, elegantly "hard" and restrained surface of the Cour is accommodated a vast new program of 650,000 square feet of much-needed support spaces for the Louvre. Poised as perfect complement and counterpoint and rising only a modest 71 feet above the ground, is the symbol of the project, the central entrance pyramid. Despite an almost ephemeral presence that derives from an ingeniously conceived triangular web of supports, clad in a wonderful warm ochre, lightly tinted glass especially drawn by St. Gobain to be compatible with the honey-colored stone of the Second Empire facades of the old Louvre, it was controversial from its announcement in 1985 as one of President Mitterand's most ambitious "grand projets." Obviously any insertion would have been anathema to those who hold sacred and untouchable the integrity of the Louvre's classical presence. Time has somewhat blunted the critics against this example of modernism at its most elegant, although it remains less than

■ I. M. Pei & Partners, Addition to the Grand Louvre, Paris, France, 1985–1989 *(Photos: Cour Napoleon view west, Serge Hambourg; pyramid and interiors, S. Couturier)*

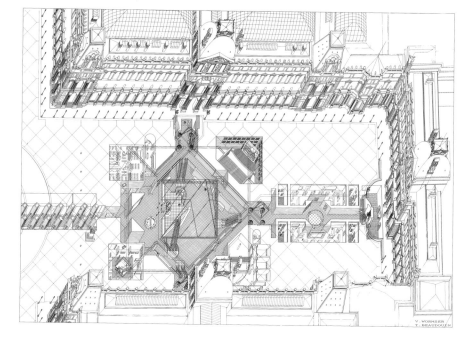

■ Louis Kahn, Kimbell Art Museum, Fort Worth, Texas, 1972 *(Photos: Marshall D. Meyers)*

successful as a sheltered entrance against the elements and the three much smaller flanking pyramids seem aesthetically gratuitous. However, at times the almost fluid, dematerialized presence of the pyramid establishes without bombast, a compellingly brave concept whose intent is to be neither aggressive nor subservient but to complement through restraint. Through simplicity the new stands with the old, each acknowledging the other.

The Kimbell Art Museum by Louis Kahn is also a disciplined, coherent, and visually clear statement, but here the aesthetics derive from the more

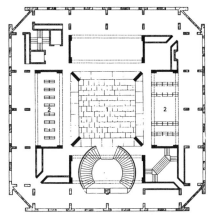

■ Louis Kahn, Library, Phillips Exeter
Academy, Exeter, New Hampshire, 1969
(Photo: Paul Heyer)

classically oriented sensibility of its architect. It has an austere yet rich simplicity that comes from the repetition of a vaultlike form, given a dull sheen from its
lead-covered exterior, and a beautifully articulated concrete structural frame
with infill paneled walls of travertine. Its classic sense of timelessness is enno-
bled by a reverence for material and detail. Its interior form, bathed in a
diffused natural light that enters the space via continuous slits at the top of the
long vaulted ceilings, is filtered through a continuous interior suspended
screen and reflected downward off the curve of the vault.

Elemental in its contemporary directness and built also with the sense
and durability of the great monuments of history is the Library at Phillips
Exeter Academy. In the spirit of the grand, classical tradition of the focal
organizing space, the reading room is a central hall encircled by balconies
containing the stacks and study alcoves. It is a space diagonally crossed by
concrete beams, reflecting light downward into the interior from windows
under the roof, which it also supports, and dramatically overlooked through
giant circular openings in the interior screen walls that define the central area.
In keeping with the campus tradition, the exterior of the building is a repetition of brick piers, wider as they approach the ground where the book loads are
greater, cut back at all four corners to subtly articulate the buildings exterior
square form. The perimeter study carrels are illuminated from windows above
the reader's eye level; smaller windows at eye level afford views to the campus or
conversely can be closed by a sliding wooden shutter for privacy and concentration. There is contact with and building upon origins in both the library and
the museum. They span time as an architecture of basic fact and of progression
as we move onward aware of both where we have come from and where we are.

While they obviously move way beyond a dependence upon geometry for
their impact, such buildings still rely upon it as an organizing tool as it becomes
a supporting idea to coherence, even to complexity within its framework.
Although the architect searches for appropriate solutions, not geometric ones,

■ Louis Kahn, Library, Phillips Exeter
Academy, Exeter, New Hampshire, 1969
(Photo: John Lobell)

geometry can be a marvelous discipliner of form, especially when ideas of geometry that grow out of the forces acting within a problem in turn suggest shape. Geometry then becomes a catalyst and clarifier in the design process, as it gives shape and expression to function and space.

Structure is framework and always derives from an organizing geometry. Space is the suggestion of plane, which is another order directly related to and interlocked with structure. Geometry is the device that not only helps bring coherence to this fundamental idea of architecture, but gives poetic rendition to parts as they seek totality, where notions of sentimentality and ingratiation are stripped away to leave suggestions of space that seem almost vulnerable for their lyricism. This has remained our constant search from the middle period of the twentieth century, regardless of the concern for coherence or inclusivity, regardless of the concern with "historicism" or "modernism" in whatever their priority. Basic, too, has been the interest in forthright solutions that inevitably manifest coherence and restraint as it was summed up so excellently in the Jean Cocteau reference that for some people style is a very complicated way of saying very simple things, for others, it is a very simple way of saying very complicated things.

8

The Inevitability
of Style

■ WHEN ARCHITECTURE MOVES toward a consensus on general attitudes and methodology, it inevitably points to common denominators of expression. This we recognize as a movement and eventually identify as a style. When the movement is broad enough and of sustained vigor, we have a period in history.

During the Renaissance period, style was, in principle, the system of putting a building together. The architect manipulated the geometries of plan configurations and the elements of a building, usually applying the Orders of architecture (the Tuscan, Doric, Ionic, Corinthian, and Composite Orders) often in combination into a formal composition, the focus being on the organization and proportion of these elements. The style of grander buildings in turn filtering down in simpler form to the more modest. The architect's search for form was not diffused but always in a formalized direction with the support of rules and precepts. There was a consensus, a recognized and accepted attitude. Even during that period however, some thinkers, such as Alexander Pope, were sarcastic and critical of the emphasis. There was the suggestion that landowners might need "real" houses designed for comfort to live in, in addition to their mansions that with their inconvenient plans derived from the symmetry of their ornate facades, presented their image to the world around.

During the revivals of the nineteenth century, artists seemed preoccupied with the need for a new style. Eclecticism as an idea also did not possess those seeds of unity that some critics of the time saw as basic to contain extremes of individualism. But with history as the primary source of reference and inspiration, there was little chance to move beyond its confines toward a new style, let alone a new way of looking at the new problems that were starting to emerge. With the likes of railroad stations and the scale of huge spaces and new ways of building, the precedent of history was being pushed to be responsive to new building types.

The Expressionistic buildings of the early twentieth century, picking up on the "new world" feel of architecture, looked at history in a fresh way, not to duplicate or emulate but rather as confirming a new expression. The history of form and element was fair game to raid, take, and transform at will. Originality was not seen as being in conflict with adopting ideas and expressions from different cultures and styles in history. The old rules, however, were dissolving and being relegated as a means of discipline.

With the International Style of the twenties, history became no longer a source of inspiration, philosophically or stylistically, the idea basically was of a new approach. There was a new set of rules and the break with the past was consciously "visible." The desire was for an idea based on moral priority: that an object worked, and that a presumed social concern was clarified within the imperative of the new machine age, technological potential and function suggesting form within the context of a new and better way of life for the many as collective fact. The promise was inspiring, if somewhat utopian. In retrospect the crisp, white, simple geometric forms of the Bauhaus expression soon became stylistically too identifiable for our new state of intellectual restlessness and, eventually, media-saturated minds. Even too "clean" for our world of social, economic, and moral turmoil. Literally, their built "cleanness" was even vulnerable to the ravages of weather. In contrast to the existing fabric of more solid in appearance and decorated buildings their style was dramatized, but in contrast to each other, or especially later where one glass facade mirrored another, a "thinness" of expression became apparent and a new thrust of experiment started to expand upon the early modernist vocabulary.

Today we are in a period developing out of this modernist edict, seeking to incorporate aspects of our historical heritage deemed pertinent. Our time has been referred to as "Post Modernism," a phrase often glibly attached to any more eclectic in spirit building, or ones less overtly utilitarian or technological in expression, and especially applied to those buildings that are more historically referential. The pitched roof is once again au courant, modern, and respectable. On the other hand structure, meaning modernist structure, is often used to supplant the word *building*. Today it is readily apparent that the rewriting of history is itself a historical process, revisionist in spirit, and that concern for "image" can never replace the resolution of problems.

With everything accessible virtually anything becomes possible. Constraint is then choice and not context by implication. Questions of style suddenly take on new meaning. The extremes of the polarity today might be categorized firstly in the ideological poles of the structural-functional aesthetic of the more orthodox modernists, to, secondly, the image-making concerns of the architects involved more with place, association, and symbolic issues—the area of common concern that of the shaping of space—evident in contrasting, for example, the work of Pei and Meier with that of Venturi and Graves. If symbol and image and questions of appropriate style seem paramount at this moment, it is because they were shown little concern by the early modernists who with their revolutionary stimulus tended to neglect many older, durable values.

This intellectual and attitudinal split was in reality present even in the early days of the modern movement; Mies van der Rohe being in the former category, Frank Lloyd Wright more the latter, with Le Corbusier somewhat a centralist between the two extremes, himself developing and refining his position through his oeuvre in his early "International Style" works, the pure "prisms" with sleek, taut exterior "skins" and planes of glass, giving way in the mid-forties in the Unité d'habitation at Marseilles, to the *béton brut*, concrete expression of elements as related sculptural form, and subsequently to their more playful and interlocking expression in the convent at La Tourette. The idea of elements serving structurally, functionally, and decoratively as an integrated attitude toward design, each being "truly what it appears to be," was subsequently elevated to something of a philosophical style by English architects of the fifties and generally referred to as the New Brutalism.

The notion that a building receives its materials "as found"—a value built into the modern movement by Moholy-Nagy at the Bauhaus—is again concomitant with the idea of exposing all *reasonable* aspects of a building's being. This contemporary historical evolution of style, through laying visible, making something of everything and making everything contribute (usually through the medium of geometry and solid-to-void relationships), presupposes an existential responsibility upon the architect and of essence remains the closest idea of responsive and responsible framework for action today. In recent years, from the more formalized, geometric, and disciplined architecture of Kahn, to the more assertedly elegant and meticulously manipulated prestigious ensembles of Roche, to the looser and seemingly spontaneous accretions of Rudolph, paralleled by forces as disparate as Meier's more spatially modernist affinity, to Graves's more historicist and illusionary approach, it has proven a variable and accommodating discipline.

To our generation the suspicion attached to concern for style per se grew out of a desire by many architects not to contrive, to avoid the transitory and fashionable, and to stay away from mannerism and the more superficial aspects of novelty. We looked into the process of problem solving rather than the gift-wrapping of solutions, with design as a more freely roving intellectual process—but with a heart. The idea that style might be any form of a consciously sought formula remains professional anathema, and style as goal rather than result, culturally alien. As numerous critics have pointed out, to create a style, to strictly try to legitimize an attitude, is to kill the need of creative intellect to search for solutions.

The concern for style basically stems from the fundamental idea that any art form needs a body of laws within which the creative process, if this is to be valid and responsible, takes place. Throughout history artists have always sought to formulate rules, which eventually might lead to method and attitude, which in turn might result in a formalization of aspects of style. The aim of contemporary architects, from Louis Sullivan on, has been that this law relate nature and art within the scope of technological fact, that this style emerge and not be imposed. That style be pertinent.

Any discussion of style today must be based on the accepted premise that the architect does not adopt a style, but matures through the experience of building and challenging his or her creative intellect with problems, to convictions about what architecture is and even the way it might look. Style as such is always in evolution. Between the hand and mind, the architect unselfconsciously stands ready to transmit the promise of style. A problem always contains and suggests the seed of its own solution and its own style. In the echoes of a context and the method of "build" there is always the imperative of style. When these fuse, like the elements of a puzzle interlocked, style becomes an act of inevitability. The collective of an architectural attitude, manifest in a work in place, *is* the inevitability of style. Architecture is then an evolving form, not an invention within any one building. It becomes accumulative energy, the transfer of vitality, and the synthesis of architecture's forward momentum. The idea—or predilection—always reveals itself and transmits the wonder of its origins with directness and lack of pretense. Style then becomes not something to consciously seek, not a simplistic idea with an impatient and false clarity, but something to let arrive. Something that is born from a new "model" of reality that parallels and derives from the facts in the world around.

The history of any art form encompasses product and the culture of the climate in which it was formed. As the intellectual focus shifts with the passage of time, an object and its philosophy is subject to reassessment within the framework of a new perspective. This new perception may clarify meaning and it will also filter views through its own emphasis and distortions. But style in any great art always endures because it has come from the very heart of any period and as such is able to transcend the peripheral and less consequential. The great painting becomes a mark in the history of painting, rather than a point of style. A building that is really *built* belongs to the history of architecture, to the idea of a right thought at a right time. As architecture touches the pulse of its time, so the maker of images can never supercede the solver of problems.

In this sense architecture exhibits its timelessness when it expresses a century whose techniques and processes unite a great epoch in architecture with its sense of tradition, where the concern for space, light, and moving people involves a response that must always be of central importance. Architecture is growth beyond any social studies, statistical diagrams, or planning generalizations because on the one hand it is immersed in the tough, rough, modest, and everyday pragmatic world of putting materials together to shape space, and, on the other, it is in the realm where it becomes one of the most potent acts and highest ideals of civilizations. Architecture also, almost contradictory, is a probing and hesitant art, so beautifully expressed in a sentence testifying to the meaning of art in a 1958 letter from Boris Pasternak to the linguist V. V. Ivanov: "Any creative activity of a personal, concentrated nature is the temporary reconciliation of imperfect awkwardness and unintentional wrong."

Index

Cooper Hewitt Museum (New York City), 257
Copley Square, 79
Corinthian order, 282
Corning Museum of Glass, 39
Corporate Training Center (Moline, Illinois), 52
Cossutta, Araldo, 159-160
Cour Napoleon (Paris), 276-277
Craft architecture, 44-46
Creative Artists Agency (Beverly Hills), 274, 275
Creative Arts Center (Middletown, Connecticut), 99-100
Crown Hall, Illinois Institute of Technology School of Architecture, 13-14, 16
Crystal Palace (London), 45, 49
Cubism, 28-29, 138, 234, 244

Daisy House (Indiana), 136
Dance Instructional Facility (Purchase, New York), 24
Daniel, Mann, Johnson & Mendenhall, 115-116, 146-149, 176
Davis, Brody & Associates, 68, 126, 189
Deane House (Long Island, New York), 73
De Armas, Raul, 56, 217
Death and Life of Great American Cities, 180
Debussy, 238
De Chardin, Teilhard, 118
Deconstructionism, 173, 234, 236
Deere Building (Moline, Illinois), 122
Deere West Building (Moline, Illinois), 51, 52
De Menil Residence (East Hampton, New York), 223
Denver Towers (Colorado), 218
Derrida, Jacques, 234
Der Scutt, 82, 213, 216
De Stijl movement, 29, 88, 138, 198
Diagonal space, 35
Disney's Swan and Dolphin Hotels, 247, 248, 249
Disney's Yacht and Beach Club Resorts, 253-254, 255
Doric order, 282
Douglas House (Harbor Springs, Michigan), 91, 166

Duany, Andres, 180-181
Duchamp, Marcel, 29, 151

Eames, Charles, 105
Eastwood, Roosevelt Island Housing, 125
Ecole des Beaux Arts (Paris), 6
Economy of means, 201
Edwardian influence, 253
Egyptian revival style, 260
Eisenman, Peter, 139-140, 232, 234
Eisenman Robertson Trott & Bean, 141
El Zoghby, Gamal, 142
Eleven Diagonal Street (South Africa), 207-208
Ellicott Complex, SUNY, 189
Elliott Residence (Bethesda, Maryland), 266-267
Ellwood, Craig, 57, 96-97, 200
Embarcadero Center (San Francisco), 30
Empire State Building, 211
Energy conservation, 54-55
Enerplex (Princeton, New Jersey), 55
Environmental ideas. *See* Nature
Exclusion, 3, 7, 199-201
Expressionism, 3, 42, 234, 282

Faceted prism, 80
Faculty Club, University of California at Santa Barbara, 164
Fargo-Moorhead Cultural Center, 245, 247
Farnsworth House (Plano, Illinois), 86
Federal Reserve Bank of Minneapolis, 62-63
Fine Arts Center (Amherst, Massachusetts), 98-99
Fire Station (Corning, New York), 23
Flavin, Dan, 200
Fodrea Community School (Columbus, Indiana), 74
Folly Farm, 250
Ford Foundation (New York City), 123
Form, 10
Foster, Norman, 242
Foxhall Crescents (Washington, D.C.), 180
Frankenthaler, Helen, 145
Franklin Court (Philadelphia), 154, 156

Franzen, Ulrich, 131, 132
Free facade, 5
Fuller, Buckminster, 61-62
Function, 10-11
Functionalism, 10-42, 129-133, 166
Futurists, 29, 42, 46

Gallery of the Twentieth Century (Berlin), 16
Gamble House (Pasadena, California), 104
Garden, 54
Garden Grove Community Church (California), 49
Gatje, Robert, 65
Gaudi, Antonio, 22. *See also* Functionalism
Gehry, Frank, 228-232, 234
General Foods (Rye, New York), 270-271
Geometry, influence of, 3, 6, 32-35, 41, 67, 80, 94, 100-101, 127-129, 136, 140-144, 149, 160-161, 172-173, 224, 274-275, 279-280
Georgian influence, 250
German Pavilion (Barcelona), 11
Getty Center (Los Angeles), 170
Gibbs, James, 6
Gill, Irving, 104, 107
Giurgola, Romaldo, 38-39, 261. *See also* Mitchell Giurgola
Glass House, 12-13
Goddard Library, Clark University, 26
Goethe, 8
Goff, Bruce, 236, 237-238
González de Leon, 101
Gothic influence, 75, 103, 114, 121, 137, 242-243
Grand Coulee Dam complex, 89
Grand Hyatt (New York City), 82-83
Grand Louvre addition (Paris), 276-278
Graves, Michael, 18, 142-143, 219-221, 244-248, 249, 283. *See also* Post-Modernism
Greek movement, 162
Greenberg, Allan, 268-269
Greene, Herb, 237
Greene Brothers, 104, 242
Green Residence (Pennsylvania), 60
Griffin, Walter Burley, 94
Gris, 244

Lehmann Court Townhouses (Chicago), 179

Les Demoiselles d'Avignon, 28

L'Esprit Nouveau, 166

Lincoln Park house (Chicago), 179

Loos, Adolph, 198

Louis, Morris, 143

Louis XIV, 70, 271

Louvre (Paris), 276–277

Lovell House (Los Angeles), 105

Lower Manhattan Expressway proposal, 186

Loyola Law School (Los Angeles), 230, 232, 234

Lugano Convention Center (Switzerland), 147, 148

Lumsden, Anthony, 115, 146

Lundy, Victor A., 62–63

Lutyens, Edwin, 250

Luxury Resort Hotel, 228

Lyles Bissett Carlisle & Wolff, 62–63

Lyndon B. Johnson Library (Austin, Texas), 67

Lyndon Buchanan & B. Beebe, 164

McKim, Mead and White, 272

McKinnell. *See* Kallmann

MacKintosh, Charles Rennie, 242

Madeira School Science Building (Virginia), 54

Magnuson House (Vashon Island, Washington), 59–60

Maison de Verre (Paris), 61

Malraux, André, 5

Manufacturer's Bank (Los Angeles), 147

Marine Midland Building (New York City), 198

Martin, A. C. & Associates, 251

Matisse, Henri, 198

Maybeck, Bernard, 104, 107–108

Mayne, Thom, 233, 234

Mediterranean influence, 102, 114, 253, 263

Meier, Richard, 91, 166–168, 169, 170, 222–227, 244, 283–284. *See also* Neoclassic movement

"Melt water," 56

Messeturm (Frankfurt), 209

Metropolitan Museum of Art (New York City), 162

Michaelangelo, 71, 121

Mies van der Rohe, Ludwig, 2, 5, 7, 11, 13–14, 16, 34, 71, 86–87, 97, 144, 198, 202, 274, 283. *See also* Modernism

Millard House (Pasadena), 106

Miller House (Lakeville, Connecticut), 139

Miró Foundation (Barcelona), 102

Mission style, 112

Mitchell Giurgola Associates, 38, 260–261, 263, 264

Mitchell Giurgola & Thorp, 94

MLTW. *See* Moore Lyndon Turnbull Whitaker

Modern classicism, 41

Modernism, 2–8, 44–84, 95, 118, 128, 134, 198–261, 275–277, 283

Moholy-Nagy, Sibyl, 26, 283

Monadnock Building (Chicago), 222

Mondrian, Piet, 29

Montreal World Fair, 61

Monumentalism, 36

Moore, Arthur Cotton, 54, 180

Moore, Charles W., 37, 108, 165, 247, 249–251

Moore Lyndon Turnbull Whitaker (MLTW), 107, 109, 114, 164

Moore-Turnbull, 109

Morphosis, 233, 235

Morris, William, 46

Morton H. Meyerson Symphony Center (Dallas), 274–275, 276

Mt. Healthy School (Columbus, Indiana), 133

Mummers Theater (Oklahoma City), 26

Murphy Jahn, 205–206, 207–210

Museum of Modern Art (New York City), 202

Mykonos, 88

Nagle, James, 178, 179

Nagle Hartray & Associates, 178–179

Nash, John, 242, 247

National Center for Atmospheric Research (Boulder, Colorado), 115

National Commercial Bank Tower (Saudi Arabia), 53

National Gallery of Art (Washington, D.C.), 40–41

Nature, 86, 87, 106, 124. *See also* Context influences

Neoclassic movement, 3, 137, 169, 241, 258

Neo-gothic, 219

Neohistoricist, 3

Neutra, Richard, 105

New Brutalist movement, 6, 242, 283

New England shingle house, 159

New Life Child Development Center (Brooklyn), 152, 155

Newman, Barnett, 200

New York Botanical Garden, 50–51

New York Townhouse, 252, 253

Noguchi, Isamu, 200

Noland, Kenneth, 89, 111, 145

"Non-directional, non-gravitational enclosure," 147

Nonstraightforward approach, 3

North Shore Congregation Israel (Glencoe, Illinois), 258, 261

North Western Terminal (Chicago), 206

Notre Dame (Paris), 50

Nude Descending the Staircase, 29

Oakland Museum (California), 123

Oeuvres Complètes, 5

Oldenburg, Claus, 238

One Liberty Place Tower (Philadelphia), 209

One Park Plaza (Los Angeles), 146

One South Wacker (Chicago), 206

Open plan, 5

Orangerie, 144

Order-disorder dialogue, 158–196

Pacific Design Center (Los Angeles), 50, 149

Paint techniques, 145

Palace of Fine Arts (San Francisco), 108

Palladian influence, 36, 110, 270

Palladio, 121

Parc La Villette, 172, 234

Parliament House (Australia), 94

Parrish, Maxfield, 108, 110, 238

Parts of Architecture, The, 6

Pasternak, Boris, 285

Paul Mellon Arts Center (New Haven, Connecticut), 273

"Pavilions," 100

Paxton, Joseph, 45